D1291706

Praise for
Leading at a Higher Level

"At Southwest Airlines, we have always strived to lead at a higher level. We truly believe that profit is the applause you get for taking care of your internal and external customers. We have always insisted upon a happy, carefree, team-spirited—yes, even fun—working environment, which we think results in motivated employees who will do the right thing for their internal and external customers. Reading this book will make a positive difference in your organization."

Colleen C. Barrett, *President Emeritus, Southwest Airlines*

"This is not just theory. It is the real stuff, tried in dozens of companies big and small. It represents the most concise, practical, and effective thinking on leadership around. Plainly said, this works."

Gary Crittenden, *Managing Director, Huntsman Gay Global Capital, former CFO of Citigroup and American Express*

"Leading at a higher level is a must today if leaders are to rebuild trust and credibility, as we are doing at Tyco. This book will teach you how."

Eric Pillmore, *Senior Vice President of Corporate Governance, Tyco International*

"*Leading at a Higher Level* translates decades of research and 40 years of global experience into simple, practical, and powerful strategies to equip leaders at every level to build organizations that produce bottom-line results. At Nissan, we have made these principles a core part of our leadership philosophy, better equipping our managers to bring out the great energies and talents of our employees."

Jim Irvine, *Vice President of Human Resources, Nissan North America*

The concepts in *Leading at a Higher Level* have been used by high performing organizations around the world, including:

Abbott Laboratories
AMF Bowling Worldwide, Inc.
Anthem Blue Cross and Blue Shield
Applebee's International, Inc.
Bayer AG
Big Lots Stores, Inc.
Biogen Idec Inc.
Bose® Corporation
Bowater® Incorporated
Burger King®
Callaway Golf Company
Caterpillar Inc.
Cellular One
Chick-fil-A®, Inc.
Children's Hospital
The Coffee Bean and Tea Leaf®
Comerica Incorporated
Compaq
CompUSA®
ConocoPhillips
Domino's Pizza
Dow Corning Corporation
Energy Northwest
Exxon Mobil Corporation
Fairmont Hotels & Resorts
FedEx Kinko's Office and Print Services
Fireman's Fund Insurance Company®
Foster Farms
Genentech, Inc.
Georgetown University
Hilton Hotels Corporation
Home Depot
Host Hotels & Resorts (formerly known as Host Marriott)
Hyatt Corporation
Jack in the Box Inc.
Kennedy Space Center
Krispy Kreme Doughnut Corporation
L'Oréal
Marriott International
Mattel, Inc.
MCI, Inc.
Merck & Co., Inc.
The Michelin Group
Microsoft Corporation
Nabisco
Nissan Motor Co.
Northrop Grumman Corporation
Novartis AG
Pepperdine University
Polaris Industries
The Ritz-Carlton Hotel Company
Royal Caribbean Cruises Ltd.®
Safeco Corporation
San Diego Padres
S.C. Johnson & Son, Inc.
Six Continents Retail
Sony Corporation of America
Staples, Inc.
Toshiba Corporation
Toyota Motor Corporation
TRW Automotive Inc.
Tyson Foods, Inc.
UCLA
UPS™
Verizon
Victoria's Secret
Wal-Mart Stores, Inc.
Washington State Criminal Justice Training Commission
WD-40 Company
Wells Fargo & Company
Wendy's International, Inc.
Yellow Pages (GTE)

LEADING AT A HIGHER LEVEL

Third Edition

Contributing Authors

Ken Blanchard

Marjorie Blanchard

Scott Blanchard

Madeleine Blanchard

Don Carew

Eunice Parisi-Carew

Randy Conley

Kathy Cuff

Garry Demarest

Claire Díaz-Ortiz

Chris Edmonds

Fred Finch

Susan Fowler

Bob Glaser

Lael Good

Vicki Halsey

Laurence Hawkins

Judd Hoekstra

Fay Kandarian

Linda Miller

Alan Randolph

Jane Ripley

Jesse Stoner

Drea Zigarmi

Pat Zigarmi

LEADING AT A HIGHER LEVEL

Blanchard on Leadership and Creating High Performing Organizations

Third Edition

The Founding Associates
and Consulting Partners of
The Ken Blanchard Companies®

Published by Pearson Education, Inc.

Many of the designations used by manufacturers and sellers to distinguish their products are claimed as trademarks. Where those designations appear in this book, and the publisher was aware of a trademark claim, the designations have been printed with initial capital letters or in all capitals. Company and product names mentioned herein are the trademarks or registered trademarks of their respective owners.

The authors and publisher have taken care in the preparation of this book, but make no expressed or implied warranty of any kind and assume no responsibility for errors or omissions. No liability is assumed for incidental or consequential damages in connection with or arising out of the use of the information or programs contained herein.

For information about buying this title in bulk quantities, or for special sales opportunities (which may include electronic versions; custom cover designs; and content particular to your business, training goals, marketing focus, or branding interests), please contact our corporate sales department at corpsales@pearsoned.com or (800) 382-3419.

For government sales inquiries, please contact governmentsales@pearsoned.com.

For questions about sales outside the U.S., please contact intlcs@pearson.com.

ISBN-10: 0-13-485753-4
ISBN-13: 978-0-13-485753-4

Library of Congress Control Number: 2018947162

1   18

Executive Editor: Laura Norman
Senior Marketing Manager: Stephane Nakib
Development Editor: Kiran Kumar Panigrahi
Managing Editor: Sandra Schroder
Senior Project Editor: Lori Lyons
Cover Designer: Chuti Prasertsith
Project Manager: Suganya Karuppasamy
Copy Editor: Gill Editorial Services
Proofreader: Christopher Morris
Indexer: Ken Johnson
Compositor: codemantra

Dedicated to all leaders in the world who are trying every day to lead at a higher level. May you keep your energy high and know that what you are doing makes a difference.

Contents at a Glance

Introduction xxii

SECTION I **Set Your Sights on the Right Target and Vision** 1

Chapter 1 Is Your Organization High Performing? . . . 3
Don Carew, Fay Kandarian, Eunice Parisi-Carew, Jesse Stoner, and Ken Blanchard

Chapter 2 The Power of Vision 17
Jesse Stoner, Ken Blanchard, and Drea Zigarmi

SECTION II **Treat Your People Right** 33

Chapter 3 Empowerment Is the Key. 35
Alan Randolph and Ken Blanchard

Chapter 4 SLII®: The Integrating Concept 53
The Founding Associates

Chapter 5 Self Leadership: The Power Behind Empowerment 69
Susan Fowler, Ken Blanchard, and Laurence Hawkins

Chapter 6 One-on-One Leadership. 81
Fred Finch and Ken Blanchard

Chapter 7 Essential Skills for One-on-One Leadership. 103
Ken Blanchard and Fred Finch

Chapter 8   Building Trust. 119
             Ken Blanchard, Cynthia Olmstead,
             and Randy Conley

Chapter 9   Coaching: A Key Competency for
             Leadership Development. 131
             Madeleine Homan Blanchard
             and Linda Miller

Chapter 10   Mentoring: The Key to Life Planning 145
             Ken Blanchard and Claire Díaz-Ortiz

Chapter 11   Team Leadership 155
             Don Carew, Eunice Parisi-Carew, Lael Good,
             and Ken Blanchard

Chapter 12   Collaboration: Fuel for High
             Performance 179
             Jane Ripley, Eunice Parisi-Carew,
             and Ken Blanchard

Chapter 13   Organizational Leadership 191
             Ken Blanchard, Jesse Stoner, Don Carew,
             Eunice Parisi-Carew, and Fay Kandarian

Chapter 14   Organizational Change: Why People
             Resist It 209
             Pat Zigarmi, Judd Hoekstra,
             and Ken Blanchard

Chapter 15   Leading People Through Change 225
             Pat Zigarmi and Judd Hoekstra

Chapter 16   Managing a Successful Cultural
             Transformation 249
             Garry Demarest, Chris Edmonds, and Bob Glaser

SECTION III   Treat Your Customers Right . . .263

Chapter 17   Serving Customers at a Higher Level 265

Ken Blanchard, Kathy Cuff, Vicki Halsey,
and Jesse Stoner

SECTION IV   Have the Right Kind
of Leadership. 285

Chapter 18   Servant Leadership 287

Ken Blanchard, Scott Blanchard,
and Drea Zigarmi

Chapter 19   Determining Your Leadership
Point of View 313

Margie Blanchard, Pat Zigarmi,
and Ken Blanchard

Endnotes 333

Acknowledgments. 347

About the Authors. 349

Services Available 371

Index. 375

Register your copy of *Leading at a Higher Level* at informit.com for convenient access to updates and corrections as they become available. To start the registration process, go to informit.com/register and log in or create an account. Enter the product ISBN (9780134857534) and click Submit.

Contents

Introduction xxii
Leading at a Higher Level xxiii
Why Did We Write This Book? xxiv
How This Book Is Organized. xxvi

SECTION I Set Your Sights on the Right
Target and Vision 1

Chapter 1 Is Your Organization High Performing? . . . 3
The Right Target: The Quadruple Bottom Line. 4
Employer of Choice 4
Provider of Choice 5
Investment of Choice. 6
Corporate Citizen of Choice. 8
A High Performing Organization Scores Every Time 9
The HPO SCORES® Model. 10
S = Shared Information and Open
Communication 10
C = Compelling Vision. 10
O = Ongoing Learning 10
R = Relentless Focus on Customer Results 11
E = Energizing Systems and Structures 11
S = Shared Power and High Involvement 11
Leadership Is the Engine 12
The HPO SCORES® Quiz: How Does Your
Organization Score? 13
HPO SCORES® Quiz 13
How Does Your Organization Score? 15
How Should I Use My Quiz Results? 15

Chapter 2 The Power of Vision 17
The Importance of Vision 17
Effective Versus Ineffective Vision Statements 18

Creating a Vision That Really Works. 19

    Significant Purpose. 20

    A Picture of the Future 21

    Clear Values 22

A Compelling Vision Creates a Culture
of Greatness. 24

Vision Is the Place to Start. 24

Vision Can Exist Anywhere in an Organization 26

Make Your Vision a Reality 27

    How It's Created 27

    How It's Communicated 28

    How It's Lived 28

Vision and Leadership. 29

SECTION II   Treat Your People Right 33

Chapter 3   Empowerment Is the Key. 35

What Is Empowerment? 36

The Power of Empowerment 37

How History Blocks Change to Empowerment. 37

Tapping People's Power and Potential:
A Real-World Example. 39

Learning the Language of Empowerment 40

The Three Keys to Empowerment 41

    The First Key to Empowerment:
    Share Information with Everyone 41

    The Second Key to Empowerment:
    Create Autonomy Through Boundaries 45

    The Third Key to Empowerment:
    Replace the Old Hierarchy with
    Self-Directed Individuals and Teams. 48

Chapter 4   SLII®: The Integrating Concept. 53

The Three Skills of an SLII® Leader. 54

    Goal Setting: The First Skill 54

    Diagnosis: The Second Skill 54

    Matching: The Third Skill 55

Enthusiastic Beginners Need a Directing Style 58

Disillusioned Learners Need a Coaching Style 59

Capable But Cautious Performers Need a
Supporting Style 60

Self-Reliant Achievers Need a Delegating Style 60

Development Level Varies from Goal to
Goal and Task to Task 61

Meeting People Where They Are .62

The Importance of Partnering with People 66

Effective Leadership Is a Transformational
Journey 67

Chapter 5   **Self Leadership: The Power
Behind Empowerment** **69**

Creating an Empowered Workforce 70

Creating Self Leaders Through Individual
Learning 71

The Three Skills of a Self Leader 72

The First Skill of a Self Leader: Challenge Assumed
Constraints. 72

The Second Skill of a Self Leader:
Activate Points of Power 73

The Third Skill of a Self Leader:
Be Proactive 77

Chapter 6   **One-on-One Leadership** **81**

Establishing an Effective Performance
Management System 81

One-on-One Leadership and the Performance
Management System 85

Performance Planning: The First Part of
a Performance Management System 85

Performance Coaching: The Second Part
of a Performance Management System 90

Performance Review: The Third Part of
a Performance Management System 100

Partnering as an Informal Performance
Management System 100

One-on-Ones: An Insurance Policy for
Making One-on-One Leadership Work 101

Chapter 7   **Essential Skills for One-on-One Leadership** **103**

One Minute Goal Setting. 103

Areas of Accountability 104

Performance Standards 105

    Performance Reviews Can Undermine
Performance. 107

    Limit the Number of Goals .108

    Good Goals Are SMART Goals 108

One Minute Praisings. 110

    Be Immediate and Specific .110

    State Your Feelings 110

    Praisings Are Universally Powerful 111

    Being Close Counts. 111

    Make Time for Praisings. 112

One Minute Re-Directs 113

    How Do One Minute Re-Directs Work? 113

    Praisings and Redirects Are Key to
One-on-One Leadership 116

The Fourth Secret of the One Minute Manager. 116

    The One Minute Apology 116

Chapter 8   **Building Trust.** **119**

The High Cost of Low Trust 119

The Benefits of Trust. 120

The Four Elements of Trust 120

Creating a High Trust Environment 121

    Step One: Know the Behaviors
That Support the ABCDs of Trust. 122

    Step Two: Assess the Current
Trust Level 122

    Step Three: Diagnose Areas
That Need Work 123

    Step Four: Have a Conversation to
Restore Trust 123

The Transparency Challenge 124

Repairing Broken Trust 126

    Step One: Acknowledge and Assure 127

    Step Two: Admit 127

Step Three: Apologize 127
Step Four: Assess 128
Step Five: Agree 128
The Ripple Effect............................128

Chapter 9 **Coaching: A Key Competency for Leadership Development. 131**
Definition of Coaching 131
Five Applications of Coaching 132
Application One: Performance Coaching 133
Application Two: Development Coaching 135
Application Three: Career Coaching.............137
Application Four: Coaching to Support Learning 140
Application Five: Creating an Internal Coaching Culture 142

Chapter 10 **Mentoring: The Key to Life Planning 145**
Obstacles to Beginning a Mentoring Relationship.....146
Choosing a Mentoring Partner......................147
Essence Versus Form..............................147
The MENTOR Model: Elements of a Successful Mentoring Partnership..................148
Mission 149
Engagement..................................149
Networking 149
Trust..149
Opportunity.................................150
Review and Renew 150
Creating a Mentoring Program in Your Organization 151
Tailoring Mentoring to Career Stages 152
Early or Entry Level..........................153
Mid-Career or Management Level..............153
Executive or Master Level 153

Chapter 11 **Team Leadership 155**
Why Teams? 156
Obstacles to High Performance 158

An Effective Team Leadership Approach 159

   Understanding the Characteristics
   That Make a High Performance Team 159

   Identifying the Team's Stage of
   Development 162

   Productivity and Morale 163

   Team Development Stage 1
   (TDS1)—Orientation 164

   Team Development Stage 2
   (TDS2)—Dissatisfaction 165

   Team Development Stage 3
   (TDS3)—Integration 166

   Team Development Stage 4
   (TDS4)—Production 167

Providing Leadership Behaviors That Match
the Team's Needs 168

   Teams at Stage 1 Need a Structuring Style 170

   Teams at Stage 2 Need a Resolving Style 171

   Teams at Stage 3 Need an Integrating Style 172

   Teams at Stage 4 Need a Validating Style 172

Strategies for Higher Team Performance 173

   Keep the Team Moving Forward 173

   Observe Team Dynamics 174

   Manage Closure 175

The Power of Teams 176

Chapter 12   **Collaboration: Fuel for
High Performance** **179**

Collaboration Is Not Coordination,
Cooperation, or Teamwork 179

Creating a Collaborative Framework 181

Collaboration Versus Competition 183

What It Takes to Be Collaborative 184

   The UNITE Model 185

   The Heart: Utilize Differences 185

   The Heart: Nurture Safety and Trust 186

   The Head: Involve Others in Crafting a
   Clear Purpose, Values, and Goals 187

The Hands: Talk Openly 188
The Hands: Empower Yourself and Others 189
Collaboration: Fuel for High Performance. 189

Chapter 13 **Organizational Leadership 191**
Real Life Examples of HPO SCORES®. 191
S—Shared Information and
Open Communication 192
C—Compelling Vision. 193
O—Ongoing Learning 194
R—Relentless Focus on Customer Results 195
E—Energizing Systems and Structures 195
S—Shared Power and High Involvement 196
Determining the Appropriate Leadership
Style for Your Organization 198
Diagnosing Your Organization's
Development Level 198
Results and Relationships: The Determinants
of a High Performing Organization. 198
Organizational Development Stage 1:
Start-Up. 199
Organizational Development Stage 2:
Improving 200
Organizational Development Stage 3:
Developing. 200
Organizational Development Stage 4:
High Performing 201
Matching Leadership Style to Your
Organization's Development Stage. 201
Applying the Appropriate Leadership Style at
Each Development Level. 203
Stage 1: Start-Up 203
Stage 2: Improving 204
Stage 3: Developing 205
Stage 4: High Performing. 206
The Importance of Diagnosis and Matching. 206
A History-Making Organizational Turnaround 207

Chapter 14 Organizational Change: Why People Resist It **209**

The Importance of Leading Change 209

Why Is Organizational Change So Complicated? 210

When Is Change Necessary? 211

Why Change Gets Derailed or Fails. 212

Focus on Leading the Journey 214

Surfacing and Addressing People's Concerns 215

Stage 1: Information Concerns 216

Stage 2: Personal Concerns 216

Stage 3: Implementation Concerns. 220

Stage 4: Impact Concerns .221

Stage 5: Collaboration Concerns 222

Stage 6: Refinement Concerns 222

Different People Are at Different
Stages of Concern 223

The Importance of Involving Those Who
Are Being Asked to Change 223

Chapter 15 Leading People Through Change **225**

Five Change Leadership Strategies 225

Change Strategy 1: Expand
Involvement and Influence .226

Change Strategy 2: Explain Why
the Change Is Needed 233

Change Strategy 3: Collaborate on
Implementation 236

Change Strategy 4: Make the
Change Sustainable 241

Change Strategy 5: Explore Possibilities. 245

The Importance of Reinforcing the Change 247

Chapter 16 Managing a Successful Cultural Transformation **249**

Gung Ho!: A Starting Point 250

One "Right" Culture? 251

Culture by Design, Not by Default. 251

Skepticism about Culture from
Senior Leaders 252

The Importance of a Compelling Vision 254

Managing a Successful Cultural Transformation 255

    Phase One: Discovery. 256

    Phase Two: Immersion. 257

    Phase Three: Alignment. 258

    Phase Four: Refinement. 260

Critical Success Factors for Cultural
Transformation 261

SECTION III   Treat Your Customers Right . . .263

Chapter 17   Serving Customers at a Higher Level 265

Getting Legendary SCORES from Your
Customers 265

Creating Legendary Service. 267

Serving Customers at a Higher Level. 272

    Decide What You Want Your
    Customer Experience to Be 272

    Discover What Your Customers
    Want 275

    Deliver Your Ideal Customer
    Service Experience 277

Permitting People to Soar 281

Wallowing in a Duck Pond 282

Giving Your People Wings 282

**SECTION IV   Have the Right Kind of
                       Leadership .285**

Chapter 18   Servant Leadership 287

What Is Servant Leadership?. .287

Applying Servant Leadership .290

Great Leaders Encourage People to
Bring Their Brains to Work 293

What Kind of Leadership Impacts
Performance the Most? 294

Being a Servant Leader Is a Question of
the Heart. 298

Driven Versus Called Leaders .299

The Plight of the Ego 300

Ego Antidotes. 302

What Servant Leaders Do 304

Servant Leadership: A Mandate or a Choice 307

Chapter 19   Determining Your Leadership
Point of View **313**

Elements of a Leadership Point of View 314

     Key People 314

     Key Events 315

     Values 317

     Expectations for Yourself and Others 321

Developing Your Own Leadership Point of View 323

Become a Higher Level Leader 332

Endnotes **333**

Acknowledgments. **347**

About the Authors. **349**

Services Available **371**

Index **375**

List of Illustrations

Illustration		Page
Figure 1.1	The HPO SCORES® Model	12
Figure 2.1	The Visionary Role of Leadership	29
Figure 2.2	The Implementation Role of Leadership	30
Figure 4.1	The SLII® Model	56
Figure 4.2	Matching Leadership Style to Development Level	57
Figure 5.1	Points of Power	74
Figure 5.2	The SLII® Model	78
Figure 6.1	The Performance Management Game Plan	86
Figure 6.2	SLII® Leadership Styles	91
Figure 9.1	The Coaching Sweet Spot	133
Figure 11.1	Characteristics of High Performance Teams	160
Figure 11.2	The Stages of Team Development	163
Figure 11.3	Team Leadership Model	169
Figure 11.4	Focus of a Participant Observer	175
Figure 12.1	The UNITE Model	185
Figure 13.1	Matching Leadership Style to Organizational Development Stage	202
Figure 14.1	The Stages of Concern Model	215
Figure 15.1	Leading People Through Change Model	226
Figure 15.2	Perceived Loss of Control Increases Resistance to Change	228
Figure 17.1	The Legendary Service Model	268
Figure 17.2	The Implementation Role of Leadership	280
Figure 18.1	The Leadership-Profit Chain	296

Introduction

Several years ago, my wife Margie and I went on a safari in South Africa with some family and friends. We had already been on many safaris, but this time I saw some things differently. The jungle appeared more vicious, competitive, and territorial than ever before. If you've ever heard a lion roar, it sends chills up your back. When our long-time guide, Gary Clarke from Topeka, Kansas, imitates the lion's roar, he shouts, "It's mine, mine, mine, mine!" That's because when the lion roars, what he's really saying is, "This is my territory. Don't mess with me." In fact, lions will kill their sons if the sons challenge their fathers' control over their territory.

The reason I saw this more vividly than ever before is that I had decided on this trip that I was going to find out as much as I possibly could about Nelson Mandela. We had been at a dinner party where people around the table were asked to share what person—of anyone in the world—they would love to have dinner with. It was a quick decision for me. I said, "Nelson Mandela. I would love to have dinner with a man who was in prison for 28 years and treated cruelly, yet came out of that experience full of love, compassion, and reconciliation." On the trip, I began to read Mandela's autobiography, *Long Walk to Freedom*.

When I compared what I saw in the jungle with how Mandela had reacted to his treatment, I realized that in many ways we as human beings are just intelligent animals. And being intelligent animals, we can choose every day whether to be self-serving or serving. Jungle animals, like the lion, can't make that choice. They have to annihilate others to protect their territory. It's not in their nature to share with other species. And yet, just as Mandela did, we as human beings can make choices to live and lead at a higher level, to be serving rather than self-serving. But when you look at the leaders around the world—whether they're running countries, businesses, churches, educational institutions, or what have you—too many people are choosing to be self-serving rather than serving. Why is that? Because they don't have a different leadership role model. They have been conditioned to think about leadership only in terms of power and control. That's what this book is all about—a different leadership paradigm. We want to help individuals and organizations lead at a higher level.

Leading at a Higher Level

What is leadership? For years we defined leadership as an *influence process.* We believed that anytime you tried to influence the thoughts and actions of others toward goal accomplishment in either your personal or your professional life, you were engaging in leadership. In recent years, we have taken the emphasis away from goal accomplishment and have defined leadership as *the capacity to influence others by unleashing their power and potential to impact the greater good.* Why did we do that? Because when the definition of leadership focuses on goal accomplishment, one can think that leadership is only about results. Yet when we talk about leading at a higher level, just focusing on goal accomplishment is not enough. The key phrase in our new definition is "the greater good"—what is best for all involved. Leadership is a high calling. It should not be done purely for personal gain or goal accomplishment; it should have a much higher purpose than that.

What is a higher purpose? It is not something as internally focused and self-centered as making money. As Matt Hayes and Jeff Stevens contend in *The Heart of Business,* when it becomes obvious that profit, which is a legitimate goal, is the driving reason for being in business, everyone—stockholders, top managers, employees, customers, suppliers, and the community—quickly becomes self-serving. They focus on their own agenda and personal enrichment. Employee loyalty and passion often go out the window as the point of work becomes simply to get as much as you can for as little effort as possible.[1]

What is the answer to this dilemma? A higher purpose—a key element of what we will refer to throughout this book as a *compelling vision.* In Hayes and Stevens's terms, it is something outwardly focused; it requires sacrifice—in other words, it takes precedence over any short-term goal like profit—and it is intrinsically honorable.

Leaders can be successful in the short run if they emphasize only goal accomplishment. What tends to fall by the wayside is the condition of the human organization. Leaders don't always take morale and job satisfaction into consideration—only results count. They forget what the point is and don't have a higher purpose. In business, with that kind of leadership, it is a short leap to thinking that the only reason to be in business is to make money. An either/or is added to people and results. Leaders falsely believe that they can't focus on both at the same time.

When you are leading at a higher level, you have a both/and philosophy. The development of people—both employees and customers—is of equal importance to performance. As a result, the focus in leading at a higher level is on long-term results and human satisfaction. *Leading at a higher level*, therefore, is a process. We define it as *the process of achieving worthwhile results while acting with respect, care, and fairness for the well-being of all involved*. When that occurs, self-serving leadership is not possible. Why?

Self-serving leaders think that leadership is all about them and not about the best interests of those they serve. They forget about acting with respect, care, and fairness toward all involved. Everything is about their own self-interest. It's only when you realize that it's not about you that you begin to lead at a higher level.

Why Did We Write This Book?

In 2006 we wrote the original edition of this book for several reasons. First, our dream was that someday everyone would know someone who is leading at a higher level. Self-serving leaders would be a thing of the past, and leadership throughout the world would be composed of people who, as Robert Greenleaf said, "serve first and lead second."[2] We wrote this book to help make our dream a reality.

Second, the vision of The Ken Blanchard Companies® is focused on leading at a higher level. This kind of leadership begins with a vision. Jesse Stoner and I wrote a book called *Full Steam Ahead!* about the power of visioning. A compelling vision tells you *who you are* (your purpose), *where you're going* (your preferred picture of the future), and *what will drive your journey* (your values).

The purpose of The Ken Blanchard Companies® is to help individuals and organizations lead at a higher level. Our mission statement reflects our new definition of leadership:

Unleash the power and potential in people and organizations for the greater good.

Our picture of the future is

- We train people to become the world's best managers. We provide the leadership language and models to help power the best-run organizations in the world—making a positive difference in the lives of leaders and the people they serve.

- We believe that great leaders have a both/and attitude toward people and results, not an either/or attitude. As a result, our company's values reflect both people and results.

Our operating *values* are

- People-oriented values:

    - **Trustworthiness**: Do the right thing.

    - **Kenship:** Value compassion, humility, and abundance.

    - **Dialogue:** Value conversion and encourage thinking.

- Results-oriented values:

    - **Ownership:** Take personal responsibility for keeping the company streamlined, nimble, innovative, and profitable.

    - **Focus & Clarity:** Set clear goals and act to achieve them.

    - **Getting to D4**: Value high-level performance and competence.

Since these values are focused on guiding the behavior of the people in our company, two of the values—Kenship and Getting to D4—use our company's internal language. Kenship is named after me—not my choice—but was meaningful to all the people who voted for these values. Getting to D4 reflects the goal of our SLII® training: mastery, the highest level of development.

Values are often rank ordered. In our case, we decided that in making decisions, we needed to consider all the values. As we strive to achieve results, we also keep human beings top of mind, honoring our relationships with our people, customers, and suppliers.

You might say that all this sounds like Pollyanna—overly optimistic. That may be, but these are the standards we have set for ourselves. And these are the same high standards we want to help you and the people in your organization reach through this book. Helping individuals and organizations lead at a higher level is our passion, both for your organization and our own.

Finally, in many ways this book spells out our leadership point of view. Extensive research shows that effective leaders have a clear leadership point of view and are willing to share with others these beliefs about leading and motivating people. We hope reading this book will impact your leadership point of view.

How This Book Is Organized

Over the years, we have found that in organizations where leading at a higher level is the rule rather than the exception, people do four things well:

- They set their sights on the right target and vision.
- They treat their people right.
- They treat their customers right.
- They have the right kind of leadership.

This book is organized into four sections. **Section I** focuses on *the right target and vision* and integrates our work on the quadruple bottom line, the characteristics of a high performing organization, and the creation of a compelling vision.

Section II focuses on *treating your people right*. In earlier editions of this book, this was Section III, following treating your customers right. But today, we believe your number-one customer is your people. If you don't empower your people and treat them right, they won't take care of what we consider to be your second most important customer—the people who use your products and services. If that happens, in the long run you won't get your desired results.

This section on *treating your people right* is the longest section of the book because your treatment of people is leadership in action. This is what The Ken Blanchard Companies® has been focusing on for 40 years. In this section, we start with empowerment and then examine four leadership domains: self leadership, one-on-one leadership, team leadership, and organizational leadership.

Section III highlights *treating the customer right* and integrates our work on legendary service, raving fans, and customer mania—all of which depend on having an empowered, motivated workforce. Without good customer service, your organization won't survive in the long run.

Section IV zeros in on *the right kind of leadership*. Here we're not talking about leadership style; we're talking about character and intentionality. My travels over the years through organizations of all shapes and sizes have convinced me of two things: Effective leadership starts on the inside, and the right kind of leadership is servant leadership. This is a leadership not based on false pride or fear, but one that's grounded in humility and focused on the greater good. With the right kind of leadership, leading at a higher level can become a reality.

This section also includes our thoughts on determining your leadership point of view. This turns the focus to you. Here we assist you in pulling together many of the concepts you have learned and help you integrate and apply that knowledge to your own leadership situation.

Writing this book has been a labor of love. Representing our best thinking from 40 years of working together, it truly is *Blanchard on Leadership*. With new chapters on trust, collaboration, mentoring, and organizational leadership, this third edition includes not only Margie's and my thinking, but also all the wonderful contributions of our founding associates—Don Carew, Eunice Parisi-Carew, Fred Finch, Laurie Hawkins, Drea Zigarmi, and Pat Zigarmi—and other fabulous consulting partners who have really made Blanchard "the home of the authors," including Randy Conley, Kathy Cuff, Garry Demarest, Claire Díaz-Ortiz, Chris Edmonds, Susan Fowler,

Bob Glaser, Vicki Halsey, Judd Hoekstra, Fay Kandarian, Linda Miller, Cynthia Olmstead, Alan Randolph, Jane Ripley, Jesse Stoner, and our son and daughter-in-law, Scott Blanchard and Madeleine Homan Blanchard. Everyone can lead at a higher level, whether at work, at home, or in the community. We hope that regardless of your position, the size or type of your organization, or the kind of customers or people you serve, you will learn some important information in this book. We also hope this book will help you lead at a higher level and create a high-performing organization that not only accomplishes your desired results but is a welcome harbor for the people you touch. May good come out of your reading of this book.

Ken Blanchard
San Diego, California
Fall 2018

SECTION I

Set Your Sights on the Right Target and Vision

Chapter 1   Is Your Organization High Performing?.......... 3

Chapter 2   The Power of Vision..17

1

Is Your Organization High Performing?

Don Carew, Fay Kandarian, Eunice Parisi-Carew,
Jesse Stoner, and Ken Blanchard

Marksmen will tell you that when you aim at a target, you should go for the bull's-eye. The reason is that if you miss the bull's-eye, you're still on the target. But if all you do is aim for the target and you miss, you're nowhere. Don Shula, who coauthored *Everyone's a Coach*[1] with Ken Blanchard, always told his Miami Dolphins football team that the target they were aiming at was to win every game. Was that possible? Obviously not, but if you don't shoot for excellence, you never have a chance of getting there. That's probably why Shula's teams won more football games than teams of any other coach in the history of the NFL. His 1972 Dolphins is still the only team in history to go undefeated for an entire season, including the Super Bowl. So the target you aim for has a lot to do with your performance.

Wall Street and the pressures of business today make many people think that the only target that counts is financial success. Yet few, if any, businesspeople would want their epitaph to include their company's bottom line—their stock price or profit margin. They might, however, want people to remember their contribution to the creation of a high performing organization.

Those who want to lead at a higher level need to understand what a high performing organization looks like and what is necessary to create one. They need to aim for the right target.

The Right Target: The Quadruple Bottom Line

In high performing organizations, everyone's energy is focused on not just one bottom line, but four bottom lines—being the *employer of choice,* the *provider of choice,* the *investment of choice,* and the *corporate citizen of choice.* This quadruple bottom line is the right target and can make the difference between mediocrity and greatness.[2] The leaders in high performing organizations know that their bottom line depends on their people, their customers, their investors, and their communities. These leaders realize the following:

> *Profit is the applause you get for caring for the community and creating a motivating environment for your people so they will take care of your customers.*

Employer of Choice

Being the employer of choice is increasingly challenging. With highly mobile, competent workers in demand, employers must find new ways to attract and keep their best people. Good pay is no longer the only answer. It is true that some competent workers will go elsewhere for a higher wage; however, today's workers generally want more. They seek opportunities where they feel like their contributions are valued and rewarded—where they are involved and empowered, can develop skills, can see advancement opportunities, and can believe they are making a difference.

You will get little argument today if you tell managers that people are their most important resource. We suggest that the customer should come second; without committed and empowered employees, a company can never provide good service. You can't treat your people poorly and expect them to treat your customers well.

In the days before cell phones, a friend of ours had an experience in a department store that illustrates this point well. He normally shopped at Nordstrom but found himself in a competitor's store. Realizing that he needed to talk to his wife, he asked a salesperson in the men's department if he could use the store's telephone. "No!" the salesperson said.

He replied, "You have to be kidding me. You can always use the phone at Nordstrom."

The salesperson said, "Look, buddy! They don't let *me* use the phone here. Why should I let *you*?"

People who are treated poorly tend to pass on that attitude to their customers.

Another reason that your people are so important today is because these days your organization is evaluated on how quickly it can respond to customer needs and problems. "I'll have to talk to my boss" doesn't cut it anymore. Nobody cares who the boss is. The only people customers care about are the ones who answer the phone, greet them, write up their order, make their delivery, or respond to their complaints. They want top service, and they want it fast. This means that you need to create a motivating environment for your people and an organizational structure that is flexible enough to permit them to be the best they can be.

Provider of Choice

Being the provider of choice is equally challenging. Competition is fierce as new competitors emerge unexpectedly. Customers are more demanding, with many more options at their fingertips. The world has changed in such a way that today the buyer, not the seller, is sitting in the driver's seat. These days, nobody has to convince anybody that providing legendary service for your customers is all important. In fact, companies are motivated to change when they discover the new rule:

---

*If you don't take care of your customers,
somebody else will.*

In *Raving Fans®: A Revolutionary Approach to Customer Service*, Sheldon Bowles and Ken Blanchard argue that to keep your customers today, you can't be content just to satisfy them.[3] You have to create raving fans—customers who are so excited about the legendary way you treat them that they want to tell everyone about you. They become part of your sales force. Let's look at a simple yet powerful example.

What's the most common wake-up call that you get in a hotel in America today? The phone rings at the allotted hour, but when you pick it up, no one is there. At least the hotel got the machine to call your room at the designated hour. The second most common wake-up call greets you with a recording. But again, no one's there. Today if you pick up the phone on a wake-up call and a human being is on the other end—someone you can actually talk to—you hardly know what to say. A while back, one of our colleagues was staying at the Marriott Convention Hotel in Orlando. He asked for a 7:00 wake-up call. When the phone rang and he picked it up, a woman said, "Good morning; this is Teresa. It's 7 o'clock. It's going to be 75 and beautiful in Orlando today, but your ticket says you're leaving. Where are you going?"

Taken aback, our colleague stammered, "New York City."

Teresa said, "Let me look at the *USA Today* weather map. Oh, no! It's supposed to be 40 degrees and rainy in New York today. Can't you stay another day?"

Now where do you think our colleague wants to stay when he gets to Orlando? He wants to stay at the Marriott so that he can talk to Teresa in the morning! Raving fans are created by companies whose service far exceeds that of the competition and even exceeds customer expectations. These companies routinely do the unexpected and then enjoy the growth generated by customers who have spontaneously joined their sales force.

Investment of Choice

Growing or expanding requires investment, regardless of whether the company is publicly owned, privately held, government, or non-profit. All organizations require funding sources, through stock purchases, loans, grants, or contracts. To be willing to invest, people must believe in the organization's viability and performance over time.

They need to have faith in the leadership, the quality of the people, the product and services, the management practices, and the organization's resilience.

If an organization's financial success is a function of revenue minus expenses, you can become more sound financially either by reducing costs or increasing revenues. Let's look at costs first, because in today's competitive environment, the prize goes to those who can do more with less. More organizations today are deciding that the only way to be financially effective is to downsize. There's no doubt that some personnel reduction is necessary in large bureaucracies where everyone just has to have an assistant, and the assistant must have an assistant. Yet downsizing is an energy drain, and it's by no means the only way to manage costs.

There's a growing realization that another effective way to manage costs is to make all your people your business partners. For instance, in some companies, new people can't get a raise until they can read their company's balance sheet and understand where and how their individual efforts are impacting the company's profit-and-loss statement. When people understand the business realities of how their organization makes and spends money, they are much more apt to roll up their sleeves and help out.

Traditionally, managers have been reluctant to share financial information. Yet these days, many organizations are responding with open-book management. That's because they realize the financial benefits of sharing previously sensitive data. For example, in working with a restaurant company, one of our consulting partners was having a hard time convincing the president of the merits of sharing important financial data with employees. To unfreeze the president's thinking, the consulting partner went to the firm's largest restaurant one night at closing time. Dividing all the employees—cooks, dishwashers, waitstaff, bus people, receptionists—into groups of five or six, he asked them to come to an agreement about the answer to a question: "Of every sales dollar that comes into this restaurant, how many cents do you think fall to the bottom line—money that can be returned to investors as profit or reinvested in the business?"

The least amount any group guessed was 40 cents. Several groups guessed 70 cents. In a restaurant, the reality is that if you can keep 5 cents on the dollar, you get excited—10 cents, and you're ecstatic! Can you imagine the attitude among employees toward such things as food costs, labor costs, and breakage when they thought their company was a money machine? After sharing that the restaurant made only a 5 percent profit margin, the president was impressed when the chef said, "That means we make only $1 profit on a $20 steak! So if I burn a steak that costs the restaurant $6, we have to sell six steaks at no net profit to make up for my mistake." He already had things figured out.

> *If you keep your people well informed and let them use their brains, you'll be amazed at how they can help manage costs.*

This is particularly important in uncertain times. If you develop committed and empowered people, not only will they help manage costs, but they'll also increase your revenues. How? By creating raving fan customers who will want to brag about you. These customers become part of your unofficial sales force or PR department, which increases your sales or visibility or both and makes your organization more attractive as an investment. Now you are a leader of a high performing organization.

Corporate Citizen of Choice

In an increasingly connected world of rising populations and shrinking resources, there's a growing consensus that organizations have responsibilities beyond making money. Businesses are expected to balance the needs of their stakeholders with the environment and to treat those affected by their activities ethically and respectfully.

The 100 Best Corporate Citizens list, published by *Corporate Responsibility* magazine, ranks companies based on publicly available information in seven categories: environment, climate change, employee relations, human rights, governance, finance, and philanthropy.

High performing organizations today must be good corporate citizens. Whether it's protecting the planet, contributing to charities, championing human rights, maintaining an ethical supply chain, or participating in public awareness campaigns, social responsibility is no longer optional for organizations striving for excellence.

A High Performing Organization Scores Every Time

Employer of choice, provider of choice, investment of choice, and corporate citizen of choice—the four elements of the quadruple bottom line—form the right target. If you aim for only one of the four elements, you won't hit the target, and your organization won't be able to sustain high performance. Once leaders understand the importance of the target, questions naturally arise, such as "What is a high performing organization?" and "What does a high performing organization that hits the target look like?"

To answer these questions, Don Carew, Fay Kandarian, Eunice Parisi-Carew, and Jesse Stoner conducted an extensive research project to define and identify the characteristics of a high performing organization.[4] Their first step was to define a "high performing organization." While many organizations rise quickly and then plateau or topple, some continue to thrive, somehow reinventing themselves as needed. The researchers focused on these kinds of organizations, creating the following definition:

High performing organizations are enterprises that over time continue to produce outstanding results with the highest level of human satisfaction and commitment to success.

Because of their flexibility, nimbleness, and responsive systems, high performing organizations (HPOs) not only remain successful and respected today but also are poised to succeed in the future. HPOs demonstrate results consistently over time.

The HPO SCORES® Model

As a result of their research, Drs. Carew, Kandarian, Parisi-Carew, and Stoner created the HPO SCORES® model. SCORES is an acronym that represents the six elements evident in every high performing organization. (Refer to Figure 1.1, later in this chapter.) A high performing organization scores—hits the target consistently—because it demonstrates strength in each of the six elements, which are described below.

S = *Shared Information and Open Communication*

In high performing organizations, information needed to make informed decisions is readily available to people and is openly communicated. Sharing information and facilitating open communication builds trust and encourages people to act like owners of the organization. Encouraging dialogue lessens the danger of territoriality and keeps the organization healthy, agile, flexible, and fluid.

C = *Compelling Vision*

A compelling vision is the hallmark of a high performing organization. When everyone supports such an organizational vision—including purpose, a picture of the future, and values—it creates a deliberate, highly focused culture that drives the desired business results toward a greater good. In these organizations, people are energized by, excited about, and dedicated to such a vision. They have a noble sense of purpose that creates and focuses energy. Their personal values are aligned with the values of the organization. They can describe a clear picture of what they intend to create. Everyone is aligned and going in the same direction.

O = *Ongoing Learning*

High performing organizations are constantly focusing on improving their capabilities through learning systems, building knowledge capital, and transferring learning throughout the organization.

Organizational learning is different from individual learning. High performing organizations engage in both. Everyone is always striving to get better, both individually and as an organization.

R = Relentless Focus on Customer Results

No matter what industry they are in, high performing organizations understand who their customers are—both internally and externally—and measure their results accordingly. They produce outstanding results, in part because of an almost obsessive focus on results. However, what is unique is the way in which they focus on those results: from the customer's viewpoint.

E = Energizing Systems and Structures

The systems, structures, processes, and practices in high performing organizations are aligned to support the organization's vision, strategic direction, and goals. This makes it easier for people to get their jobs done. Energizing systems and structures provide the platform for rapid response to obstacles and opportunities. The bottom-line test of whether the systems and structures are energizing is to look at whether they help people accomplish their jobs more easily or make them more difficult.

S = Shared Power and High Involvement

In high performing organizations, power and decision making are shared and distributed throughout the organization, not guarded at the top of the hierarchy. Participation, collaboration, and teamwork are a way of life. When people feel valued and respected for their contributions, are allowed to make decisions that impact their lives, and have access to information to make good decisions, they *can* and *will* function as valuable contributors to the organization's purpose and vision. In high performing organizations, a sense of personal and collective power exists.

The HPO SCORES® Model

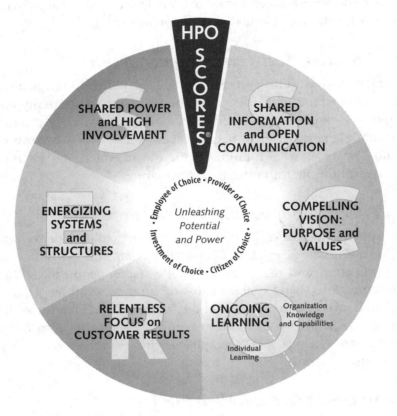

Figure 1.1 The HPO SCORES® Model

Leadership Is the Engine

If becoming a high performing organization is the destination, leadership is the engine. While the HPO SCORES® model describes the characteristics of a high performing organization, leadership is what moves the organization in that direction.

In high performing organizations, the role of formal leadership is radically different from traditional organizations. High performing organizations rely not on cultivating a great, charismatic leader, but on building a visionary organization that endures beyond the leader. The role of leadership shifts from privileged status and power for its own sake toward a more complex, participative, long-term process. As this book will continually emphasize, once leaders establish the vision, they assume the attitude and behavior of a servant leader.

In high performing organizations, leadership practices support collaboration and involvement. Leadership is assumed at every level of the organization. Top leaders live the organization's values. They embody and encourage a spirit of inquiry and discovery. They help others think systematically. They act as teachers *and* lifelong learners. They are visible in their leadership and have the strength to stand firm on strategic business decisions and values. They keep everyone's energy focused on the bull's-eye of excellence.

In high performing organizations, leadership is not the province of formal leaders or a few peak performers alone; leadership emerges everywhere. Individuals with expertise come forward as needed throughout the organization.

The HPO SCORES® Quiz: How Does Your Organization Score?

To begin to see how your organization scores, take a few moments to complete the following quiz. It is based on a few of the questions from the HPO SCORES® Profile, an organizational assessment that was developed as part of a research project.[5] We've also included some supplemental questions on leadership.

HPO SCORES® Quiz

On a scale of 1 to 7, to what extent do you disagree or agree with the following statements?

1 = Strongly disagree

2 = Disagree

3 = Slightly disagree

4 = Neutral

5 = Slightly agree

6 = Agree

7 = Strongly agree

Shared Information and Open Communication

___ 1. People have easy access to the information they need to do their job effectively.

___ 2. Plans and decisions are communicated so that they are clearly understood.

Compelling Vision: Purpose and Values

___ 1. Leadership is aligned around a shared vision and values.

___ 2. People have passion around a shared purpose and values.

Ongoing Learning

___ 1. People are actively supported in the development of new skills and competencies.

___ 2. Your organization continually incorporates new learning into standard ways of doing business.

Relentless Focus on Customer Results

___ 1. Everyone maintains the highest standards of quality and service.

___ 2. All work processes are designed to make it easier for your customers to do business with you.

Energizing Systems and Structures

___ 1. Systems, structures, and formal and informal practices are integrated and aligned.

___ 2. Systems, structures, and formal and informal practices make it easy for people to get their jobs done.

Shared Power and High Involvement

___ 1. People have an opportunity to influence decisions that affect them.

___ 2. Teams are used as a vehicle for accomplishing work and influencing decisions.

Leadership[6]

___ 1. Leaders think that leading is about serving, not being served.

___ 2. Leaders remove barriers to help people focus on their work and their customers.

How Does Your Organization Score?

It is possible to receive a total of 14 points for each of the elements and for the supplemental questions on leadership.

Add the scores for each element to determine how strong your organization is in that element:

>Score 12 to 14 = High performing

>Score 9 to 11 = Average

>Score 8 or below = Opportunity for improvement

How Should I Use My Quiz Results?

Although this quiz may help you determine if your organization is high performing, the main purpose of the quiz at this point is to guide your reading. While the sections and chapters of this book are sequenced for good reason, they may not be laid out in the order that most matters to you and your organization today. If you scored 8 or below on any element of the HPO SCORES® quiz, you might want to begin by focusing specifically on that area.

While it makes perfect sense to us to focus first on Section I, "Set Your Sights on the Right Target and Vision," it may make more sense for you to start with Section IV, "Have the Right Kind of Leadership." For example, some organizations have a long history of having the right target and vision, but in recent years, some self-serving leaders have risen to the top and have been causing a gap between the espoused vision and values and the vision and values in action. Other organizations have a real sense of the right target and vision, but a culture has emerged that is not treating its customers right. If that sounds familiar to you, you might want to start with Section III, "Treat Your Customers Right."

If you have no particular problem areas, we recommend that you start at the beginning and move through the planned sequence of sections as you learn how to create a high performing organization.

2

The Power of Vision

Jesse Stoner, Ken Blanchard,
and Drea Zigarmi

When leaders who are leading at a higher level understand the role of the quadruple bottom line as the right target—to be the employer of choice, provider of choice, investment of choice, and corporate citizen of choice—they are ready to focus everyone's energy on a compelling vision.

Vision calls an organization to be truly great, not merely to beat the competition and get big numbers. A magnificent vision articulates people's hopes and dreams, touches their hearts and spirits, and helps them see how they can contribute. It aims everyone in the right direction.

The Importance of Vision

Why is vision so important to an organization? Because

Leadership is about going somewhere. If you and your people don't know where you are going, your leadership doesn't matter.

Alice learned this lesson in *Alice in Wonderland* when she was searching for a way out of Wonderland and came to a fork in the road. "Would you tell me, please, which way I ought to go from here?" she asked the Cheshire Cat. "That depends a good deal on where you want to go," the cat responded. Alice replied that she really did not much care. The smiling cat told her in no uncertain terms: "Then it doesn't matter which way you go."

Jesse Stoner conducted an extensive study that demonstrated the powerful impact of vision and leadership on organizational performance.[1] She collected information from the team members of more than 500 leaders. The results were striking. Leaders who demonstrated strong visionary leadership had the highest-performing teams. Leaders with good management skills but without vision had average team performance. Leaders who were identified as weak in vision and management skills had poor-performing teams.

The biggest impediment blocking most managers from being great leaders is the lack of a clear vision for everyone to serve. In fewer than 10 percent of the organizations Jesse visited, members were clear about the vision. This lack of shared vision causes people to become inundated with multiple priorities, duplication of efforts, false starts, and wasted energy—none of which supports the quadruple bottom line.

A vision builds trust, collaboration, interdependence, motivation, and mutual responsibility for success. Vision helps people make smart choices because their decisions are being made with the end result in mind. As goals are accomplished, the answer to "What's next?" becomes clear. Vision allows us to act from a proactive stance, moving toward what we want rather than reactively away from what we don't want. Vision empowers and excites us to reach for what we truly desire. As the late management guru Peter Drucker said, "The best way to predict your future is to create it."

Effective Versus Ineffective Vision Statements

A lot of organizations already have vision statements, but most of them seem irrelevant when you look at the organization and where it's going. The purpose of a vision statement is to create an aligned organization where everyone is working together toward the same desired ends.

The vision provides guidance for daily decisions so that people are aiming at the right target, not working at cross-purposes.

How do you know if your vision statement works? Here's the test: Is it hidden in a forgotten file or framed on a wall solely for decoration? If so, it's not working. Is it actively used to guide everyday decision making? If the answer is yes, your vision statement is working.

Creating a Vision That Really Works

Why don't more leaders have a vision? We believe it's a lack of knowledge. Many leaders—such as former president George H. W. Bush—say they just don't get the "vision thing." They acknowledge that vision is desirable, but they're unsure how to create it. To these leaders, vision seems elusive—something that is magically bestowed only on the fortunate few. Intrigued by the possibility of making vision accessible for all leaders, Jesse Stoner teamed up with Drea Zigarmi to identify the key elements of a compelling vision—one that would inspire people and provide direction. In "From Vision to Reality," Jesse and Drea identified three key elements of a compelling vision:[2]

- **Significant purpose:** What business are you in?

- **A picture of the future:** What will the future look like if you are successful?

- **Clear values:** What guides your behavior and decisions on a daily basis?

A vision must include all three elements to be inspiring and enduring. Let's explore these elements with some real-world examples.

Significant Purpose

The first element of a compelling vision is a significant purpose. This higher purpose is your organization's reason for existence. It answers the question "Why?" rather than just explaining what you do. It clarifies, from your customers' viewpoint, what business you are *really* in.

Walt Disney started his theme parks with a clear purpose. He said, "We're in the happiness business." That is very different from being in the theme park business. Clear purpose drives everything the cast members (employees) do with their guests (customers). Being in the happiness business helps cast members understand their primary role in the company.

A wonderful organization in Orlando, Florida, called Give Kids the World, is an implementation operation for the Make-A-Wish Foundation. Dying children who have always wanted to go to Disney World, SeaWorld, or other attractions in Orlando can get a chance through Give Kids the World. Since 1986, the organization has brought more than 160,000 children and families to Orlando for a week at no cost to them. The organization thinks having a sick child is a family issue; therefore, the whole family goes to Orlando. When you ask the employees what business they are in, they tell you they're in the memory business—they want to create memories for these kids and their families.

On a visit to Give Kids the World, one of our colleagues passed a man who was cutting the grass. Curious about how widely understood the organization's mission was, our colleague asked the man, "What business are you in here at Give Kids the World?"

The man smiled and said, "We make memories."

"How do *you* make memories?" our associate asked. "You just cut the grass."

The man said, "I certainly don't make memories by continuing to cut the grass if a family comes by. You can always tell who the sick kid is, so I ask that youngster whether he or she or a brother or sister wants to help me with my chores."

Isn't that a wonderful attitude? It keeps him focused on serving the folks who come to Give Kids the World.

Great organizations have a deep and noble sense of purpose—a significant purpose— that inspires excitement and commitment.

When work is meaningful and connected to what you truly desire, you can unleash a productive and creative power we never imagined. But purpose alone is not enough because it does not tell you where you're going.

A Picture of the Future

The second element of a compelling vision is a picture of the future. This picture of the end result should not be abstract. It should be a mental image you can actually see. The power of imagery has been described by many sports psychologists, including Charles Garfield in *Peak Performance: Mental Training Techniques of the World's Greatest Athletes*. Numerous studies have demonstrated that not only does mental imagery enhance performance, but it enhances intrinsic motivation as well.[3]

Walt Disney's picture of the future was expressed in the charge he gave every cast member: "Keep the same smile on people's faces when they leave the park as when they entered." Disney didn't care whether a guest was in the park two hours or ten hours. He just wanted to keep them smiling. After all, they were in the happiness business. Your picture should focus on the end result, not the process of getting there.

At Give Kids the World, their picture of the future is that in the last week of the lives of youngsters who have been there, they will still be laughing and talking to their families about their time in Orlando.

Some people mistakenly use the Apollo Moon Project as an example of a vision. It is a wonderful example of the power of creating a picture of the future, but it's not an example of a vision. In 1961, when President John F. Kennedy articulated a picture of the future—to place a man on the moon by the end of the 1960s and bring him home safely—the United States had not even invented the technology to accomplish it. To achieve that goal, NASA overcame seemingly insurmountable obstacles, demonstrating the power of articulating a picture of the future. However, once the goal was achieved, NASA never re-created its spectacular achievement because it was not linked to a significant purpose. There was nothing to answer the question "Why?" Was the purpose to "beat the Russians" or to "begin the Space Defense Initiative" or—in the spirit of *Star Trek*—"to boldly go where no one has gone before"? Because there was no clear purpose, there was no way to guide decision making going forward and answer the question "What next?" The second element—a picture of the future—is powerful, but it alone does not create an enduring vision.

Clear Values

The third element of a compelling vision is having clear values. High performing organizations have clear values. Values define leadership and how employees act on a day-to-day basis while doing their work.

Values provide guidelines for how you should proceed as you pursue your purpose and picture of the future. They answer the questions "What do I want to live by?" and "How?" They need to be clearly described so that you know exactly what behaviors demonstrate that the value is being lived. Values need to be consistently acted on, or they are only good intentions. They need to resonate with the personal values of the members of the organization so that people truly choose to live by them.

The values need to support the organization's purpose. Robert Johnson founded Johnson & Johnson for the purpose of alleviating pain and disease. The company's purpose and values, reflected in its credo, continue to guide the company. Using its values to guide its decision making, Johnson & Johnson quickly recalled all Tylenol capsules throughout the United States during a 1982 tampering incident that was localized in the Chicago area. The immediate cost was substantial, but not knowing the extent of the tampering, the company didn't want to risk anyone's safety. In the end, Johnson & Johnson's quadruple bottom line was served, demonstrated by the company's long-term gains in reputation and profitability.

Many organizations that do have values have too many. Research done by Ken Blanchard and Michael O'Connor shows that people can't focus on more than three or four values that really impact behavior.[4] They also found that for some organizations, rank ordering values can be helpful. Why? Because life is about value conflicts. When these conflicts arise, it's helpful for people to know which value they should focus on.

For example, the Disney theme parks have four rank-ordered values: safety, courtesy, the show, and efficiency. Why is safety the highest-ranked value? Walt Disney knew that if guests were carried out of one of his parks on a stretcher, they would not have the same smiles on their faces leaving the park as they had when they entered.

The second-ranked value, courtesy, is all about the friendly attitude you expect at a Disney park. Why is it important to know that it's the number-two value? Suppose one of the Disney cast members is answering a guest question in a friendly, courteous manner, and he hears a scream that's not coming from a roller coaster. If that cast member wants to act according to the park's rank-ordered values, he will excuse himself as quickly and politely as possible and race toward the scream. Why? Because the number-one value just called. If the values were not rank-ordered and the cast member was enjoying the interaction with the guest, he might say, "They're always yelling in the park," and not move in the direction of the scream. Later somebody could come to that cast member and say, "You were the closest to the scream. Why didn't you move?" The response could be, "I was dealing with our courtesy value." In this situation, there was a value conflict, and the cast member couldn't act on two values at the same time.

While having rank-ordered values is helpful in companies like Disney, it's not always necessary. As we discussed in the introduction, in our company we have a both/and philosophy, so we have three people-oriented values and three results-oriented values. In each of those categories, one value is not more important than the other.

Therefore, we decided that all the values need to be considered when making decisions.

For a vision to endure, you need all three elements—a significant purpose, a picture of the future, and clear values—to guide behavior on a day-by-day basis. Martin Luther King, Jr. outlined his vision in his "I Have a Dream" speech. By describing a world where his children "will not be judged by the color of their skin but by the content of their character," he created powerful and specific images arising from the values of brotherhood, respect, and freedom for all—values that resonate with the founding values of the United States. King's vision continues to mobilize and guide people beyond his lifetime because it illuminates a significant purpose, provides a picture of the future, and describes values that resonate with people's hopes and dreams.

A Compelling Vision Creates a Culture of Greatness

A compelling vision creates a strong culture in which the energy of everyone in the organization is aligned. This results in trust, customer satisfaction, an energized and committed workforce, and profitability. Conversely, when an organization does not live up to its stated values, employee and customer trust and commitment erode, negatively impacting all aspects of the bottom line. For example, Ford lost credibility and market share when its stated value—"Quality Is Job One"—was tested by its hesitation to take responsibility in the recall of the defective Firestone tires on its Explorer sport utility vehicle in 2000.[5]

Vision Is the Place to Start

Research clearly demonstrates the extraordinary impact of a shared vision, or core ideology, on long-term financial performance. The cumulative stock returns of the HPOs researched by Collins and Porras were six times greater than the "successful" companies they examined and 15 times greater than the general market over a 50-year period of time![6] For this reason, vision is the place to start if you want to improve your organization's HPO SCORES® and hit the target.

Time and again research shows that an essential characteristic of great leaders is their ability to mobilize people around a shared vision.[7]

If it's not in the service of a shared vision, leadership can become self-serving. Leaders begin to think their people are there to serve them, instead of the customer. Organizations can become self-serving bureaucracies where leaders focus their energies on recognition, power, and status, rather than the organization's larger purpose and goals. The results of this type of behavior are perennially all too evident.

Once the leader has clarified and shared the vision, he can focus on serving and being responsive to the needs of the people, understanding that the role of leadership is to remove barriers and help people operate according to the vision. The greatest leaders mobilize others by coalescing people around a shared vision. Sometimes leaders don't get it at first, but the great ones eventually do.

Louis Gerstner, Jr. is a perfect example. When Gerstner took the helm of IBM in 1993—amidst turmoil and instability as the company's annual net losses reached a record $8 billion—he was quoted as saying, "The last thing IBM needs is a vision." A lot of people asked us what we thought about that statement. Our reply was, "It depends on how he defines vision. If he means a 'pie-in-the-sky' dream, he's absolutely right. The ship is sinking. But if all he's doing is plugging the holes, the ship isn't going anywhere." We were amused to read an article in the *New York Times*[8] two years later. In that article, Gerstner conceded that IBM had lost the war for the desktop operating system, acknowledging that the acquisition of Lotus signified that the company had failed to plan properly for its future. He admitted that he and his management team now "spent a lot of time thinking ahead." Once Gerstner understood the importance of vision, an incredible turnaround occurred. He became clear that the company's source of strength would be in integrated solutions and resisted pressures to split the company. In 1995, delivering the keynote address at the computer industry trade show, Gerstner articulated IBM's new vision—that network computing would drive the next phase of industry growth and would be the company's overarching strategy. That year, IBM began a series of acquisitions that positioned services to become the company's fastest-growing segment, with growth at more than 20 percent per year. This extraordinary turnaround demonstrated that the *most important thing* IBM needed was a vision—a shared vision.

If an organization's vision is compelling, the quadruple bottom line is served. Success goes way beyond mere financial rewards. Vision generates tremendous energy, excitement, and passion because people feel they are making a difference. They know what they are doing and why. There is a strong sense of trust and respect. Managers don't try to control, but rather let others assume responsibility because people know they are part of an aligned whole. People assume responsibility for their own actions. They take charge of their future, rather than passively waiting for it to happen. There is room for creativity and risk taking. People can make their contributions in their own way, and those differences are respected because people know they are in the same boat—all part of a larger whole going "full steam ahead!"

Vision Can Exist Anywhere in an Organization

You don't have to wait for an organizational vision to begin. Vision is the responsibility of every leader at every level of an organization. It's possible for leaders of departments or teams to create shared visions for their departments even when the rest of the organization doesn't have one. Consider our work helping a tax department in a Fortune 500 company. The leader of the department stated:

> "We began to understand our own and each others' hopes and dreams and discovered how close they were. We found ways to work together more effectively and began to enjoy work a lot more. We discovered what business we were really in: 'Providing financial information to help leaders make good business decisions.' As a result, we began to partner more effectively with business leaders. Our department gained more credibility in the company, and other departments began asking us what we had done to make such a turnaround. They became interested in creating a vision for their own department. It was contagious."

Too often, leaders complain that they can't have a vision because the larger organization doesn't have one. Again, it's not necessary to wait. The power of vision will work for you and your team, regardless of your level in the organization.

Make Your Vision a Reality

In their book *Full Steam Ahead! Unleash the Power of Vision in Your Work and Your Life,* Ken Blanchard and Jesse Stoner define vision as "knowing who you are, where you're going, and what will guide your journey."[9] *Knowing who you are* means having a significant purpose. *Where you're going* means having a picture of the future. *What will guide your journey* are clear values. However, vision alone is not enough. For a leader to ensure that the vision becomes a reality—a shared vision that mobilizes people—Ken and Jesse identify three important guidelines that people must follow: How the vision is created, how it's communicated, and how it's lived.

How It's Created

The process of creating the vision is as important as what the vision says. Instead of simply taking the top management to a retreat to put the vision together and then announcing it to others, encourage dialogue about the vision. While the initial responsibility for drafting an organizational vision rests with the top management, the organization needs to put in place mechanisms to give others an opportunity to help shape the vision—to put their thumbprint on it.

For a departmental or team vision, it's possible to craft the vision as a team. Although the leader must have a sense of where he's going, it's important that he trusts and utilizes the knowledge and skills of the people on the team to get the best vision.

Regardless of how you initially draft the vision, it's important that you get input from those it affects before you finalize it. Ask people these questions: "Would you like to work for an organization that has this vision? Can you see where you fit in the vision? Does it help you set priorities? Does it provide guidelines for making decisions?

Is it exciting and motivating? Have we left anything out? Should we delete anything?" Involving people will deepen their understanding and commitment and create a better vision.

How It's Communicated

Creating a vision—for your organization or department, for your work, and for your life—is a journey, not a one-time activity.

In some organizations, a vision statement may be found framed on the wall, but it provides no guidance or, worse, has nothing to do with the reality of how things actually are. This turns people off. Visioning is an ongoing process; you need to keep it alive. It's important to keep talking about the vision and referring to it as much as possible. Max Depree, the legendary former chairman of Herman Miller and author of *Leadership Is an Art*, said that in his visionary role, he had to be like a third-grade teacher. He had to keep on saying the vision over and over and over until people got it right, right, right! The more you focus on your vision, the clearer it will become and the more deeply you will understand it. In fact, aspects of what you thought was the vision may change over time, but its essence will remain.

How It's Lived

The moment you identify your vision, you need to behave as if it were happening right now. Your actions need to be congruent with your vision. As others see you living the vision, they will believe you are serious, and this will help deepen their understanding and commitment. Two strategies will support your efforts to live your vision:

- **Always focus on your vision.** Your vision should be the foundation for your organization. If an obstacle or unforeseen event throws you off-course, you may have to change your short-term goals, but your vision should be long-lasting. Change is bound to happen. Unforeseen events are bound to occur. Find a way to reframe what is happening as a challenge or opportunity on the road to living your vision.

- **Show the courage of commitment.** True commitment begins when you take action. There will be fears; feel them and move ahead. It takes courage to create a vision, and it takes courage to act on it. In the words of Goethe, "Whatever you can do, or dream you can, begin it. Boldness has genius, power, and magic in it."

Vision and Leadership

Vision always comes back to leadership. People look to their formal leaders for vision and direction. While leaders should involve people in shaping direction, the ultimate responsibility for the *visionary/direction* aspect of leadership remains with the leaders and cannot be delegated to others. This is where the traditional hierarchical pyramid is effective (see Figure 2.1).

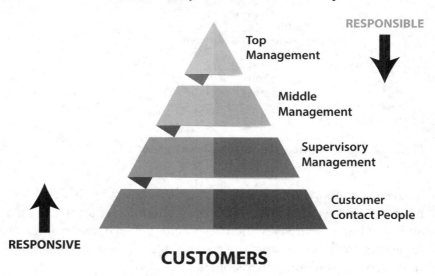

Figure 2.1 The Visionary Role of Leadership

Creating a vision is not an activity that can be checked off a list. It's one of the most critical ongoing roles of a successful leader. It means the difference between high and average performance, whether it's an entire organization, a department, or a team.

Once a vision is agreed upon, the leader's role moves to implementation to ensure that people respond to the vision. Now the traditional hierarchical pyramid turns upside-down as the leader supports people in accomplishing the vision (see Figure 2.2).

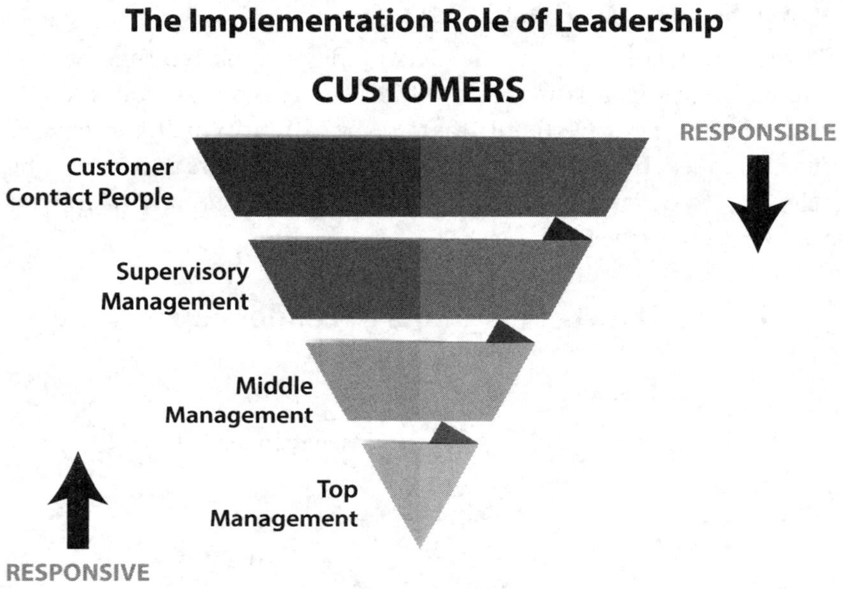

The Implementation Role of Leadership

CUSTOMERS

Customer Contact People

RESPONSIBLE

Supervisory Management

Middle Management

Top Management

RESPONSIVE

Figure 2.2 The Implementation Role of Leadership

The leader supports by removing barriers; by ensuring that policies, practices, and systems make it easier for them to act on the vision; and by holding themselves, their peers, and their people accountable for acting consistently with the vision. This way the leader assures that everyone is serving the vision, not the leader.

In their book *Gung Ho! Turn On the People in Any Organization*, Ken Blanchard and Sheldon Bowles describe the three factors that make a compelling organizational vision come alive.[6]

First, people need to have *worthwhile work*. In many ways, that's what this chapter has been all about. People need a higher purpose and shared values that guide all plans, decisions, and actions. Worthwhile work gets people up in the morning with a spring in their step.

Second, people need to *be in control of achieving the goal*. When people know why they are working and where they're going, they want to bring their brains to work. Being responsible demands people's best and allows them to learn and act like owners.

Third, to continue to generate energy, people need to *cheer each other on*. Of all the things we've taught over the years, we can't overemphasize the power of catching each other doing things right and accentuating the positive.

Being in control of achieving the goals and *cheering each other on* turn our focus to Section II, "Treat Your People Right." In this section, we will explore both aspects of leadership: the visionary/direction role—with an emphasis on goal setting—and the implementation role—with an emphasis on goal accomplishment.

Companion Online Resource

Visit www.LeadingAtAHigherLevel.com to access the free virtual conference titled *Set Your Sights on the Right Target and Vision*. Use the password "Target" for your FREE access.

SECTION II

Treat Your People Right

Chapter 3   Empowerment Is the Key 35

Chapter 4   SLII®: The Integrating Concept..................... 53

Chapter 5   Self Leadership: The Power Behind
Empowerment... 69

Chapter 6   One-on-One Leadership 81

Chapter 7   Essential Skills for One-on-One
Leadership 103

Chapter 8   Building Trust.. 119

Chapter 9   Coaching: A Key Competency for
Leadership Development 131

Chapter 10   Mentoring: The Key to Life Planning........... 145

Chapter 11   Team Leadership 155

Chapter 12 Collaboration: Fuel for High
Performance 179

Chapter 13 Organizational Leadership 191

Chapter 14 Organizational Change: Why
People Resist It 209

Chapter 15 Leading People Through Change 225

Chapter 16 Managing a Successful Cultural
Transformation 249

3

Empowerment Is the Key

Alan Randolph and Ken Blanchard

How do the best-run companies in the world beat the competition day in and day out? They have a workforce that is excited about their vision and motivated to serve customers at a higher level. So how do you create this motivated workforce? The key is *empowerment.*

Empowerment means letting people bring their brains to work and allowing them to use their knowledge, experience, and motivation to create a healthy quadruple bottom line. Leaders of the best-run companies know that empowering people creates positive results that are just not possible when all the authority moves up the hierarchy and managers shoulder all the responsibility for success.

> *People already have power through their knowledge and motivation. The key to empowerment is letting this power out.*

Ideally, people's power will be focused not only on organizational outcomes—such as outstanding customer service and financial goals—but on the greater good.

We believe organizations work best when they can depend on individual contributors who take the initiative to go beyond problem spotting to problem solving. Yet because most of us have experienced only hierarchical organizations, we all have much to learn about moving to a culture of empowerment.

What Is Empowerment?

Empowerment is the process of unleashing the power in people—their knowledge, experience, and motivation—and focusing that power to achieve positive outcomes for the organization. Creating a culture of empowerment consists of only a few key steps, yet because they challenge most people's assumptions, these steps are often difficult for managers and direct reports alike.

> *Empowerment requires a major shift*
> *in attitude. The most crucial place*
> *that this shift must occur is in the heart*
> *of every leader.*

For empowerment to succeed, leaders must take a leap of faith and fight the battle against habit and tradition. For example, most managers continue to define empowerment as "giving people the power to make decisions." Perhaps this misguided definition explains why so many companies have difficulty engaging the minds and hearts of their people. Defining empowerment as "the manager giving power to the people" still regards the manager as controller and misses the essential point: namely, that *people already possess a great deal of power*—power that resides in their knowledge, experience, and internal motivation. We prefer the following definition:

> *Empowerment is the creation of an*
> *organizational climate that releases the*
> *knowledge, experience, and motivation*
> *that reside in people.*

Unfortunately, this is easier said than done. Other players can block this release of power, and a strong force of past history often inhibits the shift to empowerment.

Direct reports, too, misunderstand empowerment. Many of them feel that if they are empowered, they will be given free rein to do as they please and make all the key decisions about their jobs. Direct reports often fail to grasp that the price of freedom is sharing risks and responsibilities. This is particularly true in a post-Sarbanes-Oxley environment of accounting oversight and corporate responsibility.[1] Indeed, an empowerment culture requires much greater accountability from direct reports than a hierarchical culture does. Yet it is precisely this frightening increase in responsibility that engages people and gives them a sense of fulfillment. The opportunities and risks of empowerment invigorate direct reports and managers alike.

The Power of Empowerment

Does empowerment work in the real world? You bet it does! Several researchers have found that when people are empowered, their organizations benefit overall. For example, Edward Lawler found that when people are given more control and responsibility, their companies achieve a greater return on sales (10.3 percent) than companies that do not involve their people (6.3 percent).[2] Trader Joe's is a niche retailer in the food industry well known for pushing decision making to the store level. Over an eight-year period its annual sales growth increased from 15 percent to 26 percent, sales per store increased 10 percent per year, and the number of stores increased by almost 100 percent. In addition, overall sales volume increased more than 500 percent. While other factors contributed to these increased sales, empowered employees were deemed a major element of Trader Joe's success.[3]

Not only is there clear evidence of a positive relationship between empowerment and performance, but scholars such as Thomas Malone believe that empowerment is essential for companies that hope to succeed in the new knowledge-based economy.[4]

How History Blocks Change to Empowerment

Most people have a history of working under external guidance and control. The following questions are all too familiar to us:

At school: "What does the teacher want me to do to get good grades?"

At work: "What does my boss want me to do?"

Having spent our lives in a framework of hierarchical thinking, we are far less accustomed to dealing with questions like these:

At school:	"What do I want to learn from this class?"
	"How will I know I have learned something I can use?"
At work:	"What do I need to do to help my company succeed?"

These are the kinds of questions that arise—and require answers—when an organizational culture begins to support empowerment. President Kennedy made a call for these kinds of questions when he challenged Americans: "Ask not what your country can do for you; ask what you can do for your country."[5]

Many of us possess hard-earned parenting, teaching, and managing skills that fulfill role expectations based on an assumption of hierarchical responsibility. Indeed, we feel it is our responsibility as parents, teachers, or managers to tell people what to do, how to do it, and why it needs to be done. We feel it would be avoiding our responsibility to ask children, students, or direct reports such questions as these:

"What do you think needs to be done, and why is it important?"

"What do you think your goals should be?"

"How do you think you should go about achieving your goals?"

Because managers know they will still be held accountable for outcomes, many are reluctant to relinquish control to direct reports. This reluctance points to one of the main sources of resistance to empowerment: managers who feel their control is threatened by empowerment. Ironically, it is through the development of self-directed individuals and teams as a replacement for the hierarchy that managers can most easily assume their new and more empowering roles as coaches, mentors, and team leaders.

Tapping People's Power and Potential: A Real-World Example

While there is a learning curve from a hierarchical to an empowerment culture, the benefits can be well worth the effort, as the following case study shows.

A management team of a large organization was struggling with a severe traffic problem on the road leading to its location. The road crossed four miles of protected wetlands, so it could not be widened without significantly impacting the environment. Each morning, the traffic leading to the site was backing up the entire four-mile length of the road, adding an hour to commuting time. The resulting delay and aggravation caused a significant drop in productivity.

Three years earlier, the management team had hired traffic consultants to solve the problem. Their work focused on a future widening of the road and looked promising, but their attempts to devise short-term solutions failed miserably. As a last resort, management decided to assemble a team of engineers, clerical personnel, line workers, and union representatives to address short-term solutions. This team met twice a week for a month. At the end of that time, the team provided a series of practical recommendations.

The simplicity of the team's recommendations surprised management. For example, the team suggested that trucks be prohibited from making deliveries to the site between the hours of 6 a.m. and 9 a.m. Since there were many deliveries to the site at this time, this recommendation immediately removed some of the slowest, most cumbersome traffic clogging the road. Other recommendations also contributed to easing the problem. The result was almost instantaneous improvement in the traffic flow.

At the outset, management had doubted that this team could solve the problem. After all, experts had been studying the dilemma for three years. Yet in turning to their own people, they tapped into a hidden reservoir of knowledge, experience, and motivation—and found a solution.

Learning the Language of Empowerment

Moving to an empowerment culture requires learning a new language. To understand the differences between the command-and-control structure and the culture of empowerment, consider the following words and phrases:

Hierarchical Culture	Empowerment Culture
Planning	Visioning
Command and control	Partnering for performance
Monitoring	Self-monitoring
Individual responsiveness	Team responsibility
Pyramid structures	Cross-functional structures
Workflow processes	Projects
Managers	Coaches/team leaders
Employees	Team members
Participative management	Self-directed teams
Do as you are told	Own your own job
Compliance	Good judgment

As you compare the words in the two lists, the differences in attitude, expectations, and associated behaviors become clear. For example, *planning* suggests a step-by-step, controlled process, while *visioning* suggests a more holistic and inclusive approach. *Command and control* suggests that the manager tells us what to think and do, while *partnering for performance* suggests that how we achieve the vision is left open for discussion and input by everyone involved. *Monitoring* suggests that someone—usually the manager—should check on each individual's performance and provide performance evaluations and feedback, while *self-monitoring* suggests that everyone possesses requisite goal clarity and measurement skills, as well as access to relevant data. Thus armed, they can check their own performance and make the behavior adjustments they need to stay on goal. *Do as you are told* exemplifies the external commitment attitude. Once you are told what to do, you can do it, but please don't use your intellect or judgment, and don't be too concerned about results—that's the manager's job. On the other hand, *own your own job* exemplifies the internal commitment attitude: You care about results and use your own intellect and judgment to decide how to achieve individual, team, and company success.

This final example may best clarify the key distinction between a culture of empowerment and a hierarchical culture. In the latter, individuals do what they are told—to a fault. Even when they know a task is not being done in the best way, or that it may be altogether the wrong task, they may continue to do it in a spirit of malicious compliance. Why? Because that is what they are rewarded for and what they are expected to do under hierarchical management.

In a culture of empowerment, individuals respond differently. They take the risk of challenging tasks and procedures that they feel are not in the best interest of the organization. They are driven by a sense of pride in their jobs and a feeling of ownership of the results. People think about what makes sense in the situation and act in ways that both serve the customer and achieve the organization's goals.

The Three Keys to Empowerment

The journey to empowerment needs strong leadership to support this change. In their book *Empowerment Takes More Than a Minute*, Ken Blanchard, John Carlos, and Alan Randolph contend that leaders must use three keys to guide the transition to a culture of empowerment: sharing information, declaring the boundaries, and replacing the old hierarchy with self-directed individuals and teams.[6]

The First Key to Empowerment: Share Information with Everyone

One of the best ways to build a sense of trust and responsibility in people is by sharing information. Giving team members the information they need enables them to make good business decisions. Sharing information sometimes means disclosing information that is

---

considered privileged, including sensitive and important topics such as future business plans and strategies, financial data, and industry issues or problem areas. Providing people with more complete information communicates trust and a sense of "we're in this together." It helps people think more broadly about the organization and the interrelationships of various groups, resources, and goals. By having access to information that helps them understand the big picture, people can better appreciate how their contribution fits in and how their behavior impacts other aspects of the organization. All of this leads to responsible, goal-related use of people's knowledge, experience, and motivation. While this runs counter to hierarchical management, it is based on the following premise:

> *People without accurate information cannot act responsibly; people with accurate information feel compelled to act responsibly.*

In an example close to home, The Ken Blanchard Companies®, like many businesses, was negatively impacted by the events of September 11, 2001. In fact, the company lost $1.5 million that month. To have any chance of ending the fiscal year in the black, the company would have to cut about $350,000 a month in expenses.

The leadership team had some tough decisions to make. One of the leaders suggested that the staffing level be cut by at least 10 percent to stem the losses and help get the company back in the black—a typical response in most companies.

As with any major decision, members of the leadership team checked the decision to cut staff against the rank-ordered organizational values at that time of ethical behavior, relationships, success, and learning. Was the decision to let people go at such a difficult time ethical? To many, the answer was no. There was a general feeling that because the staff had made the company what it was, putting people out on the street at a time like this just was not the right thing to do. Did the decision to let people go honor the high value that the organization placed on relationships? No, it did not. But what could be done? The company could not go on bleeding money and be successful.

Knowing that "no one of us is as smart as all of us," the leadership team decided to draw on the knowledge and talents of the entire staff. At an all-company meeting, the books were opened to show everyone how much the company was bleeding, and from where. This open-book policy unleashed a torrent of ideas and commitment. Small task forces were organized to look for ways to increase revenues and cut costs. This participation resulted in departments throughout the company finding all kinds of ways to minimize spending and maximize income. As the company's Chief Spiritual Officer, Ken Blanchard cheered people on by announcing they would all go to Hawaii together when the company got through the crisis. People smiled politely, although many had their doubts.

Over the next two years, the finances gradually turned around. By 2004, the company produced the highest sales in its history, exceeding its annual goal. In March 2005, the entire company—350 people strong—flew to Maui for a four-day celebration.

When important information is shared with people, they soon act like owners. They begin to solve problems creatively, which makes celebrating the wins even more special. On the other hand, leaders who are unwilling to share information will never have their people as partners in running a successful, empowered organization.

Sharing Information Builds Trust

Another powerful benefit of information sharing is raising the level of trust in the organization. Bureaucratic organizations typically are close to bankruptcy in terms of trust—direct reports do not trust managers, and managers do not trust direct reports. As a result, people exert enormous energy trying to protect themselves from each other. It's important to share information, even if the news is bad. If no decisions have been made, share information about what is being discussed. By sharing information about market share, true costs, potential layoffs, and real company performance—in other words, opening the books for everyone to see—management begins to let people know they are trusted, and people return that trust to managers.

One top-level manager told us he was initially scared to share such sensitive information, but when he took the risk, people responded with a more mature understanding and a sense of appreciation for being included. "It created such a sense of ownership," the manager commented, "far more than I could have imagined. People began to come forward with ideas to save money by changing their jobs and by reorganizing departments—ideas that previously had been met with great fear when proposed by management."

Sharing Information Promotes Organizational Learning

One of the most powerful ways to share information is through organizational learning, one of the key elements of high performing organizations.[7] What we're talking about here goes beyond merely acquiring information; it means actually learning from that information and applying that knowledge to new situations.

High performing organizations *seek knowledge* by constantly scanning the environment, checking the pulse of their customers, tracking their competition, surveying the marketplace, and following global events. They collect data continuously and use it to make corrections and develop new approaches. High performing organizations also seek knowledge about internal performance. They treat mistakes and failures as important data, recognizing that they often can lead to breakthroughs. This is why Hewlett-Packard's "H-P Way" includes the statement "We reserve the right to make mistakes."[8]

High performing organizations *transfer knowledge* by encouraging dialogue, questioning, and discussion. This runs counter to traditional organizations, where people hoard information to protect themselves and establish a power base. High performing organizations make information easy to access. They know that when data is unavailable or not easily retrieved, people have a harder time learning and lose opportunities. They create structures such as cross-functional teams that teach people how to transfer the knowledge they've gained because they know that knowledge sharing is critical to success.

New-car developers at Ford Motor Company learned this the hard way when they set out to understand why the original Taurus design team was so successful. Unfortunately, no one could tell them. No one remembered or had recorded what made that effort so special. The knowledge gained in the Taurus project was lost forever.[9]

High performing organizations continually look for ways to *incorporate knowledge into new ways of doing business.* When you don't recognize or share knowledge, you can't apply it directly to work. In the words of Michael Brown, former chief financial officer of Microsoft:[10]

The only way to compete today is to make your intellectual capital obsolete before anyone else does.

The Second Key to Empowerment: Create Autonomy Through Boundaries

In a hierarchical culture, boundaries are really like barbed-wire fences. They are designed to control people by keeping them in certain places and out of other places. In an empowered culture, boundaries are more like rubber bands that can expand to allow people to take on more responsibility as they grow and develop.

Unlike the restrictive boundaries of a hierarchical culture, boundaries in an empowerment culture tell people where they *can* be autonomous and responsible, rather than telling them what they *can't* do. Boundaries are based on people's skill level. For example, people who lack the skills to set budgets are given a boundary—a spending limit—before they are given more responsibility. In an empowerment culture, they also are given the training and skill development needed to enable greater autonomy. One of the most paradoxical aspects of creating a culture of empowerment is that managers must start by creating *more* rather than *less* structure.

*Like the lines on a tennis court,
the boundaries in an empowerment
culture help people keep score and
improve their game.*

A good example of boundary setting came up recently for a supervisor we know who was frustrated by the amount of time he spent performing tasks that, although important from an administrative viewpoint, did not maximize his talents and skills. One of his most frustrating tasks was ordering small tools and materials for the team each time a team member came to him with a request. In a spirit of empowerment, he taught them how to place the orders themselves and allowed them to submit small orders directly without his approval. Initially, he placed a boundary on the purchases—a cost limit of $100—but he later widened the boundary as the team's (and his) comfort level grew. Because they had the authority to order needed supplies without the delay of their supervisor's approval, the team members felt great. The cost of supplies decreased by 20 percent as people took more care in ordering only those materials they really needed.

Boundaries help people clarify the big picture as well as the little picture. As we saw in Chapter 2, "The Power of Vision," organizations need to **create a compelling vision** that motivates and guides people.

*The organizational vision is the big picture.
Boundaries help people see how their piece
of the puzzle fits into that picture.*

Declaring the boundaries translates the big picture into specific actions. It allows people to **set goals** that help the organization achieve that big picture. These goals are viewed not as ends, but rather as collaboratively set milestones of progress.

Declaring boundaries also requires that managers **clarify the new decision-making rules.** At first, team members may think that empowerment means, "We get to make all the decisions." Two reactions often follow. One is that team members are disappointed when managers continue to make strategic decisions and leave only the operational decisions to them. The other is that team members feel the urge to back off from decisions when they realize they will be held accountable for all the decisions they make—both the good and the bad.

Empowerment means that people have the freedom to act. It also means that they are accountable for results.

In a culture of empowerment, managers continue to make strategic decisions. Team members get involved in making operational decisions as they become more comfortable assuming the inherent risks. As people gradually begin to assume responsibility for decisions and their consequences, managers must gradually pull back on their involvement in decision making. The new decision-making guidelines allow managers and team members to operate freely within their newly defined roles.

Declaring boundaries also calls managers to **create new performance appraisal processes.** The performance appraisal process found in most companies is almost inevitably disempowering in nature and must be restructured. Focus must shift away from the *appraisal* of the team member by the manager and toward *collaboration* between the team member and the manager. As a manager once told us, "The best person to assess an employee's performance and improvement is the employee himself or herself." Of course, this cultural shift is not easy. In Chapter 7, "Essential Skills for One-on-One Leadership," we'll discuss this transition to a new performance appraisal process in considerable detail.

As we stated earlier, declaring the boundaries requires that leaders **provide heavy doses of training.** To master the new skills of empowerment—negotiation of performance plans, decision making, conflict resolution, leadership, budgeting, and technical expertise—people need regular training. Without this continuous learning, people cannot function in an evolving culture of empowerment. They have to unlearn bureaucratic habits and learn the new skills and attitudes needed in an empowered world. Ongoing learning is an integral part of a high performing organization, not an extra perk or necessary evil.

Moving from a hierarchical culture to a culture of empowerment should be a gradual process. People cannot handle too many changes at once, or large changes in one dose. We will discuss these issues further in Chapter 15, "Leading People Through Change."

The Third Key to Empowerment: Replace the Old Hierarchy with Self-Directed Individuals and Teams

As people learn to create autonomy by using newly shared information and boundaries, they must move away from dependence on the hierarchy. But what will replace the clarity and support of the hierarchy? The answer is self-directed individuals and teams—highly skilled, interactive groups with strong self-managing skills.[11] Continual downsizing, which reduces the number of management layers and increases the spans of control for managers, is forcing companies to empower individuals and teams today. The result has been a decision-making void that must be filled if companies are to be successful.

> *The perceived division between superior and subordinate is no longer very useful in business organizations. In fact, it works directly counter to success. Success today depends on individual and team effort.*

Does success today really depend on empowered individuals and teams? Our work with organizations suggests that the answer to this question is a resounding yes. Here are two examples.

The Power of Self-Directed Individuals

The leaders of Yum! Brands—one of the world's largest restaurant companies, with more than 45,000 restaurants in more than

135 nations—understand the power of self-directed individuals.[12] A significant part of training at Yum! focuses on empowering people to take care of customer problems. If a waitperson has a customer with a problem, the team member is encouraged to solve it immediately rather than talk to the manager. In fact, team members can decide how to take care of customers. That makes it a little crazier, but that's how Yum! likes it.

When Ken Blanchard spoke at a meeting of KFC (one of the companies that Yum! owns) a number of years ago, he told the story of how Ritz-Carlton gave its frontline people a $2,000 discretionary fund to solve customer problems without checking with anyone. Yum!'s chairman and CEO at that time, David Novak, loved the idea of giving people discretionary funds. He later told us, "Our customer mania program now includes empowering team members to solve customer complaints right on the spot. They used to have to get the restaurant general manager to deal with problems. Now they can use up to $10 to respond to a customer issue.

"Some people in our organization said, 'Hey, if we let our team members do that, we'll end up going broke, because we'll be giving away all our profits.' And yet we have the highest margin we've ever had in the company since we launched customer mania. So people aren't out there ripping us off. The half or 1 percent who were doing it before are probably still doing it. But this policy has had an impact on team members. They feel respected and empowered; consequently, our customers see us as much more responsive."

A $10 discretionary fund in a quick-service restaurant is a lot of money. In Ritz-Carlton, which is a much higher-end operation, $2,000 is a lot of money. The point is, a discretionary fund becomes a competitive advantage when individuals who are closest to the customer are empowered to solve problems.

The Power of Self-Directed Teams

The case of the Allied Signal fibers plant in Moncure, North Carolina, illustrates the power of self-directed teams. The shift leaders (formerly called forepersons) were frustrated, angry, and confused about their role. The plant had recently restructured its manufacturing operations to work group teams. The shift leaders were told to back off and let the teams move toward self-management. Not only were the shift leaders frustrated, but morale among team members was low. There was a decrease in production and an increase in cost per pound of products. Was the solution to go back to the old way of working? Some people wondered why not. The Moncure fibers plant had a history of excellent labor/management relationships. But leadership saw an opportunity for the organization to move to a higher level if they could figure out how to do it right.

One shift leader, Barney, and two master facilitators, Dawn and Gloria, attended a program on building high performing teams facilitated by one of the HPO SCORES® researchers, Don Carew. Excited and enthusiastic, Dawn and Gloria returned to Moncure and convinced the plant leaders to implement team skills and team leadership training throughout the plant.

Don worked with the shift leaders and master facilitators to develop a one-day classroom training program to be given to each product team by their respective shift leader. The 24 shift leaders were trained to deliver this program. Over the next two years they provided the one-day initial training program to all 59 of the plant's teams. The formerly disillusioned shift leaders now had a whole new sense of purpose and a whole new set of skills. Their role had become clear: to focus on developing people and teams, both in a classroom setting and on the shop floor. The atmosphere in the plant changed from frustration to enthusiasm. Furthermore, productivity increased by 5 percent, and costs decreased by 6 percent.[13]

Dealing with the Leadership Vacuum

As they move toward empowerment, both managers and team members go through a stage of disillusionment and demotivation. During this time, team members often feel they lack competence, and managers are often just as lost as their people about what to do next. Even the top-level managers who initiated the empowerment process are often unclear about what to do. We call this phenomenon the *leadership vacuum.* Remember that both managers and team members are emerging from the grip of bureaucratic, hierarchical practices and assumptions. Both have been accustomed to operating in a hierarchy where managers make decisions and team members implement them. They have a lot to learn, and this learning is often fraught with periods of frustration.

Once people admit this lack of management knowledge, a dramatic transformation occurs. When managers begin to admit their confusion—but continue to hold on to a clear vision of empowerment and keep communication open and information flowing—things begin to change. Small flashes of empowerment begin to appear among individual performers and teams. One person might offer a suggestion to which others gravitate; then other ideas are expressed. Almost before anyone realizes what is happening, leadership emerges from an unexpected source—team members. Over time, the glimmerings of empowerment become more frequent. The very leadership vacuum that has been so uncomfortable has drawn out team member talent and applied it to organizational problems. In the end, the leadership vacuum enhances the empowerment of people and organizations.

The journey to empowerment requires managers and direct reports alike to challenge some of their most basic assumptions about how organizations should operate. Simply announcing the destination is insufficient. People at all levels of the organization must master new skills and learn to trust self-directed individuals and teams as decision-making entities. We discuss in detail the development of self-directed individuals in Chapter 5, "Self Leadership: The Power Behind Empowerment," and Chapter 7. Chapter 11, "Team Leadership," discusses the development of high performing teams. But first let's turn to Chapter 4, "SLII®: The Integrating Concept," which explores the leader's role in empowering people.

4

SLII®: The Integrating Concept

The Founding Associates:

Ken Blanchard, Margie Blanchard,
Don Carew, Eunice Parisi-Carew, Fred Finch,
Laurence Hawkins, Drea Zigarmi, and Pat Zigarmi

Empowerment is the key to treating people the right way and motivating them to treat your customers right. Therefore, having a strategy to shift the emphasis from leader as boss and evaluator to leader as partner and cheerleader is imperative. But what, exactly, is the right strategy or leadership style?

For a long time, people thought there were only two leadership styles—autocratic and democratic. In fact, people used to shout at each other from these two extremes, insisting that one style was better than the other. Democratic managers were accused of being too soft and easy, while their autocratic counterparts were often called too tough and domineering.

We believe that managers who restrict themselves to either extreme are bound to be ineffective "half managers." Whole managers are flexible and can adapt their leadership style to the situation. This strategy is the essence of Situational Leadership®*, a leadership model originally created by Paul Hersey and Ken Blanchard at Ohio University in 1968. This leadership model gained prominence in 1969 in the authors' classic text, *Management of Organizational Behavior*, now in its tenth edition.

---

*Situational Leadership® is a registered trademark of Leadership Studies, Inc., dba The Center for Leadership Studies.

In the early 1980s Ken Blanchard and the founding associates of The Ken Blanchard Companies—Margie Blanchard, Don Carew, Eunice Parisi-Carew, Fred Finch, Drea Zigarmi, and Patricia Zigarmi—created a revised model, calling it SLII®. This model has endured as an effective approach to managing and motivating people.[1] It opens communication and fosters a partnership between the leader and the people the leader supports and depends on. SLII® can be summed up by a familiar phrase:

Different strokes for different folks.

SLII® is based on the beliefs that *people can and want to develop,* and *there is no best leadership style* to encourage that development. You should tailor leadership style to the situation.

The Three Skills of an SLII® Leader

To become effective in using SLII®, you must master three skills: *goal setting*, *diagnosis*, and *matching.* None of these skills is particularly difficult; each simply requires practice.

Goal Setting: The First Skill

The first skill of an SLII® leader is *goal setting.* This means aligning on what needs to be done, and when. All good performance starts with clear goals. Clarifying goals involves making sure that people understand two things: first, what they are being asked to do—their areas of accountability—and second, what good performance looks like—the performance standards by which they will be evaluated.

Diagnosis: The Second Skill

To be an effective SLII® leader, you must diagnose the development level of your direct reports on each of their goals or tasks. But how, exactly, do you accomplish that? The key is to look at two factors— competence and commitment.

Competence is the sum of knowledge and skills that an individual brings to a goal or task. The best way to determine competence is to look at a person's performance. How well can your direct reports plan, organize, problem-solve, and communicate about doing a particular task? Can they accomplish the stated goal accurately and on time? Competence can be gained through formal education, on-the-job training, and experience, and it can be developed over time with appropriate direction and support.

The second factor to look for when diagnosing development level is *commitment:* a person's motivation and confidence about a goal or task. How interested and enthusiastic are your direct reports about doing a particular job? Are they self-assured? Do they trust their own ability to do the goal or task? If their motivation and confidence are high, your direct reports are committed.

It is important to remember two things:

First, there are different combinations of competence and commitment. To be precise, four combinations of competence and commitment make up what we call the four development levels: the *Enthusiastic Beginner* (D1: low competence, high commitment), the *Disillusioned Learner* (D2: low to some competence, low commitment), the *Capable But Cautious Performer* (D3: moderate to high competence, variable commitment), and the *Self-Reliant Achiever* (D4: high competence, high commitment). (See bottom of Figure 4.1.)

Second, it's important to recognize that development level is goal or task specific. People can be at one level of development on one task and at another level of development on the next task. That's why diagnosis is so important.

Matching: The Third Skill

To be an effective SLII® leader, you must also match your leadership style to the development level of the person you are leading. As illustrated in Figure 4.1, the SLII® model has four basic leadership styles: directing (S1), coaching (S2), supporting (S3), and delegating (S4). Is your direct report new and inexperienced with the task at hand? Then more guidance and direction are called for (S1). Is the direct report motivated, highly experienced, and skilled? That person requires less hands-on supervision (S4). The truth is, all of us are at different levels of development depending on the task we are working on at a particular time.

Over supervising or under supervising—that is, giving people too much or too little direction—has a negative impact on people's development. That's why it's so important to match leadership style to development level.

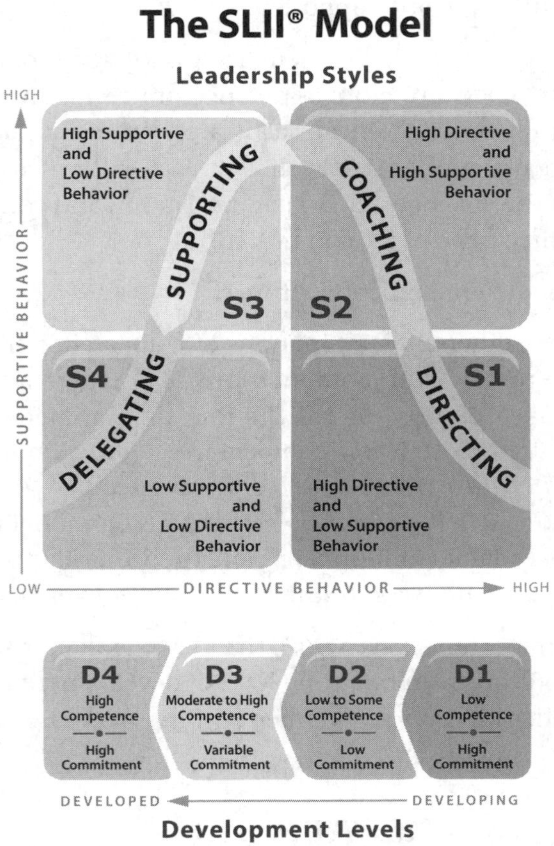

The SLII® Model

Leadership Styles

Figure 4.1 The SLII® Model

To help you determine the appropriate leadership style to use with each of the four development levels, draw a vertical line up from a diagnosed development level to the leadership curve running through the four-quadrant model. As illustrated in Figure 4.2, the appropriate leadership style—the match—is the quadrant where the vertical line intersects the curved line.

Using this approach, the Enthusiastic Beginner (D1) would get a directing (S1) leadership style. The Disillusioned Learner (D2) would get a coaching (S2) leadership style. The Capable But Cautious Performer (D3) would get a supporting (S3) leadership style, and the Self-Reliant Achiever (D4) would get a delegating (S4) leadership style.

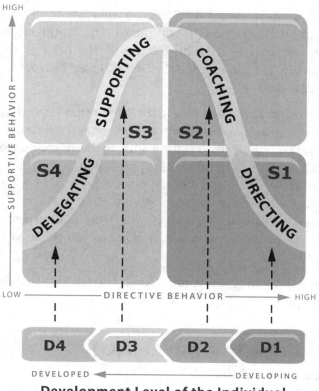

Matching Leadership Style to Development Level

Figure 4.2 Matching Leadership Style to Development Level

In determining what style to use with what development level, just remember this:

Leaders need to do what the people they supervise currently can't do for themselves.

To show you how the model works in the real world, we'll start with an example from your childhood. Can you remember when you started learning how to ride a bicycle? Sometimes you were so excited that you couldn't sleep at night, even though you didn't know how to ride yet. You were a classic *Enthusiastic Beginner* who needed *directing.*

Remember the first time you fell off your bike? As you were picking yourself up off the pavement, you might have wondered why you wanted to learn to ride in the first place and whether you would ever really master it. You had reached the *Disillusioned Learner* stage, and you needed *coaching.*

Once you could ride your bike with your mom or dad cheering you on, that confidence probably became shaky the first time you decided to take your bike out for a spin without your cheerleader and supporter close at hand. At this point, you were a *Capable But Cautious Performer* in need of *support.* Finally, you reached the stage where your bicycle seemed to be a part of you. You could ride it without even thinking about it. You were truly a *Self-Reliant Achiever,* and your parents could *delegate* to you the job of having fun on your bike.

Now let's see how the development levels and leadership styles apply to the workplace.

Enthusiastic Beginners Need a Directing Style

Suppose you recently hired a 22-year-old salesperson. Three key responsibilities are required of an effective salesperson besides selling: service, administration, and team contribution. Having worked in the hotel industry during the summer, your new salesperson seems to have good experience in service. Since he was the treasurer of his fraternity and captain of his college soccer team, it looks like he also has some experience in administration and team contribution. As a result, your initial training focus with him will be in the sales part of his job, where he is an *Enthusiastic Beginner.* In this area, he is excited and ready to learn, despite his lack of skills. Because of his high commitment to becoming a good salesperson, he is curious, hopeful, optimistic, and excited. In this area of his job, a *directing* leadership style is appropriate. You teach your new hire everything about the sales process, from making a sales call to closing the sale. You take him on sales calls with you so that you can show him how the sales process works and what a good job looks like. Then you lay out a step-by-step plan for his self-development as a salesperson. In other words, you not only pass out the test, but you also are involved in teaching him the answers. You provide specific direction and closely supervise his sales performance, planning and prioritizing what has to be accomplished for him to be successful. Teaching and showing him what experienced salespeople do—and letting him practice in low-risk sales situations—is the appropriate approach for this Enthusiastic Beginner.

Disillusioned Learners Need a Coaching Style

Now, suppose that your new hire has a few weeks of sales training under his belt. He understands the basics of selling but is finding it harder to master than he expected. You notice that his step has lost a little of its spring, and sometimes he looks a bit discouraged. While he knows more about sales than he did as a beginner and has flashes of real competence, he's sometimes overwhelmed and frustrated, which has put a damper on his commitment. A person at this stage is a *Disillusioned Learner.* What's needed now is a *coaching* leadership style, which is high on direction and support. You continue to direct and closely monitor his sales efforts, but you now engage in more two-way conversations, going back and forth between your advice and his questions and suggestions. You also provide a lot of praise and support at this stage because you want to build his confidence, restore his commitment, and encourage his initiative. While you consider your salesperson's input, you are the one who makes the final decisions since he is learning on actual clients.

Capable But Cautious Performers Need a Supporting Style

Fast-forward a couple months. Now the young man you hired knows the day-to-day responsibilities of his sales position and has acquired some good sales skills. Yet he still has some self-doubt and questions whether he can sell well *on his own,* without your help or the support of other colleagues. While you say he's competent and knows what he's doing, he is not so sure. He has a good grasp of the sales process and is working well with clients, but he's hesitant to be out there completely on his own. He may become self-critical or even reluctant to trust his own instincts. At this stage, he is a *Capable But Cautious Performer* whose commitment to selling fluctuates from excitement to insecurity. This is when a *supporting* leadership style is called for. Since your direct report has learned his selling skills well, he needs little direction but lots of support from you to encourage his wavering confidence. Now is the time to stand behind his efforts, listen to his concerns and suggestions, and be there to support his interactions not only with clients, but also with others on your staff. You encourage and praise, but rarely do you direct his efforts. The supporting style is more collaborative; feedback is now a give-and-take process between the two of you. You help him reach his own sales solutions by asking questions that expand his thinking and encourage risk taking.

Self-Reliant Achievers Need a Delegating Style

As time passes, your former new salesperson becomes a key player on your team. Not only has he mastered sales tasks and skills, but he's also taken on challenging clients and has been successful with them. He anticipates problems and is ready with solutions. He is justifiably confident because of his success in managing his own sales area. Not only can he work on his own, but he inspires others. At this stage, he is a *Self-Reliant Achiever* in the sales part of his job. You can count on him to hit his sales goals. For a person at this level of development, a *delegating* leadership style is best. In this situation, it is appropriate to turn over responsibility for day-to-day decision making and problem solving to him by letting him run his own territory. Your job now is to empower him by allowing and trusting him to act independently. What you need to do is acknowledge his excellent performance and provide the appropriate resources he requires to carry out his sales duties. It's important at this stage to challenge your high performing salesperson to continue to grow in his sales ability and cheer him on to even higher levels of sales.

Development Level Varies from Goal to Goal and Task to Task

The preceding example reemphasizes that development level is not a global concept—it's task-specific. We could have tracked the salesperson's progress in service, administration, or team contribution, and it would have been a different journey. It's important to remember not to pigeonhole people into any particular development level. In reality, development level applies not to the person, but to the person's competence and commitment to do *a specific goal or task*. In other words, an individual is not at any one development level overall. Again, development level varies from goal to goal and task to task. An individual can be at one level of development on one goal or task and be at a different level of development on another goal or task.

For example, Casey works in the consumer products industry. In the marketing part of her job, she is a genius when it comes to rolling out new products and opening new markets. She is clearly a **Self-Reliant Achiever**, as demonstrated by the success of her past marketing plans. However, when it comes to setting up a database to track demographics and buying patterns, Casey has little experience beyond email and word processing. Depending on her motivation for the task, she could be an **Enthusiastic Beginner** or a **Disillusioned Learner.**

This example shows that you need to use not only *different strokes for different folks*, but *different strokes for the same folks*, depending on what goal or part of their job you are focused on at any given time.

Meeting People Where They Are

Some people think that it's inconsistent to manage some people one way and other people in a different way. However, we don't define consistency as "treating everybody the same way." We define it as "using the same leadership style in similar situations." To those who argue that it's unfair to treat direct reports differently, we agree with U.S. Supreme Court justice Felix Frankfurter:

> *There is nothing so unequal as the equal treatment of unequals.*

When you can comfortably use a variety of leadership styles, you have mastered *flexibility.* As your direct reports move from one development level to the next, your style should change accordingly. Yet our research shows that most leaders have a preferred leadership style.[2] In fact, 54 percent of leaders tend to use only one style, 35 percent tend to use two styles, 10 percent tend to use three styles, and only 1 percent use four styles. To be effective, leaders must be able to use all four leadership styles.

Friends of ours experienced the downside of inflexible leadership when their son was eight years old and in the third grade. They got word from the school that he was way ahead of his class in reading but far behind in math. Initially, they thought, "How can that be? How could a kid be so good in reading and so bad in math?" But after they thought about it for a while, it made sense. Some kids are great in social studies but poor in science. People are good at some things and not others. When the father of the child in question understood the reality of the situation and how it was possible, he met with one of his son's teachers. We say "one of his son's teachers" because their son was in an open-style school with 110 kids in the class and four or five teachers working with them in a large, open space.

"Look, I don't want to cause any problems," he said, "but what I'd like to know is, why is our son doing so well in reading and so poorly in math? How do you treat him differently in reading versus math?"

The teacher said, "Over here on this wall we have a group of files. Each kid has his or her own reading file. When it's time for reading, the kids go get their reading files, come back to their desks, and continue to do their reading where they left off. If they have a question, they raise their hand, and one of us comes over and sees them."

Our friend asked, "How is that working with our son?"

The teacher said, "Super. He's one of our best readers."

Our friend said, "Keep it up. You're doing a great job teaching him reading."

What leadership style were they using with this youngster in reading? They were using a *delegating* leadership style. He picks out his folder, and he decides when he needs help. Why was it working? Because the kid was a *Self-Reliant Achiever* in reading. He loved it, and he had skills.

Our friend said, "Now tell me what you're doing with our son in math."

The teacher said, "Over on the other wall we have a group of files for our math program. When it's time for math, the kids go get their folders, bring them back to their desks, and continue to do their math where they left off. If they have any problems, they raise their hand, and a teacher comes to see them."

Our friend said, "How is that working with our son?"

The teacher said, "Not very well. He's falling behind the class."

What leadership style were they using with the boy in math? They were using a *delegating* leadership style, the same style they were using to teach him reading. In fact, that was the teaching style generally used in this open school. The problem with using a delegating style with this youngster in math was that the kid was at a much lower development level in math than he was in reading. He was a *Disillusioned Learner.* He didn't have the competency, the interest, or the confidence. The teachers were leaving him alone.

Our friend knew all about SLII®, so he said to the teacher, "Didn't they ever teach you in teacher education that with the same kid on a different subject you need to use a different leadership or teaching style?" Then our friend asked all the teachers in this open classroom, "Which one of you has the reputation of being a traditional teacher?" An older woman smiled. She had been a teacher for 35 years in this school system. Our friend had heard about her. Her close supervision of kids had given her a reputation for being too tough. Recognizing that this was just what his son needed, our friend asked her, "How would you deal with our son's math problem? He's not doing very well." Before we tell you what she said, let us tell you a bit about this teacher. One of our associates had gone to the elementary school where this teacher taught before she moved to the open school. In this school, the teacher had thirty third graders all by herself. The kids had to eat lunch in the classroom because the school wasn't big enough to have a lunchroom. Our associate walked by her classroom one day at 12:15. The door was wide open, and thirty third graders were quietly sitting and eating their lunches while our teacher friend was playing Beethoven on the recorder. Our associate smiled when he saw this and said to himself, "That's what I call control."

Across the hall was the other third grade teacher. The door to the classroom was shut, but our associate could see in through a window. The place looked like a zoo. Kids were running all over the place, up on the desks, while the teacher was dancing and hugging them. It looked like a fun place to be. Would that teacher be a good reading teacher for our friend's son? Absolutely, because the boy didn't need a reading teacher. If you don't need a manager, you might as well have a nice, warm, supportive one. Would this teacher be any good teaching the youngster math? No, she wouldn't.

Now, back to the directive teacher's response to our friend. She said, "It would have been a lot easier if I'd had your son from the beginning. I think he's discouraged now because it's harder than he thought it would be, and he's not doing well. So when it's time for math, I would go over to him and say, 'It's time for math.' Then I'd lead him by the hand over to his file. Sometimes I don't think he even gets his own file—he gets absent kids' files so he can goof them up. Then I would take him back to his desk, sit him down, and say, 'Do problems 1 through 3, and I'll be back in five minutes to check on you. If we work on this together, I know you'll get better at math.'"

Our friend said, "You're beautiful. Would you take over his math?" She did. Do you think their son got any better with her *coaching* style? You'd better believe it. Do you think he liked it? Not particularly. It is much easier to loosen up than tighten up. He had been used to working on his own. Even though working alone was not effective, he didn't welcome the sudden shift to close supervision. Yet if people don't know what they're doing and are discouraged, somebody has to direct and coach them. Notice that our effective math teacher *clarified expectations and goals, observed and monitored performance,* and *gave him feedback.*

Luckily, there were only three months left in the school year. Why do we say luckily? Because it was difficult for this teacher to move from a *directing/coaching* style to a *supporting/delegating* style. She was great at start-up work, but once the kids got the skills, she had problems letting the students take responsibility for their own learning. After three months, our friend's son was able to get out from under her. He moved on to a more humanistic, supporting teacher who could work with him now that he had the skills—like the warm, friendly teacher we described earlier. Teachers like these are super in their particular role, but you have to make sure they are working with the right kid at the right time. Both the directive teacher and the humanistic teacher would have been more effective if they could have used a variety of leadership styles. It's the same with managers and leaders. You have to be flexible enough to vary your leadership style depending on the skill level of your people; otherwise, your effectiveness will be limited.

All people have peak performance potential—you just need to know where they are coming from and meet them there.

The Importance of Partnering with People

SLII® is about developing a partnering relationship with your people. Partnering opens communication between you and your direct reports and increases the quality and quantity of your conversations. We call these *alignment conversations*—where you agree on goals, development level, and leadership style.

When we first started to teach SLII®, managers would leave our training excited and ready to apply and use the concepts. Yet we found that problems developed because the people managers were applying the model to didn't understand what the managers were doing and often misinterpreted their intentions.

For example, suppose that you diagnosed one of your people as predominantly a Self-Reliant Achiever. As a result, you decided basically to leave that person alone, but you didn't tell her why. After a while—when she hardly ever saw you anymore—she could become confused. "I wonder what I've done wrong," she might think. "I never see my manager anymore."

Suppose another one of your people is new, and you decide that he needs, at a minimum, a directing style. As a result, you're in his office all the time. After a while, he might start to wonder, "Why doesn't my boss trust me? He's always looking over my shoulder."

In both cases, you might have made the right diagnosis, but since your people didn't understand your rationale, they misinterpreted your intentions. Through these kinds of experiences, we realized this:

---

*Leadership is not something you do **to** people, but something you do **with** people.*

That's where creating a partnering relationship comes in. This is about gaining your direct reports' permission to use the leadership style that is a match for their development level. As you will learn in the next chapter, "Self Leadership: The Power Behind Empowerment," creating a partnership with your people allows them to ask you for the leadership style they need. Since this kind of partnering involves give-and-take between leader and follower, we will wait until you fully understand Self Leadership before going into depth on this subject in Chapter 6, "One-on-One Leadership."

Effective Leadership Is a Transformational Journey

SLII® is an integrating concept. Why? Because over time we realized that these strategies applied not only when you were leading an individual, but also when you were leading a team, an organization, and, most importantly, yourself. In fact, we have found that leadership is a four-stage transformational journey that includes self leadership, one-on-one leadership, team leadership, and organizational leadership.[3]

Self leadership comes first because effective leadership starts on the inside. Before you can hope to lead anyone else, you have to know yourself and what you need to be successful. Self knowledge gives you perspective.

Only when leaders have had experience in leading themselves are they ready to lead others. The key to *one-on-one leadership* is being able to develop a trusting relationship with others. If you don't know who you are—or what your strengths and weaknesses are—and you are unwilling to be vulnerable, you will never develop a trusting relationship. Trust between you and the people you lead is essential for working together.

The next step in the transformational journey of a leader is *team leadership.* Once leaders develop a trusting relationship with people in the one-on-one leadership arena, they are better prepared for team development and building a community. Effective leaders working at the team level realize that to be good stewards of the energy and efforts of those committed to working with them, they must honor the power of diversity and acknowledge the power of teamwork. This makes the leadership challenge more complicated, yet the results can be especially gratifying.

Organizational leadership is the final stage in the transformational journey. Whether a leader can function well as an organizational leader—someone supervising more than one team—depends on the perspective, trust, and community attained during the first three stages of the leader's transformational journey. The key to developing an effective organization is creating an environment that *values both relationships and results.*

One of the primary mistakes that leaders make today is that when they are called to lead, they spend most of their time and energy trying to improve things at the organizational level before ensuring that they have adequately addressed their own credibility at the self, one-on-one, or team leadership levels.

As you take time at each of the leadership stops along your transformational journey, SLII® will play a major role. The next chapter examines how the model applies to the first step of the transformational journey: self leadership.

Self Leadership: The Power Behind Empowerment

Susan Fowler, Ken Blanchard,
and Laurence Hawkins

As we discussed in Chapter 3, "Empowerment Is the Key," the traditional hierarchy of leadership has evolved into a new order: empowerment of individuals. When self leaders take the initiative to get what they need to succeed and leaders respond to those needs, they unleash the power in empowerment. The proverbial pyramid turns upside down, and leaders serve those who are being led.

Managers must learn to let go of command-and-control leadership styles because soon they will have no choice. In the 1980s, a manager typically supervised five people; in other words, the span of control was one manager to five direct reports. Today, companies have more lean-and-mean organizational structures, where spans of control have increased considerably. Now, it is common to find one manager for twenty-five to seventy-five direct reports. Add to that the emergence of virtual organizations—where managers supervise people they seldom, if ever, meet face to face—and an entirely different work landscape emerges. The truth is that most bosses today can no longer play the traditional role of telling their people everything they need to do, and when and how. Managers just don't have the time, and in many cases, their people know more about the work than they do. More than ever before, the success of organizational initiatives depends on the proactive behavior of empowered individuals.[1]

Many people are taking to this empowered environment like ducks to water. But some are becoming immobilized, unsure of how to take action without being told directly what to do by their manager. How can you get people to grab hold and run with the ball they're being handed?

Creating an Empowered Workforce

Just as leaders must move from command and control to a partnering relationship with their people, so too must those who are being led move from "waiting to be told" to taking the initiative to lead themselves. If the key role of SLII® leaders is to become partners with their people, the new role of people is to become partners with their leaders. This is what self leadership is all about.

> If empowerment is to be successful,
> organizations and leaders must develop
> self leaders in the workforce who have the
> skills to take initiative.

People need to be trained in self leadership. While many organizations teach managers how to delegate and "let go," there is less emphasis on developing individuals to solve problems and make decisions. Organizations on the leading edge have learned that developing self leaders is a powerful way to positively impact the quadruple bottom line.

For example, one of our clients, Bandag Manufacturing, experienced the value of self leadership after a major equipment breakdown. Rather than laying off the affected workforce, the company opted to train them in self leadership. A funny thing happened. Direct reports began holding their managers accountable and asking them to demonstrate their leadership capabilities. They were asking managers for direction and support and urging them to clarify goals and expectations. Suddenly, managers were studying up on rusty skills and working harder.

When the plant's ramp-up time was compared to the company's other eight plants that had experienced similar breakdowns in the past, the California plant reached pre-breakdown production levels faster than any other in history. The manufacturer studied other measures, too. It concluded that the determining factor in the plant's successful rebound was the proactive behavior of the workers, who were fully engaged and armed with the skills of self leadership.

> *An organization filled with self leaders is an organization with an empowered workforce.*

Creating Self Leaders Through Individual Learning

Individual learning—one of the key elements of a high performing organization—is essential to self leadership.[2] Organizations that do not encourage people to learn are less likely to be high performing because the skills of an organization are no greater than the skills of its people. Unless its individuals learn, the organization cannot.

High performing organizations appreciate that supporting people's growth, experience, and knowledge is not only the right thing to do, but also a competitive advantage. These organizations use formal training, mentoring, and on-the-job support to develop the skills and competencies of their people.

While self leaders should be responsible for their own learning, they shouldn't bear the burden alone; management should support the development of knowledge and skills. Fortunately, examples of organizations that support individual learning and the development of self leaders are plentiful. Yum! Brands—the parent company of Pizza Hut, Taco Bell, and KFC, among others—supports Yum! University. Here, associates learn the technical, business, and interpersonal skills that are related to creating customer mania.[3] Johnsonville Foods promotes continuous learning by encouraging all employees to attend any training class, regardless of its direct applicability to their current jobs.[4] GE's learning initiative broke down barriers to learning through cross-functional work on real applications.[5] Other examples abound.

> *Empowerment is what leaders give to their people. Self leadership is what people do to make empowerment work.*

The Three Skills of a Self Leader

You cannot invert the hierarchical pyramid and simply tell self leaders to accept responsibility and take initiative. Self leaders must be actively developed by teaching people skills and mental attitudes that foster empowerment.[6] In *Self Leadership and The One Minute Manager*, Ken Blanchard, Susan Fowler, and Laurence Hawkins teach the three skills of self leadership: *challenge assumed constraints, activate points of power,* and *be proactive.*[7] These three skills need to be encouraged in individual contributors and role modeled by managers.

The First Skill of a Self Leader: Challenge Assumed Constraints

The first skill of a self leader is to *challenge assumed constraints.* What, exactly, do we mean by an assumed constraint?

> *An assumed constraint is a belief, based on past experience, that limits current and future experiences.*

The classic example of an assumed constraint is illustrated by the training of elephants. The trainer takes a baby elephant and ties him to a stake with a big, heavy chain. Although the baby elephant pulls and tugs, he can't break the chain. Eventually he stops trying. He is now a six-ton elephant. He could easily pull the entire stake out of the ground, but he doesn't even try. His inability to move beyond the length of the chain isn't real; it's an assumed constraint.

Consider how the elephant's story relates to your own work experience. Do any of the following statements sound familiar? "Why should I bother? My boss won't approve anyway. They never listen to anyone's ideas around here. A woman has never held that position before. I've never been any good at that." These are all examples of assumed constraints that might be true at some level but are not the truth that should define your experience.

Indicators that an assumed constraint may be holding you hostage are negative internal dialogue, excuses, and blaming statements. At one time or another, most of us have assumed that because we did not have direct authority or position power, we could not be leaders or influence outcomes. This is one of the most common assumed constraints in the workplace. People who have become legendary for their effectiveness—from Bill Gates to Mother Teresa—are those who go beyond assumed constraints to reach their goals. For example, Mother Teresa—a minority Albanian who spoke broken English—did not begin her amazing career with a high position and authority. She used her personal power to achieve her goal of bringing dignity to the destitute. Status and recognition came later.

This is not to say that all of us aren't constrained by outside forces, whether it's a lack of time, money, or position of authority. Yet self leadership teaches that the constraints are not the problem; the problem is that we think these things are the only sources of power that are available to us. Successful people can almost name the time and date when they decided to let go of an assumed constraint and acknowledge their own power, which leads to the second skill of a self leader.

The Second Skill of a Self Leader: Activate Points of Power

The second skill of a self leader is to *activate points of power*. Everyone has points of power, although many are unaware of them.

People of all ages struggle with the mere notion of power. The abuse of power, the use of status and position to coerce others, and the egoism associated with people who have social and political power have turned people off to the acceptance of—let alone use of—power. Self leadership teaches people that we all have points of power. In helping people recognize and accept their points of power, we suggest that "the sole advantage of power is the ability to do more good."[8] Self leaders can do more good for themselves, their families, their communities, their organizations, and their coworkers when they accept and tap into their power.

The five sources of power are *position power, personal power, task power, relationship power,* and *knowledge power* (see Figure 5.1).

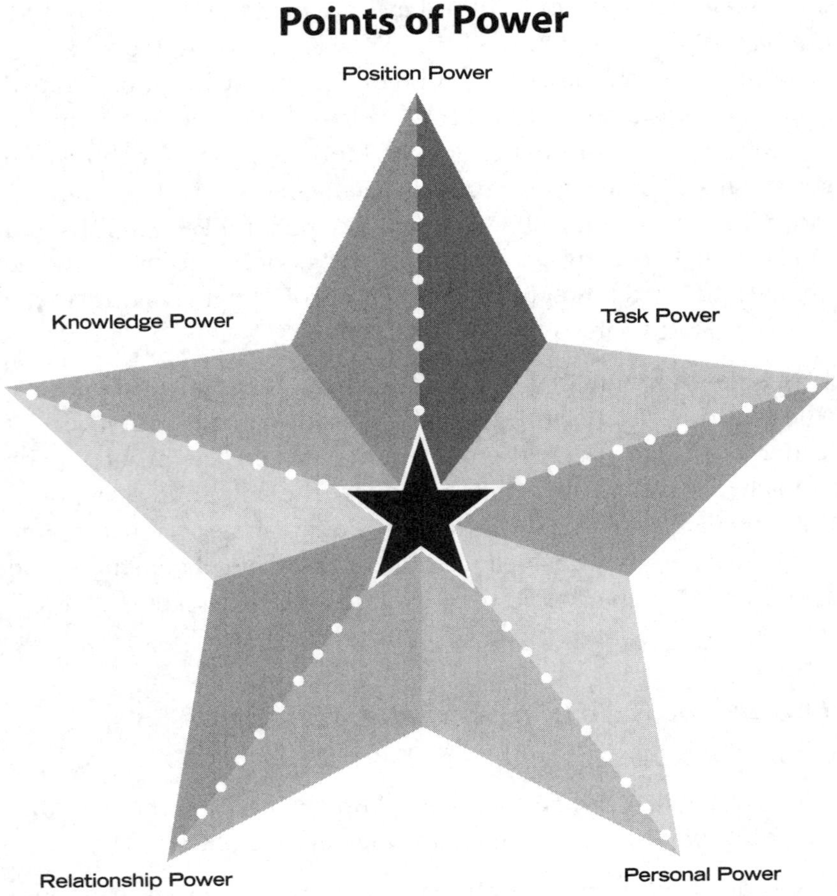

Points of Power

Position Power

Knowledge Power

Task Power

Relationship Power

Personal Power

Figure 5.1 Points of Power

Position power is the most recognized point of power. It is inherent in the authority of one's position. You have position power when your business card has a title printed on it that indicates you have the power to manage people or command resources.

Personal power comes from personal attributes such as strength of character, passion, persistence, charisma, or wisdom. Personal power is further enhanced by strong interpersonal skills, such as an ability to communicate well and be persuasive. If people like to be around you, you have personal power.

Task power relates to a task or particular job. This is power you have in being able to help others with a process or procedure they need to do or, conversely, to block or delay others from doing a task. For example, an executive assistant for a president or CEO often has the power to influence who gets added to or deleted from the executive's agenda.

Relationship power comes from the power of association with others—through building a friendship, understanding a colleague, cultivating a relationship, or knowing someone who owes you a favor. Having a mentor or champion can give you power through a relationship, as can being the relative of someone in power.

Knowledge power comes from having special expertise or skills but is also evidenced by having certain degrees or certifications indicating special training. You can often transfer knowledge power from job to job or from company to company. We're all good at something, so we all have some form of knowledge power.

Everyone has some degree of each of these forms of power, and typically the distribution is uneven. We find that few people ever think about what points of power they have. Fewer still have asked others for their perceptions on this topic. If they did, they might be surprised at how others view them—their job, position, personality, and abilities.

Getting feedback on your points of power can be an enlightening experience. Chances are good that you'll be surprised and gratified by the responses you get. With raised awareness of and attention to your own power, you come to realize how to use your points of power to better advantage. You will probably also realize that while you have been taking some points of power for granted, you have been oblivious to others. The best way to increase your power base is to gather people around you who have points of power you don't have.

---

*Don't buy into the assumed constraint
that position power is the only
power that works.*

Once you learn what your points of power are, you are ready to activate them. If you are strong in some points of power or weak in others, don't accept the assumed constraint this will be true the rest of your life. For example, if you have high knowledge power due to computer expertise but low personal power due to weak interpersonal skills, consider taking a Dale Carnegie course on "How to Win Friends and Influence People." Or perhaps you're a person who has good interpersonal skills but lacks technical skills. Be a self leader and ask someone to help you learn.

Using the Power of "I Need"

You can maximize your points of power when you combine them with two powerful words: "I need." Instead of directly stating what we need, many of us get trapped in asking dumb questions, like the woman in the subway. Let us explain: A man got on a subway in New York City and discovered there was only one seat left. There was something on the seat he didn't want on his slacks, so he laid down his newspaper and sat on it. A few minutes later, a woman tapped him on the shoulder and said, "Excuse me, sir. Are you reading your newspaper?" The man thought that was one of the dumbest questions he'd ever heard. He couldn't help himself. He stood up, turned the page, sat back down on the paper, and replied, "Yes, ma'am, I am."

While that story is amusing, you might wonder if you ask any dumb questions. We all do. For example, suppose that a coworker is running around like a chicken with her head cut off, but you need some help. So you ask, "Are you busy?" That's a dumb question. Of course she's busy! So she says something like, "There just aren't enough hours in the day." You feel guilty, so you get flustered and leave her alone, not wanting to add to her burden.

The alternative to dumb questions is to simply state your needs to your coworker truthfully: "I need 15 minutes to discuss this project. If this isn't a good time, I could come back at 3 o'clock."

What makes the "I need" phrase so powerful? When you tell somebody you want something, that person's first thought is usually, "We all want things we can't have." However, when you use the "I need" phrase, you're coming from a position of strength. You've thought about what it will take to succeed, and you are requesting someone's help. Human beings love to feel needed. They love to think they can help you.

Don't be afraid to ask for what you need from people who have points of power you don't have. By being proactive in this way, you will eliminate "being a victim" from your vocabulary. Remember, if you ask for what you need, you will either win or break even. How excited would you be about going to Las Vegas if the worst you could do was win or break even? You would catch the next plane. If you ask for what you need and you get it, you win. If you ask and don't get it, you break even because you didn't have it in the first place. Most people are afraid to ask for what they need for fear of rejection. Remember, when people say no to you, they are only turning down your idea. The only person who can turn you down is you.

"I need" is compelling. This is a key phrase for being proactive.

The Third Skill of a Self Leader: Be Proactive

The third skill of a self leader is to *be proactive.* This is where self leaders take the initiative to get the direction and support they need to achieve their goals.

In Chapter 4, "SLII®: The Integrating Concept," we introduced the four development levels and the appropriate leadership styles for each.

With self leadership, direct reports can diagnose their own development levels on a particular goal or task and take the initiative to get from their managers the leadership style they need to succeed (see Figure 5.2).

The SLII® Model

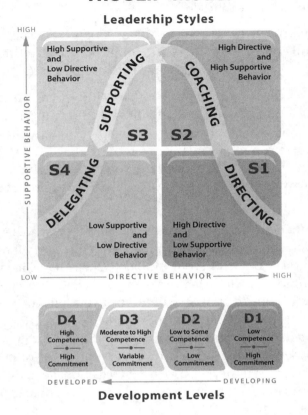

Figure 5.2 The SLII® Model

To illustrate how this works, let's return to our example in Chapter 4 of the recently hired 22-year-old salesperson. Suppose that the first thing his manager did with him was train him in self leadership. Now when he and his manager set goals around his four key areas of responsibility—sales, service, administration, and team contribution—the young salesperson can *be proactive* by playing an active role in diagnosing his own development level. He can determine the leadership style he needs for each rather than relying on his manager to do all the work. Not only will this increase his self-esteem and speed his journey to empowerment, but by being a good partner, he also will alleviate some of the management load for his boss. In the process, his manager can more easily invert the hierarchal pyramid and become more of a cheerleader and supporter than a director and controller.

Because the salesperson knows self leadership, he can diagnose himself as an *Enthusiastic Beginner (D1)* in the area of selling to existing clients. He knows that he has not yet demonstrated competence in this area and that he hasn't gained the knowledge and skills he needs to achieve his sales goals. Yet the thought of providing superior service to existing clients excites him, and his commitment is high. The salesperson should recognize that he needs a *directing (S1)* style, with high direction and low support. He should *be proactive* by asking his manager to teach him all about this part of the sales process, from making the first contact to completing the job.

In the area of administration—specifically, filing electronic reports—the salesperson realizes that he is a *Disillusioned Learner (D2)* in need of *coaching (S2)*. After taking some classes on how to use his company's sales software, he thought he was on his way. Yet using the software without the instructor at his side, his confidence is waning. The salesperson should admit to his manager that while he's comfortable with some functions, he's baffled by others. Recognizing that he needs a lot of direction and support in this area, the salesperson should *be proactive* by asking his manager for someone to answer questions that arise as he applies what he's learning in real time. He also should ask his manager for support to build his confidence and encourage him to keep learning.

The salesperson is having some trouble with cold calling. He has been well trained in this area and knows the step-by-step process for cold calling. During his training and for the first few weeks afterward, he had several successes. During the past couple of weeks, however, he's made hardly any sales through cold calls. His self-doubt has come roaring back, and he's beginning to wonder if he has what it takes to succeed in cold calling on his own. Remembering how excited and competent he felt about cold calling just a few weeks ago, he realizes that he is a *Capable But Cautious Performer (D3)* who needs a *supporting (S3)* leadership style. He should *be proactive* by asking his manager to listen to his concerns and questions and encourage his flagging confidence.

In the area of customer service, the salesperson knows full well he's a *Self-Reliant Achiever (D4)*. Having worked in the hospitality industry, he brings all kinds of customer-pleasing skills to his new position, and delighting customers comes as naturally to him as breathing. He has already won the hearts of some of the company's biggest clients by anticipating their needs and delivering more than they ever dreamed of receiving. In this area, the salesperson should *be proactive* by letting his manager know that what would work best for him would be a *delegating (S4)* leadership style. He should ask his manager to let him do the day-to-day decision making in this area. He also should let his manager know that the best way to support him is to trust him to do his job well, provide him with the resources he needs, and challenge him to deliver even higher levels of raving fan service.

Being proactive doesn't have to be restricted to your manager. You can diagnose your development level and ask for the appropriate leadership style from any number of leaders. *A leader is anyone who can give you the direction and support you need to achieve your goal.*

Are you assuming that people won't have the time or inclination to help you achieve your goals? By moving beyond that constraint and asking for help anyway, you can unleash the power of self leadership.

Now that you know about self leadership, the next chapter introduces one-on-one leadership, which will help you on your journey to becoming an effective SLII® leader.

6

One-on-One Leadership

Fred Finch and Ken Blanchard

A t its best, SLII® is a partnership that involves mutual trust between two people who work together to achieve common goals. Both leader and follower influence each other. Leadership shifts between them, depending on the task at hand and who has the competence and commitment to deal with it. Both parties play a role in determining how things get done.

This chapter provides a guide for creating such side-by-side leadership relationships. What we call one-on-one leadership is a process for increasing the quality and quantity of conversations between managers and direct reports—the people they support and depend on. These alignment conversations not only help people perform better, but they help everyone involved feel better about themselves and each other.

Establishing an Effective Performance Management System

When one-on-one leadership is done well, it becomes an integral part of an effective performance management system.

This system consists of three parts:

- **Performance planning:** After everyone is clear on the organizational vision and direction, performance planning begins. During this time leaders agree with their direct reports about the goals and objectives they should be focusing on. At this stage it's okay for the traditional hierarchy to be alive and well because if there's a disagreement between a manager and a direct report about goals, who wins? The manager does because that person represents the organization's goals and objectives.

- **Performance coaching:** This is where the hierarchy is turned upside down on a day-to-day basis. Now leaders do everything they can to help direct reports be successful. Managers work for their people, praising progress and redirecting inappropriate performance.

- **Performance review:** This is where a manager and direct report sit down and assess the direct report's performance over time.

Which of these three—performance planning, performance coaching, or performance review—do most organizations devote the greatest amount of time to? Unfortunately, it's performance review. We go into organization after organization, and people say to us, "You'll love our new performance review form." We always laugh because we think most of them can be thrown out. Why? Because these forms often measure things nobody knows how to evaluate, such as "initiative" and "willingness to take responsibility." Or "promotability"—that's a good one. When no one knows how to win during a performance review, they focus most of their energy up the hierarchy. After all, if you have a good relationship with your boss, you have a higher probability of getting a good evaluation.

Some organizations do a good job on performance planning and set very clear goals. However, after goal setting, what do you think happens to those goals? Most often they get filed, and no one looks at them until they are told it's time for performance reviews. Then everybody runs around, bumping into each other, trying to find the goals.

Of the three aspects of an effective performance management system, which one do people spend the least time on? The answer is performance coaching. Yet this is the most important aspect of managing people's performance because it's during performance coaching that feedback—praising progress and redirecting inappropriate behavior—happens on an ongoing basis.

In *Helping People Win at Work: A Business Philosophy Called "Don't Mark My Paper, Help Me Get an A,"* Ken Blanchard and WD-40 Company CEO Garry Ridge discuss in detail how an effective performance management system works.[1] The book was inspired by Ken's ten-year experience as a college professor. He was always in trouble. What drove the faculty crazy more than anything was that at the beginning of every course he gave students the final exam. When the faculty found out about that, they asked, "What are you doing?"

Ken said, "I thought we were supposed to teach these students."

The faculty said, "You are, but don't give them the final exam ahead of time!"

Ken said, "Not only will I give them the final exam ahead of time, what do you think I'll do throughout the semester? I'll teach them the answers so that when they get to the final exam, they'll get A's. You see, life is all about getting A's—not some stupid normal distribution curve."

Do you hire losers? Do you go around saying, "We lost some of our best losers last year, so let's hire some new ones to fill those low spots"? No! You hire either winners or potential winners. You don't hire people to fit a normal distribution curve. You want to hire the best people possible, and you want them to perform at their highest level.

Giving people the final exam ahead of time is equivalent to performance planning. It lets people know exactly what's expected of them. Teaching direct reports the answers is what performance coaching is all about. If you see people doing something right, you give them an "attaboy" or "attagirl." If they do something wrong, you don't beat them up or save your feedback for the performance review. Instead, you say, "Wrong answer. What do you think would be the right answer?" In other words, you redirect them. Finally, giving people the same exam during the performance review that you gave them at the beginning of the year helps them win—get a good evaluation. There should be no surprises in an annual or semiannual performance review. Everyone should know what the test will be and should get help throughout the year to achieve a high score on it. When you have a forced distribution curve—where a certain percentage of your people must be average or less—you lose everyone's trust. Now all people are concerned about is looking out for number one.

After learning about this philosophy, Ridge implemented "Don't Mark My Paper, Help Me Get an A" as a major theme in his company. He is so emphatic about this concept that he fired a poor performer's manager rather than the poor performer when he found out that the manager had done nothing to help that person get an A.

Not all managers are like Garry Ridge. Many still believe you need to use a normal distribution curve that grades a few people high, a few people low, and the rest average. The reason these managers and their organizations are often reluctant to discard the normal distribution curve is that they don't know how they will deal with career planning if some people don't get sorted out at a lower level. If they rated a high percentage of their people as top performers, they wonder how they can possibly reward them all. As people move up the hierarchy, aren't there fewer opportunities for promotion? We believe that question is quite naïve. If you treat people well and help them win in their present position, they often will use their creativity to come up with new business ideas that will expand your vision and grow the organization. Protecting the hierarchy doesn't do your people or your organization any good.

Ralph Stayer, coauthor with Jim Belasco of *Flight of the Buffalo,* tells a wonderful story that proves this point. Stayer was in the sausage manufacturing business. His secretary came to him one day with a great idea. She suggested that they start a catalog business because at the time they were direct-selling their sausages to only grocery stores and other distributors. He said, "What a great idea! Why don't you organize a business plan and run it?" Soon the woman who used to be his secretary was running a major new division of his company and creating all kinds of job opportunities for people, as well as revenue for the company.[2]

Leadership that emphasizes judgment, criticism, and evaluation is a thing of the past. Leading at a higher level today is about helping people get A's by providing the direction, support, and encouragement they need to be their best.

One-on-One Leadership and the Performance Management System

To give you a better sense of how this works, we want to share with you a game plan that will help you understand how one-on-one leadership fits into the formal performance management system we just described. While you can put this game plan into action with no prior training, it is much more powerful when everyone involved—both leaders and direct reports—understands SLII® and Self Leadership. That ensures that everyone is speaking the same language.

Performance Planning: The First Part of a Performance Management System

As you can see in Figure 6.1, there are four steps in the Performance Management Game Plan—*goal setting, diagnosis, matching,* and *delivering.* You'll notice that the first three steps are the same as the three skills needed to be an effective SLII® leader, as we described in Chapter 4.

Goal setting is the first step in the Performance Management Game Plan. This is such an important concept that we discuss it in detail in Chapter 7, "Essential Skills for One-on-One Leadership." To summarize here, good goal setting ensures that people are clear about the tasks they are responsible for and the standards by which their work will be measured.

Diagnosis is the second step in the Performance Management Game Plan. It starts with the leader and direct report individually diagnosing the direct report's development level for each of the goals agreed on. When we say individually, we mean that both leader and direct report go to a quiet place and separately diagnose the development level for each goal area. Both determine the level of competence and commitment by asking two questions:

- To determine *competence,* each should ask, "Does this person/do I know how to do this task?"

- To determine *commitment,* each should ask, "How excited is my direct report/am I about taking this on?"

The Performance Management Game Plan

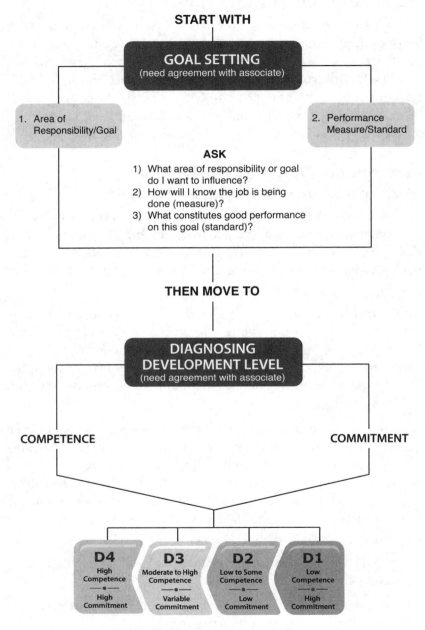

Figure 6.1 The Performance Management Game Plan

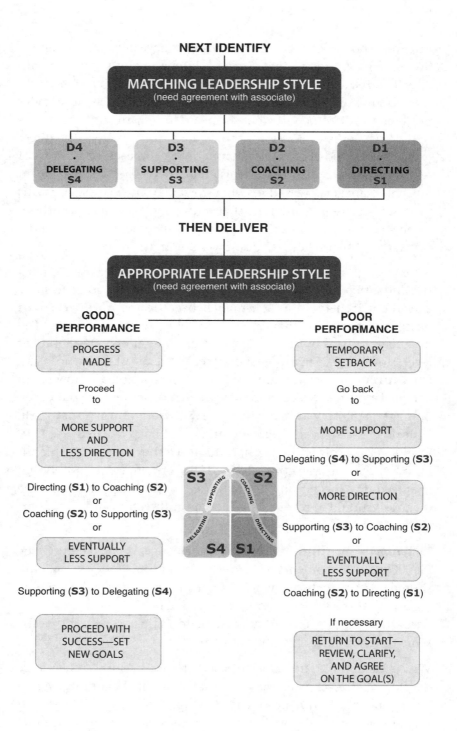

After both people in the partnering process have done their diagnostic homework, they should come back together and agree on who goes first. If the direct report goes first, the leader's job is to listen to that person's diagnosis. Then, before saying anything else, the leader must tell the direct report what she heard him saying until he agrees that's what he said. When it's the leader's turn, she tells the direct report her diagnosis of his development level on each of his areas of responsibility. His job is now to listen and feed back what he heard until his manager agrees that's what she said. Why do we suggest this process? Because it guarantees that both people are heard. Without some structure like this, if one of the two people involved is more verbal than the other, that person will dominate the conversation.

After both people have been heard, they should discuss similarities and differences in their diagnoses and attempt to come to some agreement. If there is a disagreement between leader and direct report on development level that cannot be resolved, who should win? The direct report. It is not the manager's job to fight over development level. However, the manager should make the direct report accountable. This means asking him, "What will you be able to show me in this goal area in a week or two that will demonstrate that your development diagnosis was right and mine was wrong?" You want to help your people win, even if agreement has not been reached. We have found that people will work hard to prove they are right, which is exactly what you want them to do. If performance does not live up to agreed-on expectations, it will be clear to the direct report that the diagnosis should be reconsidered and more direction and/or support should be given.

Matching is the third step in the Performance Management Game Plan. Once development level is clear, both parties, if they know SLII®, should be ready to discuss which leadership style is needed. Matching ensures that the leader provides the kind of behaviors—a leadership style—that the direct report needs to perform the task well and, at the same time, enhances his commitment.

While the appropriate leadership style to use should be clear once development level is determined, that's just the beginning. When you're engaged in one-on-one leadership, you don't just leave it at saying you'll use a delegating or coaching style. You must be more specific. For the leader, this provides an opportunity for what we call "getting permission to use a leadership style."

The purpose of getting permission to use a leadership style is twofold. First, checking to make sure that the style proposed is what the direct report agrees he needs creates clarity. Second, getting permission ensures the direct report's buy-in on the use of that style and increases his commitment. For example, if a direct report is an *Enthusiastic Beginner* who does not have much in the way of task knowledge and skill but is excited about taking on the task, this person obviously needs a *directing* leadership style. The leader might say, "How would it be if I set a task goal that I believe will stretch you but is attainable and then develop an action plan for you that will enable you to reach the goal? Then I'd like to meet with you on a regular basis to discuss your progress and provide any help you need as you get started. Does this make sense as a way for you to get up to speed as quickly as possible?" If the direct report agrees, they are off and running.

On the other hand, suppose a direct report is a *Self-Reliant Achiever* on a particular goal and therefore can handle a *delegating* leadership style. The leader might say, "Okay. The ball is in your court, but keep me in the loop. If you have any concerns, give me a call. Unless I hear from you, or the information I receive tells me otherwise, I'll assume everything is fine. If it isn't, call early. Don't wait until the monkey is a gorilla. Does that work for you?" If the direct report says yes, he is on his own until his performance or communication suggests differently. If in either of the two examples—the Enthusiastic Beginner or the Self-Reliant Achiever—the direct report doesn't agree, what should happen? Further discussion should take place until a leadership approach is agreed on.

As you can tell from the examples, once an appropriate leadership style is agreed on, the leader still needs to provide work direction. *Providing work direction* might involve establishing clear performance expectations, creating an action plan, putting in place a process for checking progress, and expressing confidence that the person can deliver on the performance plan.

As part of that process, it's important to establish a monitoring process based on the agreed-on leadership style. This is where the leader and direct report commit to holding scheduled meetings—called progress-check meetings—to discuss how performance is going.

For example, if you agree that your direct report needs a *directing* style, you would meet quite frequently and maybe have the direct report attend some formal training. If a *coaching* style is chosen, you might say, "Let's schedule two meetings a week for at least two hours to work on the goal you need help with. How about Mondays and Wednesdays from 1 to 3 p.m.?" With a *supporting* leadership style, you might ask, "What's the best way for me to recognize and praise the progress you are making? At lunch every week or so?" If you agree to have lunch together, your role would be to listen and support her actions. With a *delegating style,* it would be up to the direct report to request help since she's a Self-Reliant Achiever.

Performance Coaching: The Second Part of a Performance Management System

Once it's determined, the agreed-on leadership style establishes the number, frequency, and kind of progress-check meetings that leaders and their direct reports have with each other. The implementation of these meetings begins performance coaching. That's where leaders praise progress or redirect the efforts of their partners—their direct reports.

Leaders often assume that their work direction conversations are so clear that there is no need for follow-up or that they are so busy that they can't take the time. If you want to save yourself time and misery, schedule and hold progress-check meetings. You will be able to catch problems before they become major and significantly increase the probability that your direct report's performance on the goal will meet your expectations. If they didn't schedule progress-check meetings, leaders could set up their people for failure. That's why one of our favorite sayings is this:

You can expect more if you inspect more.

While this might sound intrusive, it really isn't. As Ken Blanchard, Thad Lacinak, Chuck Tompkins, and Jim Ballard point out in *Whale*

Done!: The Power of Positive Relationships, inspecting should emphasize catching people doing things right, not wrong. Praising progress
and redirecting efforts begins with accentuating the positive. Redirection follows praising to keep progress going. If no progress is being
made—in other words, if performance is not improving—leaders should
move straight to redirection to stop any further decline in performance.

Delivering the appropriate leadership style is the fourth step in the
Performance Management Game Plan. Let's look at the model again
and see what happens when performance is improving.

As you reexamine SLII® Figure 6.2, you might be wondering
what the curve running through the four styles means. We call it a
performance curve, and for good reason.

SLII® Leadership Styles

Leadership Styles

Figure 6.2 SLII® Leadership Styles

*Performance is what triggers a
change in leadership style.*

As development level moves from *Enthusiastic Beginner (D1)* to *Self-Reliant Achiever (D4),* the curve shows how a manager's leadership style moves from *directing (S1)* to *delegating (S4),* with first an increase in *support (S2)*, and then a decrease in *direction (S3)*, until eventually there's also a decrease in *support (S4)*. At *Self-Reliant Achiever (D4)*, the person can direct and support more and more of his or her own work. Your goal as a manager, then, should be to help your direct report improve performance by changing your leadership style over time.

To help yourself do that as a leader, imagine that the performance curve is a railroad track. Each of the four leadership styles depicts a station along the performance curve. If you start with an *Enthusiastic Beginner (D1)* using a *directing style (S1),* and you want to eventually get to *delegating (S4),* appropriate for a *Self-Reliant Achiever (D4),* what two stations do you have to stop at along the way? *Coaching (S2)* and *supporting (S3).*

You'll notice that no railroad tracks go straight from *directing (S1)* to *delegating (S4).* What happens to a fast-moving train if it goes off the tracks? People get hurt. It is important for managers not to skip a station as they manage people's journey to high performance. By staying on track and stopping at all the stations, you will lead your direct reports to perform well on their own, with little or no supervision. Lao Tzu said it well:

> When the best leader's work is done, the
> people say, "We did it ourselves!"

An experiment we did at the University of Massachusetts illustrates the power of SLII® in one-on-one leadership. We worked with four instructors teaching a basic course in management. The first two instructors only lectured or led discussions—in other words, they used *directing* and *coaching* styles. These two traditional instructors became our control group.

We taught the other two instructors SLII® and showed them how to change their teaching style over the course of eight weeks. The first two weeks we asked them to use a *directing* style: lecturing. The next two weeks we asked the instructors to lead discussions, in essence using a *coaching* style. During the following two weeks we showed them how to move to a *supporting* style by restricting their involvement in the class; they sat back and made only process comments like, "Has everybody had a chance to speak?" or supportive comments like, "This is a really interesting class." During the last two weeks, we showed them how to go to a *delegating* leadership style; they asked their students to run the class themselves, letting them know that they would be in the classroom next door writing an article for a business journal.

On the last day of class, a secretary came into all four classes and wrote a note on the whiteboard: "The instructor is sick tonight and won't be here. Carry on as usual."

What do you think happened to the students in the first two classes, where the control group instructors lectured or led discussions? Within five minutes, those students were gone. Without the instructor there, they didn't know what to do.

In the classes with the changing leadership style, nobody left. Students made comments like, "The instructor hasn't been here for the past two weeks. Big deal. What did you think about that case?" One of the two classes even stayed a half hour beyond the scheduled time.

At the end of the semester, the experimental classes with the changing teaching style outperformed the other two classes. The students knew more, they liked the course better, and they weren't late or absent. How was that possible when their instructors weren't even there for the last two weeks? Because the instructors stayed on the railroad tracks and gradually changed their teaching style from directing to coaching to supporting to delegating, the students over time moved from dependence to independence, from Enthusiastic Beginners to Self-Reliant Achievers.

Declining Performance

We rarely find decreases in performance resulting from a decline in competence. Unless you can cite cases of Alzheimer's at work, people generally don't lose their competency if they had it in the first place or were trained to have it. Changes in performance occur either because the job and the necessary skills to perform it have changed or because people have lost their commitment.

Dealing with decommitment—a change in motivation or confidence—is one of the biggest challenges facing managers.

For the most part, leaders avoid dealing with their decommitted people, largely because it is such an emotionally charged issue and they don't know how. When they do address it, they usually make matters worse: They turn the not-engaged into the actively disengaged. The core perception on the part of these decommitted people is that either their leader or the organization has treated them unfairly.

We believe that the primary reason for loss of commitment is the behavior of the leader or the organization. More often than not, something the leader or organization has done or failed to do is the primary cause of the eroded commitment.

Decommitted people are not provided with the kind of leadership that matches their needs—they are under- or over supervised. Decommitment has numerous other potential causes: lack of feedback, lack of recognition, lack of clear performance expectations, unfair standards, being yelled at or blamed, reneging on commitments, and being overworked and stressed out. The loss of commitment can affect most, if not all, of the person's job functioning.

People often assume that decommitment occurs mainly at the bottom of the organization, with individual contributors. Not so. It occurs at every organizational level.

Current literature and training programs for addressing what is called "handling performance problems" are overwhelmingly focused on frontline leaders. This literature and these programs assume that the frontline employee is the problem. The language itself—"handling performance problems"—implies that the person with the problem is the problem. The literature and training programs emphasize issues such as employees' unacceptable performance or behavior, documenting performance problems, developing organizational policies

---

to deal with them, employee counseling, removing poor performers, corrective counseling, and discipline.[3]

In general, these are lose-lose strategies that intensify decommitment and that should be used only as a last resort. This approach is commonly called "blaming the victim." A process that does not address all the causes of the problem is guaranteed not to work, particularly if the person who is blaming the performer has a hand in causing it. If the leader and the organization have a role in causing the problem, their role must be identified and resolved as part of the solution.

Placing Blame: Not a Good Strategy

First, let's assume that either the leader or the organization has contributed to the cause of an individual's decommitment. This is not always the case, but the evidence suggests that it is in the substantial majority of instances where decommitment has occurred. Next, let's assume that the issue has been going on for some time. Again, evidence supports this assumption. When we ask leaders in organizations to identify the people they lead who have "performance problems" and to tell us how long this has been going on, the responses range from six months to ten years. These responses alone identify the leader as part of the problem; the issues are not being addressed.

Dealing with decommitment is a difficult and usually highly emotionally charged undertaking. If the situation has been going on for some time, a high level of emotional tension probably exists in the relationship between the leader and the direct report. The leader blames the direct report, and the direct report blames the leader or the organization.

A sophisticated set of interpersonal skills and the ability not to let your ego get in the way are required to effectively address the problem. If you are unwilling to own up to any behavior on your or the organization's part that has contributed to the cause of the problem, resolution is unlikely.

Dealing with Decommitment

Decommitment occurs when a gap exists between the direct report's performance or behavior and the leader's expectations. This gap occurs for two primary reasons. First, a gap occurs when the person has demonstrated the ability to perform or behave appropriately, and now his performance has declined or his behavior has changed in a negative way. Second, a gap occurs when the person is unwilling to gain knowledge or skills that would lead to improved performance or behavior.

We see three possible strategies for addressing decommitment:

- Keep on doing what you've always done.

- Catch it early.

- Go to a supporting leadership style (high supporting/low directing leader behavior).

The first alternative—keep on doing what you've always done—will get you what you've always gotten: escalating anger, frustration, and no resolution.

The most effective alternative is to catch decommitment early—the first time it is observed, before it gets out of control and festers. Early detection makes it easier for both you and your direct report to identify the causes and resolve them.

Just as improvements in performance prompt forward shifts in style along the curve, decreases in performance require a shift backward in leadership style along the performance curve. If a person you are delegating to starts to decline in performance, you want to find out why. So, you would move from a delegating style to a supporting style, where you listen and gather data. If both of you agree that the direct report is still on top of the situation, can explain the decline in performance, and can get performance back in line, you can return to a delegating leadership style. However, if you both agree that this performance situation needs more attention from you, you now can go to a coaching style where you can provide closer supervision. Seldom, if ever, do you have to go all the way back to a directing style.

The third alternative for addressing decommitment when the problem has been going on for some time is to cautiously go to a supporting leadership style. That may seem inappropriate to impatient managers who would like to get off the railroad tracks and head straight back to a directing leadership style. Let's explore why and how a supporting leadership style is a better choice.

Step 1: Prepare

Preparation should involve selecting a specific performance or behavior that you believe you have a chance of jointly dealing with. Do not attempt to address everything at once.

After you have pinpointed the performance or behavior you want to focus on, gather all the facts that support the existence of the performance or behavior from your point of view. If it is a performance issue, quantify the decline in performance. If it is a behavior issue, limit your observations to what you have seen. Don't make assumptions or bring in the perceptions of others. This is a sure way to generate defensiveness. And you probably won't be able to specifically identify these "others" anyway because they usually don't want to be named. Also, use the most recent information possible. Next, identify anything you or the organization might have done to contribute to the decommitment. Be honest. Owning up is the most important part of moving toward resolution.

Ask yourself questions to determine your role in the situation. Were performance expectations clear? Have you ever talked to the person about his or her performance or behavior? Does the person know what a good job looks like? Is anything getting in the way of performance? Have you been using the right leadership style? Are you giving feedback on the performance or behavior? Is the person being rewarded for inappropriate performance or behavior? (Often people in organizations are rewarded for poor behavior—that is, nobody says anything.) Is the person being punished for good performance or behavior? (Often people are punished for good performance or behavior—that is, they do well and someone else gets the credit.) Do policies support the desired performance? For example, is training or time made available to learn needed skills?

Once you have done a thorough job of preparing, you're ready for Step 2.

Step 2: Schedule a Meeting, State the Meeting's Purpose, and Set Ground Rules

Scheduling a meeting is vital. It is important to begin the meeting by stating the meeting's purpose and setting ground rules to ensure that both parties will be heard in a way that doesn't arouse defensiveness. Decommitted people with serious performance or behavior issues are likely to be argumentative and defensive when confronted. For example, you might open the meeting with something like this:

"Jim, I want to talk about what I see as a serious issue with your responsiveness to information inquiries. I would like to set some ground rules about how this discussion proceeds so that we can both fully share our perspectives on the issue. I want us to work together to identify and agree on the issue and its causes so that we can set a goal and develop an action plan to resolve it.

"First, I would like to share my perceptions of the issue and what I think may have caused it. I want you to listen but not to respond to what I say except to ask questions for clarification. Then I want you to restate what I said, to make sure you understand my perspective and I know you understand it. When I am finished, I would like to hear your side of the story, with the same ground rules. I will restate what you said until you know I understand your point of view. Does this seem like a reasonable way to get started?"

Using the ground rules you have set, you should begin to understand each other's point of view on the performance issue at hand. Making sure that both of you have been heard is a wonderful way to reduce defensiveness and move toward resolution.

Once you have set ground rules for your meeting, you are ready for Step 3.

Step 3: Work Toward Mutual Agreement on the Performance Issue and Its Causes

The next step is to identify where there is agreement and disagreement on both the issue and its causes. Your job is to see if enough of a mutual understanding can be reached so that mutual problem solving can go forward. In most conflict situations, it is unlikely that both parties will agree on everything. Discover if there is sufficient common ground to work toward a resolution. If not, revisit those things that are getting in the way, and restate your positions to see if understanding and agreement can be reached.

When you think it is possible to go forward, ask, "Are you willing to work with me to get this resolved?"

If you still can't get a commitment to go forward, you need to use a directing leadership style. Set clear performance expectations and a time frame for achieving them; set clear, specific performance standards and a schedule for tracking performance progress; and state consequences for nonperformance. Understand that this is a last-resort strategy that may resolve the performance issue but not the commitment issue.

When you get a commitment to work together to resolve the issue, it is normal to feel great relief and assume that the issue is resolved. Not so fast.

If you or the organization has contributed to the cause of the problem, you need to take steps to correct what has been done. Anything you have done to cause or add to the problem needs to be addressed and resolved. Sometimes you have no control over what the organization has done, but just acknowledging the organization's impact often releases the negative energy and regains the other party's commitment.

If you finally get a commitment to work together to resolve the issue, you can go to Step 4 and partner for performance.

Step 4: Partner for Performance

Now you and the direct report need to have a partnering for performance discussion in which you jointly decide the leadership style you will use to provide work direction or coaching. You should set a goal, establish an action plan, and schedule a progress-check meeting. This step is crucial.

Resolving decommitment issues requires sophisticated interpersonal and performance management skills. Your first try at one of these conversations is not likely to be as productive as you would like. However, if you conduct the conversation in honest good faith, it will reduce the impact of less-than-perfect interpersonal skills and set the foundation for a productive relationship built on commitment and trust.

Performance Review: The Third Part of a Performance Management System

The third part of an effective performance management system is *performance review.* This is where a person's performance over the course of a year is summed up. We have not included performance review in the traditional sense in our Performance Management Game Plan. Why? Because we think effective performance review is not an annual event, but an ongoing process that takes place throughout the performance period. When progress-check meetings are scheduled according to development level, open, honest discussions about the direct report's performance take place on an ongoing basis, creating mutual understanding and agreement. If these meetings are done well, the year-end performance review will just be a review of what has already been discussed. There will be no surprises.

Partnering as an Informal Performance Management System

What we have been talking about so far is how one-on-one leadership could fit in with a formal performance management system. Unfortunately, most organizations don't have a formal performance management system. Organizational goals are usually set, but often no system is established to accomplish them. As a result, the management of people's performance is left to the discretion and initiative of individual managers. While annual performance reviews are usually done, they tend to be haphazard at best in most organizations. Managers working in that kind of environment can implement one-on-one leadership on an informal basis in their own areas, even when it comes to performance review. As we stated earlier, we believe that an effective performance review is an ongoing process that should take place throughout the performance period, not just once a year. If managers do a good job with an informal performance review system, perhaps through their good example, a formal performance management system will emerge organization-wide, with one-on-one leadership as a core element.

One-on-Ones: An Insurance Policy for Making One-on-One Leadership Work

How can people close the gap between learning about one-on-one leadership and really doing it?

Margie Blanchard and Garry Demarest developed a one-on-one process that requires managers to hold 15- to 30-minute meetings a minimum of once every two weeks with each of their direct reports.[4] The manager is responsible for scheduling the meeting but the direct report sets the agenda. This is when people can talk to their managers about anything on their hearts and minds—it's their meeting. The purpose of one-on-ones is for managers and direct reports to get to know each other as human beings.

In the old days, most businesspeople had a traditional military attitude that said, "Don't get close to your direct reports. You can't make hard decisions if you have an emotional attachment to your people." Yet rival organizations will come after your best people, so knowing and caring for them is a competitive edge.

Too often, talented people report that their executive recruiter knows and cares more about their hopes and dreams than their manager does.

Don't let this be said about you. One-on-one meetings not only deepen the power of one-on-one leadership, they create genuine relationships and job satisfaction. In the next chapter, we'll reveal the final secrets of leading people one-on-one.

Essential Skills for One-on-One Leadership

Ken Blanchard and Fred Finch

We are firm believers in the 80/20 rule: Eighty percent of the results that leaders need to get in working with their people come from about 20 percent of the leadership activities they could do. The three secrets of *The New One Minute Manager*[1] are a perfect example. In this updated version of their original book, Ken Blanchard and Spencer Johnson focus on three basic concepts: One Minute Goals, One Minute Praisings, and One Minute Re-Directs. While these three skills probably represent only 20 percent of the activities that managers engage in, these skills could provide managers with the outcome they desire (the 80 percent). These three skills are core to effective partnering for performance.

One Minute Goal Setting

As we have emphasized, without clear goals, SLII® doesn't work. Why not? Because development level is task specific. As we've indicated, people are not globally Enthusiastic Beginners, Disillusioned Learners, Capable But Cautious Performers, or Self-Reliant Achievers. It all depends on which goal area of their job you're talking about.

According to research, goal setting is the single most powerful motivational tool in a leader's toolkit.[2] It provides purpose, challenge, and meaning. Goals are the guideposts along the road that make a compelling vision come alive. Goals energize people. Specific, clear, challenging goals lead to greater effort and achievement than easy or vague goals do.

Of course, people must have the knowledge, skills, and commitment necessary for goal achievement. That's what SLII® focuses on. When dealing with Enthusiastic Beginners and Disillusioned Learners, it's probably better to set learning goals than outcome goals. For example, it is better for beginning golfers to hit balls into a net than on a driving range because if the outcome of their efforts is evident, they could get discouraged after every shot. When they hit into a net, all they are focused on is whether they are learning how to swing properly. When these golfers begin to demonstrate a competent swing, they can go out onto the driving range.

Distinguishing between learning goals and outcome goals is important because some people contend that they never go through the Disillusioned Learner stage. This is because they are more focused on learning than goal achievement. Still, it is appropriate to move from a directing, to a coaching, to a supporting, and finally, to a delegating style with people as they improve their development level, whether they are focused on learning or goal accomplishment.

If all good performance starts with a clear goal, how do you know a clear goal when you have one? For a goal to be clear, people need to know what they are being asked to do (their areas of accountability) and what good performance looks like (the performance standards by which they will be evaluated).

Areas of Accountability

One of the biggest obstacles to productivity improvement is the problem of unclear organizational expectations and accountability. For example, when people are asked what they do and their managers are asked what their people do, they both typically give widely divergent answers, particularly if the group is asked to prioritize responsibilities. As a consequence, individuals in organizations often are punished for not doing what they didn't know they were supposed to do.

At times, the people managers believe are most responsible for a specific activity may be completely unaware of their role. For example, a group of restaurant managers concerned about sales were asked,

"Who is responsible for generating sales in your organization?" They said the waiters and waitresses were. But when the waiters and waitresses were asked what their primary responsibilities were, their reply was consistently "Serving food and taking orders." They made no reference to selling. So, although it may seem very basic, managers need to make sure their people know what is expected of them.

Performance Standards

People must also know what good performance looks like. Performance standards help managers and direct reports more easily monitor performance, and they serve as a basis for evaluation. Whether an organization has clear performance standards can be determined by asking people, "Are you doing a good job?" Most people will respond by saying either, "I don't know" or "I think so." If they answer, "Yes, I think so," a revealing follow-up question would be, "How do you know?" Typical responses are, "I haven't been chewed out by my boss lately" or "No news is good news." Such answers imply that people receive little feedback on their performance until they make a mistake. This is a sad state of affairs. That habitual practice by managers leads to the most commonly used management style in the United States: leave-alone-then-zap. This style of management can also be called "seagull management." When someone makes a mistake, seagull managers fly in, make a lot of noise, dump on everyone, and fly out. Since this is the predominant style of management in organizations, it is no wonder that motivating people is a major organizational problem today.

Scott Meyers, a longtime consultant in the field of motivation, made the same point using a novel analogy.[3] Meyers was struck by the number of unmotivated people in organizations. Yet he had never seen an unmotivated person after work. Everyone seemed to be motivated to do something.

One night when Meyers was bowling, he saw some of the "problem" employees from the last organization where he worked. One of the least motivated people—someone he remembered all too well—took the bowling ball, approached the line, and rolled the ball. The employee started to yell and jump around. Why do you think he was so happy? The answer was obvious to Meyers: The employee got a strike. He knew he had performed well—he had knocked down all the pins.

Remember that goals need to be clear. The reason people are not jumping for joy in organizations, Meyers contended, is that, in part, it is not clear what is expected of them. To continue his bowling analogy, when people approach the alley, they notice there are no pins at the end; that is, they don't know what their goals are. How long would you want to bowl without pins? Yet, every day in the world of work, people are bowling without pins, and, as a result, they cannot tell how well they are doing. Managers know what they want their people to do; they just don't bother to tell them. They assume people know. Never assume anything when it comes to goal setting.

To reach their goals, people require feedback. When managers assume that their people know what's expected of them, they are creating a second ineffective form of bowling. They put up the pins, but when the bowler goes to roll the ball, he notices there is a sheet across the alley. When he rolls the ball and it slips under the sheet, he hears a crack but doesn't know how many pins he knocked down. When asked how he did, he says, "I don't know, but it felt good."

It's like playing golf at night. A lot of our friends have given up golf. When we ask them why, they say, "The courses are too crowded." When we suggest they play at night, they laugh; who would ever play golf without being able to see the flags? To move toward goals, people need feedback on their performance.

The number one motivator of people
is feedback on results.

As former colleague Rick Tate often said, "Feedback is the breakfast of champions." Can you imagine training for the Olympics with no one telling you how fast you ran or how high you jumped? The idea seems ludicrous, yet many people operate in a vacuum in organizations, not knowing how well they are doing on their jobs.

Money motivates people only if it is feedback on results. Have you ever gotten a raise that you were pleased with, only to find out that somebody else who you didn't think worked as hard as you got the same or even a better raise? Not only was that increase in money not *motivating*, it became *demotivating* once you knew it had nothing to do with results. Suddenly, it didn't matter how hard you worked.

Once managers are convinced that the number one motivator of people is feedback on results, they usually set up a third form of bowling. When the bowler goes to the line to roll the ball, the pins are up and the sheet is still in place, but now the game has another ingredient: a supervisor standing behind the sheet. When the bowler rolls the ball, he hears the crash of the falling pins. The supervisor holds up two fingers and says, "You knocked down two." In fact, most bosses would not phrase the feedback so positively but would say, "You missed eight."

Performance Reviews Can Undermine Performance

Why don't managers lift the sheet so that everyone can see the pins? Because organizations have a strong tradition known as the *performance review*. We call it NIHYYSOB ("Now I have you, you S.O.B."). Sadly, many managers use the performance review as a once-a-year opportunity to get even with their people.

As we indicated in the last chapter, the performance review process is often used to spread people over a normal distribution curve, thereby categorizing them and distorting their performance. Having a set budget or percentage for a group's salary increases often encourages this practice. In most organizations, if six or seven people report to you, the practice of rating them all high—even if they all deserve it—is discouraged. It doesn't take managers very long to realize that if they rate all their people high, they subsequently get rated low by their managers. The only way they can get rated high is if they rate some of their people low.

One of a manager's toughest jobs is deciding who gets the low ratings. Most Americans grow up with this win-lose mentality, in which some people in every group must lose. It pervades our educational system. For example, a fifth-grade teacher giving a test on state capitals would never consider making atlases available during the test to allow the students to look up the answers. Why? Because all the children would get 100 percent. Can you imagine what would happen to American education if kids who had to take vocabulary tests were allowed to access dictionaries? There would be an uproar!

Limit the Number of Goals

Three to five goals are the ideal number on which peak performers can concentrate, according to most research.[4] Once these goals are established, they should be written down so that they can be frequently used to compare actual behavior to targeted behavior.

Often, goal setting is considered a paperwork activity—a necessary evil in getting the job done. When this is the case, goals are filed and people go off and do whatever they want until a performance review draws near. With One Minute Goal setting, the philosophy is that you should keep your goals close at hand and be able to read each in a minute or less.

Good Goals Are SMART Goals

Although most managers agree with the importance of setting goals, many do not take the time to clearly develop goals with their people and write them down. As a result, people tend to get caught in the "activity trap," where they become busy doing things, but not necessarily the right things. To focus on what is important, you should set SMART goals with your people. SMART is an acronym for the most important factors in setting quality goals:

- **Specific and measurable:** You must be specific about the area that needs improvement and what good performance looks like. Being specific reinforces the old saying, "If you can't measure it, you can't manage it." Therefore, goals must be specific, observable, and measurable. If somebody says, "But my job can't be measured," offer to eliminate it to see if anything will be missed.

- **Motivating:** Not every job people are asked to do will be super exciting, but having motivating goals helps. Sometimes all people need to know is why the task is important. People want to know that what they do makes a difference. That's motivating.

- **Attainable:** What really motivates people is to have moderately difficult but achievable goals. This has been proven time and again by setting up a version of the old ring toss game. People are asked to throw rings at a stake from any distance they choose. Unmotivated people, it has been found, stand either very close to the stake, where the goal is easily accomplished, or far away, where their chances of success are minimal. High achievers, based on classic research on achievement motivation conducted by David McClelland, find the appropriate distance from the stake through experimentation.[5] If they throw the rings from a certain spot and make most of their tosses, they move back. Why? It's too easy a goal. If they miss most of their tosses, they move forward. Why? It's too difficult a task. McClelland found that high achievers like to set moderately difficult but attainable goals—that is, goals that stretch them but are not impossible. That's what we mean by attainable.

- **Relevant:** As we stated earlier, we believe in the 80/20 rule. Eighty percent of the performance you want from people comes from the 20 percent of the activities they could get involved in. Therefore, a goal is relevant if it addresses one of the 20-percent activities that make a difference in overall performance.

- **Trackable and time-bound:** To praise progress or redirect inappropriate behavior, managers must be able to measure performance frequently. This means using a record-keeping system and timeline to track performance. If a goal consists of completing a report by June 1, the chances of receiving an acceptable, even outstanding, report will increase if interim reports are required and progress is praised along the way.

One Minute Praisings

Once your people understand what they are being asked to do and what good behavior looks like, you are ready for the second key to obtaining desired performance: the One Minute Praising. Praising is the most powerful activity a manager can do. In fact, it is the key to training people and making winners of everyone working for you. A praising focuses on reinforcing behavior that moves people closer to their goals.

> *Of all the keys of the One Minute Manager, One Minute Praisings are the most powerful.*

Look around your organization and see if you can "catch people doing something right." When you do, give them a One Minute Praising that is immediate and specific and that states your feelings.

Be Immediate and Specific

For a praising to be effective, it must be *immediate* and *specific*. Tell people exactly what they did right as soon as possible. For example, "You submitted your report on time Friday, and it was well written. In fact, I used it in a meeting today, and that report made you and me and our whole department look good." Comments that are too general, such as, "I appreciate your efforts" and "Thank you very much," are less likely to seem sincere and thus are unlikely to be effective.

State Your Feelings

After you praise people, tell them how what they did impacted you. Don't intellectualize. State your gut feelings: "I felt so happy and proud after hearing your financial report presentation at the Board of Directors meeting. I'm delighted you're on our team. Thanks so much." Although praisings do not take very long, they can have lasting effects.

Praisings Are Universally Powerful

Praisings drive all effective human interaction. These same concepts apply to any relationship, not only making people better managers, but also making them better parents, spouses, friends, and customers. Consider marriage, for example.

When you first fall in love, everything is right. You seldom see the faults or limitations of your loved one. Love is blind—you see only the positive. When you decide to get married or commit to some permanency in your relationship, you often start to see things wrong with each other. You begin to say such things as, "I didn't know you thought that" or "I can't believe you would do something like that." Your emphasis shifts to what's wrong with the other person, rather than what's right. The ultimate demise of a loving relationship is when you do something right and you get yelled at anyway because you didn't do it right enough. You hear things like, "I shouldn't have to ask" or "You should have done it earlier."

How do two people go from being excited about each other to squabbling? It's really quite simple. Good relationships are all about the frequency with which you catch each other doing something right.

Being Close Counts

This discussion brings up one of the important points to remember about praising: Don't wait for exactly the right behavior before praising someone. Catch people doing things approximately right. We want exactly right behavior, but if we wait for exactly right behavior before we recognize it, we'll probably never get it. We must remember that exactly right behavior is made up of a whole series of approximately right behaviors. We all know that with animals and little people—we just forget it with big people.

For example, suppose you want to teach a child who is learning to speak to say, "Give me a glass of water, please." If you wait until the child says the whole sentence before you give her any water, the child will die of thirst. So you start off by saying, "Water! Water!" All of a sudden one day the child says "waller." You jump all over the place, hug and kiss the child, and get Grandmother on the phone so the child can say, "Waller, waller." It isn't "water," but it's close.

You don't want a kid going into a restaurant at the age of 21 asking for a glass of waller, so after a while you only accept the word "water," and then you start on "please." So in training someone, you should emphasize catching that person doing something right—in the beginning, approximately right—and then gradually moving the person toward the desired behavior.

Bob Davis, former president of Chevron Chemical, has as one of his favorite mottos "Praise progress—at least it's a moving target." What we need to do in all our interactions at work and at home is accentuate the positive and catch people doing things right, even if it's only approximately right.

If you are having difficulty with a spouse, child, team member, boss, or friend, you must first ask yourself, "Do I want this relationship to work?" Examine your gut feelings. If deep down you don't want to make the relationship work, you won't. Why? Because you have control of the qualifier—the "Yes, but..." If you want to make the relationship work, you will catch the other person doing things right or approximately right. But if you don't want to make it work for whatever reason, you can easily undermine another person's best efforts to please you. No matter what that person does right, you will say, "Yes, but you didn't do this or that right."

Make Time for Praisings

We ask people all the time, "How many of you are sick and tired of all the praisings you get at work or at home?" Everybody laughs because most of us do not naturally think of cheering each other on. Yet we all know people who carry around in their wallet or pocketbook a praising note they got years ago. It seems "gotcha"—catching people doing things wrong—comes more easily to most of us than "well done." How do we break this pattern? Maybe we need to be more intentional about it.

You should set aside at least two hours a week for cheering people on. Write it on your calendar, just as you would any other appointment. Then use the Hewlett-Packard philosophy of Management by

Wandering Around.[6] Wander around your operation, catch people doing things right or approximately right, and tell them about it. Do the same with your spouse, children, and friends. At home, you may not need two hours a week, but ten minutes surely wouldn't hurt.

One Minute Re-Directs

If One Minute Praisings are focused on catching people doing things right and accentuating the positive, the question that inevitably arises is, "That's all well and good. What do you do if somebody's performance is not up to snuff?"

There are two strategies for dealing with poor performance: reprimand and redirection.

A reprimand works best with people who have "won't do" or attitudinal problems. These people are winners, and they know how to do what they are being asked to do, but for some reason they're not doing it. Redirection is appropriate for people with "can't do" or experience problems. These people are learners and therefore do not yet know how to do what they are being asked to do.

When *The One Minute Manager* was originally published in 1982, the third secret of the One Minute Manager was the One Minute Reprimand. That was an appropriate label when the world of work was not as complicated and organizational leadership was considered a top-down process. But today leadership is more of a side-by-side process. Also, things are changing so fast today in most fields that people's competency to do a job is often short lived. Ongoing learning is necessary for all of us to keep up today. Even if you're an expert, the next day your area might be eliminated. Redirection helps people learn in this fast-changing environment. Reflecting these changes, the third secret of the One Minute Manager has been renamed One-Minute Re-Directs.

How Do One Minute Re-Directs Work?

If a person makes a mistake or her performance isn't up to par, a One Minute Re-Direct is appropriate.

Before we get into how to do One Minute Re-Directs, it's important that the manager makes sure that the goal the person was working on was clear. If it wasn't, the manager needs to accept responsibility for that and clarify the goal.

If the goal was clear and a performance problem exists, the leader should proceed with a re-direct.

There are two parts of a re-direct. The first half focuses on the performance. The second half focuses on the performer.

The first half of a re-direct:

1. As with One Minute Praisings, re-direct as soon as possible after an incident. Do not save up your feelings. The longer you wait to give someone feedback, the more emotional it can become. So give feedback as soon as possible.

2. Confirm the facts and review with the person what has gone wrong. Be specific. For example, if a customer did not receive the correct order, make that clear to the person responsible.

3. Express how you feel about the mistake and its impact on results. You might say, "I'm concerned. One of our best customers was really upset. She needed that order for a sales presentation, and because it didn't arrive on time, her event was less than stellar."

Pause. At this point you might want to be quiet for a moment to allow the person to feel the impact of the error.

The second half of a re-direct:

4. Remember to let the person know that they are better than their mistake and you still think well of them as a person. "Everyone makes mistakes. I still think you're a great contributor to this team."

5. Remind them that you have confidence and trust in them and you don't expect a repeat of this mistake. "I have a lot of confidence in you, and I trust this won't happen again."

The goal of redirection is not to tear people down but to build them up in a way that they will return to top performance and stay motivated to learn.

Matt Peterson, managing director at Aethos Consulting Group, gives an excellent example of redirection and why it works. An otherwise competent server at the famous Hotel del Coronado in San Diego—who was well aware of the hotel's standards for excellence—had messed up an order and handled it so dismissively that a longtime customer complained that she would not be returning to the hotel. His manager had to decide: Should he fire the server or just rake him over the coals?

The manager did neither. Instead, this manager sat down with the employee, reviewed exactly what he had done wrong, and redirected him to change his behavior in the future. Then he pulled out a piece of paper and, together, he and the employee wrote an apology to the guest. The note was delivered to the guest that evening.

As Matt reports, the next day the server happened upon the guest in the lobby. Feeling horrible about the negative effect his carelessness had on both the customer and the hotel's reputation, the server approached the guest. With tears in his eyes, he apologized for his poor service. The guest accepted his apology and they made a genuine connection. Before she left the hotel, the guest booked her next stay.

This story illustrates the ripple effect of an effective redirection. By treating the server's lapse in performance as a learning moment rather than a punishable offense, the manager was able to positively impact the employee, the customer, and the organization. The manager's firm but compassionate approach did not place the employee on the defensive, so he was open to learning a valuable lesson. More important, the employee was able to pass that compassion on to the customer—who in turn remained loyal to the brand.

This story also demonstrates how effective one-on-one leadership can impact profitability. When people are well served by their immediate manager, they in turn serve their customers well. A well-served customer is a repeat customer, which creates a healthy bottom line.

Praisings and Redirects Are Key to One-on-One Leadership

The fourth step in effective one-on-one leadership is delivering the appropriate leadership style. Again, as a leader you are constantly looking for opportunities to move your leadership style forward so that you can eventually get to delegating. As people's performance increases, praising their progress is key to supporting their efforts. If at any time their performance stalls or moves backward, rather than reprimanding or punishing them, the best strategy is to redirect and get them back on course. As managers manage by wandering around, it behooves them to praise progress or redirect. That is how you help people accomplish their goals and live according to the organization's vision.

The Fourth Secret of the One Minute Manager

Shortly after Ken Blanchard and Spencer Johnson's *The One Minute Manager* came out, a top manager wrote to Ken and expressed how much he enjoyed the three secrets of the One Minute Manager. But he suggested that managers aren't always right. He insisted that managers make mistakes all the time. "I think the fourth secret of the One Minute Manager should be the One Minute Apology," he said.

That resonated with Ken because his mother always said, "Two phrases that are not used enough in the world that could make it a better place are 'Thank you' and 'I'm sorry.'" The One Minute Praising covered thank-you, but the three secrets didn't cover I'm sorry. That's when Ken and Margret McBride decided to write *The Fourth Secret of the One Minute Manager: A Powerful Way to Make Things Better.*[7]

The One Minute Apology

As with praisings and redirections, the One Minute Apology has several key aspects:

- A One Minute Apology *begins with surrender*. That starts with your being truthful and admitting to yourself that you've done something wrong and need to make up for it. The key here is a willingness to take full responsibility for your actions and any harm done to anyone else.

- A One Minute Apology *ends with integrity*. This involves recognizing that what you did or failed to do is wrong and inconsistent with who you want to be. It is important that you reaffirm that you are better than your poor behavior and forgive yourself.

- Once these two things are done, your focus must be on making amends to that person for the harm you caused.

- Finally, commit to yourself and others not to repeat what you did wrong, and keep this commitment by changing your behavior.

What would an apology look like? Suppose at a meeting you kept interrupting a colleague, not permitting her to finish a thought. When another of your associates pointed this out after the meeting, you had a big aha, realizing that what you did was wrong and not beneficial to your team.

As soon as possible, go to the offended person and say something like, "I got some feedback about how I kept interrupting you at the meeting today and not letting you finish. I want to apologize because I recognize the truth in that feedback, and I feel bad. That's not who I want to be. In fact, I think I'm better than that. I promise I will never do that again. How can I make amends for what I did today?"

A One Minute Apology can be an effective way to correct a mistake you have made and restore the trust needed for a good relationship. Adding the One Minute Apology to goal setting, praising, and redirection makes one-on-one leadership a real give-and-take process where admitting your vulnerability can be more of a rule than an exception. Effective one-on-one leadership relationships depend on trust, and trust can occur only when we can get out of our own way and be authentic as we work with our people.

In the next chapter, you'll see that trust—a teachable skill—is essential not only for effective one-on-one relationships, but for teams and organizations as well.

8

Building Trust

Ken Blanchard, Cynthia Olmstead, and Randy Conley

Trust is the foundation of all healthy relationships, so it comes as no surprise that a leader's ability to build trust is the key to effective one-on-one partnerships, teams, and organizations.

Without trust, it is impossible for an organization to function effectively. Studies show that productivity, income, and profits are positively or negatively impacted depending on the level of trust in the work environment.[1]

Unfortunately, levels of trust have been dwindling in organizations. A poll by Maritz indicates that only 7 percent of workers strongly agree that they trust their senior leaders to look out for their best interests.[2] And a survey by MasteryWorks indicates that a lack of trust correlates strongly to employee turnover.[3]

The High Cost of Low Trust

Blanchard's research confirms that employees will leave an organization where trust is lacking. In a study of more than 1,000 leaders, 59 percent of respondents indicated they had left an organization due to trust issues, citing lack of communication and dishonesty as key contributing factors.[4]

Untrustworthy leaders rob an organization of the best employees have to offer. When people perceive that an organization—or its leaders—are less than forthcoming, they become unwilling to contribute discretionary energy or make commitments to their organization's well-being beyond the absolute minimum.

Because they need a paycheck, employees will often stay with the organization and do their jobs, but not much more. Work becomes purely a transactional relationship with employees asking themselves, "If the organization does not do right by me, why should I do right by them?"

The Benefits of Trust

When people believe they are working for trustworthy leaders, they are willing to invest their time and talents in making a difference in an organization. They feel more connected and invest more of themselves in their work. High trust levels lead to a greater sense of self-responsibility, deeper interpersonal insight, and more collective action toward achieving common goals.

Trustworthy leaders are rewarded by employees who stretch, push their limits, and volunteer to go above and beyond. When leaders create a high-trust environment, collaboration increases and organizations leap forward.

Recognizing the benefits of a high trust workplace, organizational decision makers are making the building of trust a top priority.

The Four Elements of Trust

Building trust is a teachable skill that begins with communication. Because trust means different things to different people, decision makers must first find a common language of trust—qualities they agree are consistent with trustworthiness. In *Trust Works!: Four Keys to Building Lasting Relationships*, Ken Blanchard, Cynthia Olmstead, and Martha Lawrence identify four qualities leaders can use to define and discuss trust with the people they lead.[5] These four qualities make up the ABCD Trust Model™.

Able is about demonstrating competence. Do the leaders know how to get the job done? Are they able to produce results? Do they have the skills to make things happen—including knowing the organization and equipping people with the resources and information they need to get their job done?

Believable means acting with integrity. Leaders must be honest in their dealings with people. In practical terms, this means creating and following fair processes. People need to feel that they are being treated equitably. It doesn't necessarily mean that everyone has to be treated the same way in all circumstances, but it does mean that people are being treated appropriately and justly based on their unique circumstances. Believability is also about acting in a consistent, values-driven manner that reassures people they can rely on their leaders.

Connected is about demonstrating care and concern for other people. It means focusing on people and identifying their needs. It is supported by good communication skills. Leaders need to openly share information about the organization and about themselves. This allows direct reports to see their leaders as real people and more easily identify with them. When leaders are vulnerable and share information about themselves, it creates a sense of connection.

Dependable is about honoring commitments by following through on what the leaders say they are going to do. It means being accountable for their actions and being responsive to the needs of others. If leaders promise something, they must deliver. It also requires being organized and predictable so that people can see that the leaders have things in order and are able to keep their promises.

Creating a High Trust Environment

Using the ABCD Trust Model™ as a guideline, leaders can create high-trust environments that foster involvement and energy by taking four steps:

1. Know the behaviors that support the ABCDs of trust.

2. Assess the current trust level.

3. Diagnose areas that need work.

4. Have a conversation to restore trust.

Step One: Know the Behaviors That Support the ABCDs of Trust

With the ABCD Trust Model™, we define trust in behavioral terms. Leaders who understand how their behaviors affect others find it much easier to gain respect, earn trust, and accomplish mutual goals. Consistent with the ABCD Trust Model™, the following behaviors encourage, build, and sustain trust:

Able

Get quality results.

Resolve problems.

Develop skills.

Be good at what you do.

Use skills to assist others.

Connected

Listen well and ask for input.

Praise and show interest in others.

Share about yourself.

Work well with others.

Show empathy for others.

Believable

Keep confidences.

Admit when you're wrong.

Be honest and sincere.

Don't talk behind people's backs.

Be nonjudgmental and show respect.

Dependable

Do what you say you'll do.

Be timely and responsive.

Be organized and accountable.

Follow up.

Be consistent.

Defining trust in behavioral terms allows everyone to talk openly about this sensitive subject. Now, instead of pointing out individuals as "untrustworthy," people can use the model to identify the behaviors that are undermining trust.

Step Two: Assess the Current Trust Level

The second step is to assess yourself in the areas of Able, Believable, Connected, and Dependable. You can find an online assessment at http://leadership.kenblanchard.com/trustworks/.

Because trust is a two-way street, your self-assessment is only part of the picture. Ask people to rate you in the ABCD areas. Again, you can find the "How Trustworthy Do You Think I Am?" assessment at http://leadership.kenblanchard.com/trustworks/.

It is important to set up the process correctly so that people will be candid in their assessments and won't fear retaliation for their answers. Encourage them to leave their names off the assessment unless they choose to be identified with their feedback. Explain that their responses will help you become more aware of how your behavior is perceived by others. Remember to thank people for their responses and tell them what you have learned about yourself.

Step Three: Diagnose Areas That Need Work

The next step is to learn how to diagnose low-trust situations to find out what behavior or behaviors are causing any breakdowns in trust. Your self-assessment and the assessments of others should give you a good idea about where your strengths and weaknesses are—that is, which of your behaviors are building trust, and which are undermining trust.

It's important to note that many of the behaviors that undermine trust are not intentional or even conscious. For example, when Ken Blanchard was assessed by his team at work, his highest score was in the *Connected* behaviors and his lowest score was in the *Dependable* behaviors. When he and his team looked at why people felt *Dependable* was his weak area, they determined it was because Ken never really heard a bad idea—in other words, he said yes too easily. Despite his good intentions, he often became overcommitted, and that put stress on both him and his team.

Step Four: Have a Conversation to Restore Trust

While it might be uncomfortable to discuss trust issues, ignoring them will not make these issues go away. In many cases, avoidance only makes matters worse. A candid conversation will not only clear the air but serve as a catalyst to improve results and relationships.

To help Ken become more *Dependable,* he and his team talked about various strategies to mitigate his tendency to become overcommitted. Margery Allen, his executive assistant at that time, suggested that when Ken went on business trips he should pass out her business card instead of his so she could help screen callers and talk with Ken about which business proposals were realistic considering his time, energy, and the team's resources. The strategy has been highly successful in making Ken more **Dependable.**

Leaders with an autocratic management style might be uncomfortable with this strategy, perhaps feeling that it gives direct reports too much authority. Yet to be effective, leaders must admit that they, too, are human and make mistakes. The ability to acknowledge and repair breaches in trust not only builds stronger relationships, but models effective behavior for future leaders.

Leaders must think about the four core elements in the ABCD Trust Model™ and how people in their organization would rate them in these areas. If they find themselves lacking in a particular area, they need to tackle this head-on.

Again, the key is to exhibit the trust-building behaviors that people look for in their leaders. This is critical, because people need to see trust in action more than they need to hear about it. For example, business leaders who tell it straight—who are open and honest even about bad news—develop the trust essential for strong, long-term relationships both inside and outside the company.

It is also important to demonstrate trust in others. Establishing rules, policies, and procedures to protect against a few bad apples sends the wrong message to the majority of people in your organization who need and deserve to be trusted.

Apple cofounder Steve Jobs emphasized the importance of trust in an interview in *Rolling Stone* magazine, stating, "Technology is nothing. What's important is that you have a faith in people, that they're basically good and smart, and if you give them tools, they'll do wonderful things with them."[6]

The Transparency Challenge

Information is power. One of the best ways to build a sense of trust in people is by sharing information. This is the heart of transparency. But knowing this and acting upon it can be two different things.

Sharing information sometimes means disclosing information that is considered privileged, including sensitive and important topics such as the competition's activities, future business plans and strategies, financial data, industry issues or problem areas, competitors' best practices, the way group activities contribute to organizational goals, and performance feedback. Providing people with more complete information communicates trust and a sense of "we're in this together." It helps people think more broadly about the organization and the interrelationships of various groups, resources, and goals.

For example, Berrett-Koehler Publishers in Oakland, California, makes its author contracts and publication memo open to the public through a Creative Commons license that is linked on the publisher's website.[7]

A famous example of transparency is the outerwear company, Patagonia. The company newsletter, the *Footprint Chronicles*, reveals the farms, textile mills, and factories in Patagonia's supply chain, as well as the materials it uses that may be harmful to the environment. Patagonia's website states: "It is remarkably hard to reduce the environmental impact associated with our technical gear, especially our shells. Unlike other products we make, a shell is a lifesaving piece of equipment that absolutely must perform in the world's worst weather. Unfortunately, to meet that standard of functionality we rely on fossil fuels."[8]

While Patagonia's transparency may not please all stakeholders, it does garner trust. The leadership challenge with transparency is to behave in ways that support vulnerability and share information at a level that is comfortable for your organization.

When deciding on issues of transparency, organizational leaders should consider the following questions: What does transparency mean in your organization? Should employees be getting all the information? Who should be included in meetings? If you have been a very tight-lipped organization in the past, you must answer these questions and communicate candidly about what you are going to do to become a more transparent organization.

Leaders in low trust organizations with little transparency are faced with a challenge. To turn things around, they must take a hard look in the mirror and examine their own behaviors. Are they being trustworthy? Is there transparency and honesty with people at all levels of the organization?

Bipul Sinha, cofounder and chief executive of the cloud data-management start-up Rubrik, operates under a strict code of radical transparency. For example, the company's board meetings are open to all 600 of the company's employees, and a majority of them attend either physically or virtually. Except for confidential client information, no relevant business topics are off the table, and employees are encouraged to question and challenge the board.

Such openness "can be scary," Sinha admits. "But if you are true and transparent it creates trust. It creates empowerment."[9]

Repairing Broken Trust

Despite our best intentions, at one time or another all of us break trust with others. In fact, misunderstandings and relationship strains due to trust issues are fairly common. The good news is that if trust has been broken, your professional or personal relationship can recover. It takes hard work to build trust, especially after it has been betrayed, but it can be done.

Having a conversation using the ABCD Trust Model™ as a guide—as we saw with Ken and his team—can help in these circumstances. But what do you do when a breach of trust is so severe that the relationship is strained to the breaking point—or breaks completely? We call this damaged trust. If you are avoiding another person because you feel there is no safe way to communicate openly, you are probably experiencing damaged trust. If the very thought of approaching this person fills you with dread, anger, or fear, that's another sign that you're dealing with damaged trust.

Contending with damaged trust requires fortitude and forethought. A conversation with the party in question is likely to be challenging. Emotions will be volatile and the stakes will be high. Additionally, the conversation could have consequences you would rather avoid. If you feel a situation is so explosive—or the stakes are so perilous—that a conversation could cause further damage, you probably need to engage the services of a qualified mediator or therapist. If, on the other hand, you have assessed the challenges and decided that the risks are manageable, you can use the following five-step process created by Randy Conley to begin rebuilding the relationship and restoring trust.

Step One: Acknowledge and Assure

To begin the rebuilding process, the first step is to acknowledge that a problem exists and needs to be addressed. If you are initiating the trust conversation, this will require courage. As you acknowledge the problem, assure the other party that your intention is to restore trust between the two of you and that you are willing to take the time and effort to get the relationship back on track. It is important to find out if your goal of rebuilding the relationship is mutual. If it is not, there is little you can do other than thank them for their honesty. You may—or may not—want to let the person know that if they change their mind, you will be open to a conversation in the future.

Step Two: Admit

The next step is to admit your part in causing the breach of trust. Own up to your actions and take responsibility for whatever harm was caused. Even if you don't feel you are entirely at fault, admit to your part in the situation. In cases where you feel the other party is mostly to blame, your part might be as simple as, "I admit I haven't let you know what's been bothering me." Admitting your part in the situation is a crucial step that should not be overlooked. Refusing to admit your mistakes undermines your believability.

Step Three: Apologize

The third step in repairing damaged trust is to apologize for your role in the situation. This takes humility. Again, even if you don't feel you were entirely at fault, apologize for your part in the situation. Express regret for any harm you may have caused and assure the other person you will change the undesirable behavior. ("I apologize for avoiding you. In the future I will let you know right away when I have a problem.") It's important that your apology is sincere and that you feel authentic remorse. If it's contrived or forced, the other person will pick up on that and question your believability. Avoid making excuses, shifting blame, or using qualifying statements, as these will undermine your apology.

Step Four: Assess

Invite feedback from the other party about how he or she sees the situation. Together, assess which elements of the ABCD Trust Model™ were violated. Discussing the behaviors that damaged the relationship is bound to bring up uncomfortable emotions, so be prepared. It will be helpful to affirm that the purpose of this step is not to point fingers, but rather to identify problem behaviors so they can be avoided in the future. The more specific you can be about the behaviors that damaged the trust, the easier it will be to repair the breach, as you'll each have a clear idea about what needs to change.

Step Five: Agree

The final step in rebuilding damaged trust is to work together to create an action plan. Now that you have discussed each other's perceptions and identified the specific negative behaviors at the root of the problem, you can mutually identify the positive behaviors you'll use going forward. This is the time to clarify your shared goals for the relationship and make requests about what you'd like to see both more and less of in the future.

The Ripple Effect

Higher level leaders personify trust. By role modeling trustworthy behaviors, they set an example for others to follow. Employees who experience this concern for their well-being see how they should be treating others, which creates a ripple effect of trust throughout the organization. The result is an organization where people assume the best of each other. This trusting atmosphere is telegraphed to clients and customers, resulting in greater results and relationships.

Leaders must regularly assess trust levels in their organizations and watch for signs that trust is eroding. If they find trust is lacking, they need to find out where the breakdowns are occurring and immediately begin a process to rebuild trust.

Synovus Financial, a bank that consistently ranks high in the Survey of Bank Reputations and the *Forbes* list of America's Most Trustworthy Financial Companies, experienced fluctuating levels of trust in the aftermath of the 2007 recession. By being transparent about the tough choices they had to make to keep the business viable—including branch closures and job cuts—Synovus CEO Kessel Stelling and his management team quickly restored the bank's reputation. Keeping in mind the company's stated value of "keeping people first in every decision they made," the Synovus leadership team made the decision to work with several debt-laden customers who had experienced job losses and other setbacks, allowing them more time to pay off loans.

"I saw people lose their life savings, their businesses, their homes," Stelling told *American Banker.* "I saw good people get hurt and still try as hard as they could to honor their obligations. We want to lend to people with good credit, but we have to look at the circumstances and be willing to give people a second chance."[10] This is how higher level leaders maintain both results and relationships.

The ability to inspire trust is a key competency for any leadership position, but especially for those who coach. In the next chapter, we'll explore how coaching can be used to build an organization's leadership bench strength.

Coaching: A Key Competency for Leadership Development

Madeleine Homan Blanchard and Linda Miller

I n companies all over the world, surveys are showing that a leadership shortage is coming soon. Future leaders are needed in all industry sectors and functional areas and at all levels within organizations. The development of new leaders is becoming an important focus for executives and senior managers. More and more, coaching is being recognized as one of the key competencies that effectively develops future leaders.

A 2008 American Management Association study found that coaching is associated with higher performance in organizations, yet it is used by only about half of today's companies. Coaching continues to gain in popularity, and the field offers great growth opportunities.[1] The AMA concluded its report by stating: "We expect that coaching will become one of the keys to developing and retaining scarce talent in the future, and we think companies that learn to leverage it well will have a significant competitive advantage in the global marketplace."

Definition of Coaching

When we talk about coaching in this context, we are expanding our definition far beyond the *coaching* leadership style described in SLII®. In the narrow definition, a coaching leadership style involves providing the appropriate direction and support needed when disillusionment sets in, either because a task is more complicated than anticipated or circumstances have caused a change in attitude. Coaching as we describe it in this chapter is a broader term that encompasses several applications. We define this broader term as follows:

> *Coaching is a deliberate process using focused conversations to create an environment that results in accelerated performance and development.*

Regardless of people's function or position, successful coaching encourages them to be deliberate, purposeful, and fully aligned with team and organizational objectives as they make decisions and take action. Central to coaching is a focus on self responsibility, forward movement, and taking intentional action.

Five Applications of Coaching

Coaching can be provided for leaders in organizations by the use of external coaches or managers and HR professionals trained to provide coaching as one of their job responsibilities. In our discussion, all the examples used focus on internal coaches. Regardless of who performs the coaching, it has five common applications:

- **Performance coaching** is used when individuals need help returning their performance to acceptable standards.

- **Development coaching** is used when high performing individuals are ready to become more fully rounded in their current role.

- **Career coaching** is employed when individuals are ready to plan their next career moves.

- **Coaching to support learning** occurs when managers or direct reports need support, encouragement, and accountability to sustain recent training and turn insights into action.

- **Creating an internal coaching culture** is what happens when leaders recognize the value of coaching and use it to develop others.

After working with thousands of people in organizations, we have found that many managers and leaders spend most of their time dealing with performance challenges. With the leadership shortage ahead, it is important to shift from managing performance to focusing on development. As shown in Figure 9.1, while coaching sometimes involves discussions or conversations about performance and career, the coaching sweet spot centers on development.

The Coaching Sweet Spot

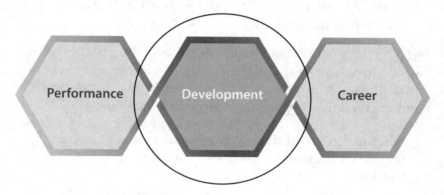

Figure 9.1 The Coaching Sweet Spot

Let's take a deeper look at the five applications of coaching.

Application One: Performance Coaching

Performance coaching is needed when individuals have been capable and confident about goals or tasks in the past, but their present performance no longer reflects that. Often, they seem to be regressing. This usually results from a change in attitude, not skills.

Let's take the example of Erin and Max.

> For the past two years, Erin knew that Max could deliver on his key responsibility areas without much direction. However, over the past three months Erin has noticed that Max isn't completing projects the way he used to. Being

extremely busy, Erin hadn't scheduled regular one-on-ones to check in with Max. Finally, she called him into her office.

"You missed that last deadline," Erin said to Max. "What's going on?"

With a shrug he said, "What's the big deal with missing one deadline? We have lots of time to take care of it. I'll get it by next week."

Surprised by his comment, Erin asked Max where he was in his development level around the project and what he needed to complete it. Again, he just shrugged.

The purpose of performance coaching is to reignite past competence and confidence about the goals or tasks, thus regaining momentum and improving performance. SLII® is useful for diagnosing development level and matching the leadership style that's needed.

Erin was concerned about Max's response. After observing him for several months, she decided it was time to give him feedback.

"Max, I want to share with you what I've noticed the past few months. Prior to January, you seemed to enjoy the team and the work we were doing. On most of the projects and goals, you have been either a Capable But Cautious Performer or a Self-Reliant Achiever. You certainly haven't needed much direction from me. You've been a major contributor to this team's work for years, but you've been missing deadlines and keeping your door closed." Erin paused to look him in the eye. "What's going on?" she asked.

Max did not respond.

Erin continued, "We have a lot at stake with this project. I'm happy to give you more direction if that's what you need to continue moving forward. If we don't get the project done this week, our unit will hold up others who are relying on us for the next step. I need you to step back in, or I will have to get someone else involved."

Max raised his eyes and looked at Erin. "You don't have to do that. I admit I've gotten a little disillusioned about the project, but now that I hear from you how important it is, I'm ready to roll up my sleeves and tackle it."

Erin said, "Wonderful. You've been a great contributor to our team in the past, and I value your work. Let's keep in touch with the steps you're taking this week because I want for you and for us to be successful with the deadline. When would be a good time for our next meeting?"

Tips for Performance Coaching

Managers and HR professionals who use coaching when performance is dropping need to be comfortable giving accurate and objective feedback. They need to be clear about what is at stake and who is accountable for what.

It's important to remain neutral when giving feedback and talking about consequences. It's also important to be clear that the person has a choice whether to make the changes. Come to an agreement about the changes that are needed. This step may take time and is not always as easy as it sounds.

Beware of being pulled off focus. Stay on track with the points you want to make. Take care not to come across as punishing. As much as possible, be positive and encouraging. Also, be certain to clearly state the consequences if the agreed-upon goals are not met. To avoid confusion and misunderstandings, it's important to be clear in your mind about the consequences before you begin performance coaching conversations.

Application Two: Development Coaching

Most managers are so busy putting out fires that they overlook development conversations. They may forget that team members, like themselves, are energized and encouraged when their development is kept in mind.

Development coaching is useful when direct reports are doing well and are ready for the next steps. They may be functioning at a

Self-Reliant Achiever level (D4) on most of their projects and goals. They are ready to be more fully rounded in their current role. The responsibility remains primarily on the direct report for keeping development top of mind. Yet when the manager focuses on it too, it conveys an underlying message of trust and support to the team member.

> Becca loved her job. She had been in it for four years, often taking on new responsibilities and projects. She also knew that she needed to be challenged more often so that she wouldn't get bored. One day she noticed that Oliver, her manager, had requested a meeting on her calendar. Because their company had many locations, she called Oliver at the meeting time.
>
> "Hi, Becca. Thanks for calling and for being so prompt. I've always liked that about you. I've been thinking of you recently and realized we haven't talked about your development lately. You consistently are such a Self-Reliant Achiever with your responsibilities and projects that I sometimes forget to talk with you about what's next for you in this role. Can we talk about that for a few minutes?"
>
> Becca felt a rush of excitement. "That would be great," she said.

Development coaching is focused on encouraging and increasing opportunities that lead to further development in the same role. To keep people engaged and growing, it's important for managers to keep expanding people's capability whenever possible. This helps develop them as future managers or leaders.

When using coaching for development, a supporting style (S3) is useful. Be sure to listen for what's most important to the person and to ask probing questions. Be sure to ask what the team member thinks is a developmental opportunity and what ideas he has. Think about the conversation as a way of challenging and inspiring the person to think more broadly.

When Oliver heard the enthusiasm in Becca's voice, he continued. "Becca, what do you see as some development opportunities ahead?"

Becca replied, "You know, I would love to know more about the budgeting process for our team. I've always been fascinated by that area."

Oliver was pleased to hear that Becca had been thinking about her development, even though she hadn't brought it up before. "Becca, I think it's very timely that you're interested in budgeting, especially since we're about to start our budgeting process for next year. I've got a couple of people who might be good for you to connect with."

Tips for Development Coaching

When thinking about coaching to develop others, remember that either the team member or the manager can begin these conversations. When identifying a person's strengths and weaknesses, keep the emphasis on maximizing strengths. Focus broadly on developmental opportunities for the person, but beware of making specific promises. Don't forget that introducing your direct reports to your network of professionals may be as important as finding a new project for them.

Application Three: Career Coaching

Career coaching is taking off in organizations as the need for leaders continues to increase. It's a strategy that retains talent and increases bench strength over time. Even in flat organizations that don't have a lot of upward mobility, it's energizing for people to talk about their future.

When should a manager broach these discussions? When a direct report is consistently functioning at a Self-Reliant Achiever level, it's time to begin conversations about that person's career. Coaching at this time can help the direct report look ahead to where he or she wants to be in the next few years, and the leader, as coach, can assist in planning the next career moves.

Several signals can indicate that it's time to have a career discussion. When direct reports continually exceed expectations, they might be ready to grow. Has one of your direct reports told you he or she wants more responsibility? That can also be a sign. An obvious signal is when a direct report brings up the topic. But just because high performers haven't asked to talk about their careers doesn't mean they don't want to. In most cases, they do.

Leaders and managers might find career coaching conversations threatening, since they could lead to losing an important team member. Be sure to curb your anxiety about losing the person and move bravely into the discussion. Marshall Goldsmith's research shows that one of the reasons top performers leave a company is because nobody asked them to stay.[2] Conversations about career are opportunities to show your direct reports how valued they are. In the end, it's important to think about what's best for the direct report as well as for the organization.

Don't avoid career coaching conversations because you think they take too much time. These are exactly the conversations that high performers want to have to stay in the organization. A gentle transition generally is less time-consuming than having to fill a position that's been vacated without discussion.

Career conversations are a time to challenge and encourage high-potential employees to keep developing as they look ahead. Focusing on the future creates a win for the organization as well as the direct report. When part of the career strategy includes bringing people into a role that may be vacated, it creates a win for the manager, too.

As the following example shows, most employees look to their leaders for guidance and support in the career area.

> Hannah had been with her company for eight years when she started wondering what might be ahead. She knew it was time to talk with her manager, Niki. Niki had also been thinking about Hannah's development, but she hadn't said anything yet, except in conversations with colleagues.

Hannah brought it up at their next one-on-one meeting. "Niki, I'd really like to talk with you about what's next for me. I've worked with you for several years, and most of the time I feel like I'm a Self-Reliant Achiever in my tasks and goals. What's next?"

Niki knew this conversation had been coming. She also knew that she didn't want to lose Hannah. Yet she knew that keeping her would stunt Hannah's growth, which ultimately wouldn't be good for their company.

"Hannah," Niki said, "I'm glad you're thinking about this. I've thought about it, too, and I apologize for not talking with you sooner. I'd love to hear your thoughts about your goals and how they support our corporate goals. Thanks for starting the conversation."

Hannah began by telling Niki about the things she was doing, being sure to mention that she was ready for new challenges and opportunities.

Niki listened carefully, thinking about where Hannah's skills and passion aligned with their organization's needs. "Hannah, I'm thinking that a cross-functional project would be perfect for you and will expand your skills and network." Niki went on to describe the project.

"I'd love to get involved in that," said Hannah.

"Who could you be training to take over your job if this leads to a career change for you?" Niki asked.

Hannah thought for a moment. "I have a couple of people in mind."

Niki said, "Great. You'll have to reach out to them and see if they are ready and willing to take on your old role. Let's keep talking about this, okay?"

"Absolutely," said Hannah. Both she and Niki were pleased when the meeting ended.

Tips for Career Coaching

Hold career coaching conversations on a regular basis with your high performing direct reports. Again, when a manager brings up the subject of careers, it's a proactive move that makes direct reports feel cared about. During these conversations, it's important to explore what the employee is thinking and how his or her ideas align with organizational objectives. Familiarize yourself with the career services your HR department offers and what information is available about job roles and their corresponding competencies. Share this information with your direct report as you talk about all aspects of the next steps: when, where, and how the person's career will move forward. Finally, be sure to offer resources and make introductions when needed.

Application Four: Coaching to Support Learning

People learn through training, and training is one of the best ways to develop people in your organization. Training can enhance any number of areas: management, leadership, skills, processes, communication, and a host of other job-related areas. As we said at the end of the last chapter, a major challenge with training is narrowing the learning-doing gap—getting people to use what they've learned after the training. One of the best ways to maximize an organization's investment in training is to do follow-up coaching.

We have found that coaching to support learning is most effective when the learning process is followed by at least three follow-up coaching conversations. These are conversations that managers, HR professionals, and internal or external coaches can have immediately after the training.

With as few as three coaching sessions during the eight-week period following a training event, participants consistently apply what they've learned. Having the first follow-up coaching session within two weeks of the training and continuing with a coaching session once every two to three weeks generates the best results. Each coaching conversation should be focused on how to apply information from the training to the workplace.

Here's an example of what it might look like to follow up training with coaching:

> Morgan loved to learn as part of her new manager training. Her company offered excellent training. She was pleased when her manager told her she could attend an advanced management course that focused on SLII®. What she didn't know was that this course would be different in that it included six months of follow-up coaching with an external professional coach.
>
> During their first call, her coach, Kyle, asked Morgan what she had learned that would be helpful to implement on the job. This caused her to think about the material and revisit her notes. She realized that some of her interactions with her team members had not been going well. Kyle asked her what she could immediately apply from the training that would help with those conversations. First, Morgan realized that she tended to use the same leadership style with all her people. Diagnosing the specific development levels of her team members and determining the appropriate leadership style for each was eye-opening for her. She learned that having one-on-one meetings with her people would not only help their relationships, but help her apply what she had learned.
>
> Kyle asked Morgan what actions she was willing to take between this call and the next to move forward in these areas. Morgan agreed to schedule one-on-one meetings with each of her people before her next call with Kyle.

Tips for Coaching to Support Learning

It's important to get started with the coaching as soon as possible after the training event. Have a system in place to get people scheduled with their first and subsequent sessions. Focus on how your direct reports can apply their new learning to their jobs. Help them identify action items and obstacles to action.

Don't fall into the trap of debating the point of the training. The purpose of the coaching is to help your people apply the learning, not to debate the learning itself. Stay focused on action. Coaching to support learning is a time to talk about how to use the material in the real world.

Finally, don't use the excuse that you don't have time for coaching to support learning. Remember that time spent coaching maximizes the investment in training, empowers you and your direct reports, and saves time down the road.

Application Five: Creating an Internal Coaching Culture

The best way for coaching to positively impact an organization is to create your own internal coaching culture. This can happen only when leaders and managers recognize the value of coaching and use it to develop people for much-needed future leadership roles.

In *Coaching in Organizations*, Madeleine Blanchard and Linda Miller contend that creating an internal coaching climate has many benefits.[3] Not only does coaching emphasize leadership development, but it also fosters a mentality of taking ownership for work that is done. A coaching culture is a culture of self responsibility rather than blaming or pointing to others when things go awry. Even though it takes a while to cultivate, this type of culture creates a wonderful work environment that supports productivity and boosts morale.

It can take twelve to eighteen months to roll out an internal coaching culture. The ramp-up and rollout process may include coach training for managers and leaders, mentor coaching for those who are learning how to coach others, and time to develop the support systems and measurement strategies that ensure success.

The following example shows the extent of thinking that must be done prior to establishing an internal coaching culture:

> When Rob realized how much he loved coaching and how important it could be for his manufacturing company, he wasted no time in interviewing coaching companies with which he could partner. The company he hired assigned

a team lead, Alec, to work with Rob because Alec knew coaching and had experience setting up coaching systems in other companies. When Rob and Alec first met face to face, Alec began asking questions.

"Rob, we need to address several areas before we go any further with this project. First, what does coaching mean to you, and what do you expect coaching to do for your company?"

Rob responded, "Since I've been working with my coach over the past year, I've experienced such great growth. My team has become much more productive than it was, and this has gained the attention of senior leadership. They're asking me what I'm doing differently. The only thing I'm doing differently is coaching my team. I think it's time for others to get the same experience, and I want to lead the way here in our company."

"How will you get senior-level sponsorship and clarity from that level on the objectives for the coaching?" Alec asked.

Rob replied, "Our CEO and COO have already bought in. Your question about the objectives is interesting. I think I need to do a bit more work on that. I'm not sure we're clear enough on the objectives."

Alec nodded. "While you're talking about the objectives, be sure to ask how they want the outcomes measured. Many organizations are measuring the success of coaching by thinking about ROE, return on expectations, rather than ROI, return on investment."

Rob agreed. "Yes, it would be good to figure that out now. We're a company that's big on ROI, so I'll start talking about the difference. I know that measuring this type of thing can be challenging, and we'll need to talk more about it down the road."

"That's for sure," said Alec. "The clearer you can be on what you want to measure and how you'll go about measuring it, the better. You'll also want to agree with senior leaders on what information is shared and what is kept confidential. Keeping confidential the content of the coaching conversations is a critical part of coaching."

Rob nodded. From his own coaching experience, he knew immediately what Morgan was talking about.

Tips for Creating an Internal Coaching Culture

In creating an internal coaching culture, it's important to first define the purpose and objectives, and make sure they fit with the organization's purpose and values. Next, find senior leadership advocates who can role-model the coaching culture, and be sure to get administrative help to roll out the initiative. Reward coaching behaviors and activities, and set up an internal communication about the coaching to help cascade it throughout the organization. Depending on who is available, it may be appropriate to provide professional coaches from outside the organization.

As you take steps to create an internal coaching culture, you should watch for several things. First, be sure to define and honor confidentiality. One breach of confidentiality from coaching conversations can severely damage the entire coaching initiative. Second, remember that a coaching culture isn't established overnight. Allocate plenty of time to get started. Third, remember to stay flexible. If something isn't working, you can always change it.

*****

When you talk about coaching, people often ask about mentoring and how they fit together. In the next chapter, we'll answer that question.

10

Mentoring: The Key to Life Planning

Ken Blanchard and Claire Díaz-Ortiz

When people look back on their lives and the successes they've had, almost without exception they talk about the people along the way who've guided their journey. That's because successful people do not reach their goals alone. Behind even the most independent achiever is a person or group of people who helped that person succeed.

Like coaching, mentoring is a one-to-one process. But the relationship between an individual and a coach has specific objectives and goals focused on developing potential, improving relationships, and enhancing performance. Mentoring, on the other hand, has big-picture objectives and goals. As the subtitle of this chapter suggests, mentoring is about more than goal accomplishment; it's about life planning.

Does mentoring work? Absolutely. As Michael Hyatt says, "Nothing drives success faster than the right mentoring relationship."

Mentoring is a mutually beneficial relationship. Yet when most people think about mentoring, they focus on the impact the mentor can have on the mentee—in other words, on the person supposedly doing the teaching. Very little is said about the impact the mentee can have on the mentor. In fact, most mentor-mentee relationships are win-win: Both parties learn and gain from the experience.[1]

Another common perception is that mentors are older people with established careers and well-honed skill sets who provide guidance to younger mentees. This isn't always the case. A mentor can be older or younger. The key to success is selecting the mentor or mentee who best suits your needs, regardless of age.

How do you determine if mentoring might be right for you? Consider the following three questions:

- Where are you in your life—are you on an upward trajectory, or have you hit a plateau?
- Do you feel uncertain about the direction you're heading?
- Are you open to learning from others?

These questions are important to ask, regardless of your age.

Suppose your gut feeling says, "Yes, I should be a mentor" or "Yes, I could use a mentor." What concerns might stop you from developing a mentoring relationship?

Obstacles to Beginning a Mentoring Relationship

There are three primary concerns people have about getting involved in mentoring.

The first is *time.* Many people believe that mentoring is too time-consuming. Yet being a mentor or mentee isn't a full time job. If you're a mentee, the right mentor can save you from making costly mistakes that can set your career back years. Having a mentor will improve the quality of your decisions and provide opportunities that simply wouldn't be available to you otherwise.

If you're a mentor, a mentee can give you new perspective about where you are in your own career.

The second concern has to do with *fear.* A lot of people are afraid to approach potential mentors, and a lot of potential mentors are afraid they don't really know how to be a mentor. It's natural to feel anxious about beginning a mentoring relationship, but that's no reason to miss out on the potential advantages of mentoring.

The third concern about mentorship has to do with *confusion.* Uncertainty about what mentoring is and what it means to be a mentor or mentee prohibits people from pursuing mentoring relationships. In *One Minute Mentoring: How to Find and Work with a Mentor—and Why You'll Benefit from Being One*, Ken Blanchard and Claire Díaz-Ortiz clarify what mentoring is and what it involves.[2]

Choosing a Mentoring Partner

Before selecting a mentoring partner, you must determine the type of mentoring relationship you're seeking. The following is a partial list of various mentor-mentee relationships:

New hire mentoring: Many organizations have formal mentoring programs for newly hired employees. The concept is simple: pair up a new hire with an experienced performer, and watch the new hire learn and grow.

Peer-to-peer mentoring: These relationships involve partnering with someone of the same status or ability so that you can mentor one another and improve each other's effectiveness.

Cross-generational mentoring: This involves two people from different generations pairing up for mutual benefit and growth. The older person might be a role model with wisdom to impart to the younger person, or the younger person might be a teacher of cutting-edge skills—such as technology—to the older person.

Essence Versus Form

It's important to bear in mind that there are two aspects of working with someone in a mentoring relationship—essence and form. *Essence* is all about sharing heart-to-heart and finding common values. *Form* is about structure—how you will work together.

Once you've identified a potential mentor or mentee, meet with that person first to find out if it's a good match in terms of *essence*. Do your values align? Do your personalities click? Does the conversation flow?

If you and your potential mentor or mentee have passed the essence test, you can move on to the *form* aspect of working together—what you intend to accomplish, how you intend to achieve your mission, when you'll communicate, and where you'll work together.

The importance of essence versus form really became clear to Ken Blanchard before he developed a mentoring coauthor relationship with Norman Vincent Peale. Ken initially had an idea of writing a book called *The Power of Positive Management,* and he met to discuss coauthoring the book with an author who was considered a leader in positive thinking. At the meeting, all his potential coauthor wanted to talk about was form: who was going to do what, how they were going to divide the royalties, and the like. He quickly redirected any discussion of essence to form. So Ken decided to pass on working with him.

Shortly afterward Ken got a call from his publisher, who said, "I understand you had a disappointing talk with your potential coauthor. Have you considered writing a book with Norman Vincent Peale?" Ken's reaction was, "Is he still alive?" His parents had gone to Norman's church before Ken was born. "Not only is he still alive at 86, but he's also a fabulous human being," said his publisher.

After Ken agreed to meet with Norman and his wife, Ruth, he was amazed that the entire conversation was about essence. Norman and Ruth were quick to tell Ken all about who they were and their values and asked him about the same things. At the end of a three hour lunch, Norman turned to his wife, Ruth, and said, "Well, Ruth, do you think we should write a book with this young man?" It was the first time the subject of form—business—had come up. Ruth said, "Absolutely, under one condition. That from now on, whenever we meet, he will bring his wife Margie."

Not only did Ken write a book with Norman, *The Power of Ethical Management*, but they developed a wonderful mentoring relationship that was cross-generational: Ken and Margie were in their mid-forties and Norman and Ruth were well into their mid-eighties.

The MENTOR Model: Elements of a Successful Mentoring Partnership

Once you and your mentor or mentee have decided to work together, putting some structure around the relationship will make your time together more productive. That's why Ken Blanchard and Claire

Díaz-Ortiz developed The MENTOR model: six guidelines for an effective mentoring relationship.[3] Following these guidelines will keep your mentoring partnership on track.

Mission

Take time to craft a mutually agreed-upon mission statement for the mentorship. What do each of you intend to get out of your partnership? A mentoring mission is a picture of how things will be if everything goes as planned. While this at first may seem like overkill, you'll be surprised by how the process of creating a mission will clear up assumptions and make your time together more productive.

Engagement

Agree on ways to engage that work for your personalities and schedules. Particularly at the beginning of your mentorship, make a commitment to regular meetings, even if they are virtual. By deciding how often you will communicate with each other and by what means, you will be building the structure that will make your mentoring partnership a reality.

Networking

Both mentor and mentee will bring a network of connections to each other. These connections will become a pipeline to new knowledge, skills, and opportunities. However, care must be taken so that you are not being reckless with each other's connections. There is a fine line between following up with a contact that is offered to you and taking undue advantage of the people in your partner's network. Be careful not to cross that line.

Trust

It takes time to establish the deep communication and give-and-take that happens in a mature mentoring relationship. Trust can be destroyed in an instant, so address any mistakes and communication breakdowns right away. By telling the truth, staying connected, and being dependable, you can build the kind of trusting relationship that leads to significant personal and professional growth.

Opportunity

For both of you, the relationship will open up opportunities—events, learning experiences, connections, and career options. Digital media makes potential networks bigger than ever, allowing for more opportunities for partners. Stay on the lookout for potential opportunities you can share with each other, and follow up on the opportunities offered to you.

Review and Renew

Mentoring relationships don't necessarily last indefinitely. Once your mission is established, a regular review—perhaps annually or biannually—will help you keep the relationship on track and let you know when the mission for your mentorship has been accomplished. At that point, you can renew the relationship and create a new mission, or you can bring the mentorship to a close.

In their mentoring partnership, Norman Vincent Peale and Ken Blanchard touched on all the elements of The MENTOR model.

Their **mission** was to write a book that would have a positive impact on ethics and integrity in business and organizations, showing that people didn't have to cheat to win.

They agreed on **engagement** early on, deciding where and how often to meet, and how they would communicate with each other.

When it came to **networking,** their mentorship was mutually beneficial. Norman introduced Ken to Truett Cathy, the founder of Chick-fil-A. Ken introduced Norman to Bob Buford, the author of *Halftime*, and other younger spiritual leaders.

The **trust** that developed between Ken and Norman was deep and authentic. They both realized that they didn't just write about their ideals; they did their best to live by them. Norman was the most positive person Ken had ever met. And Norman often said that when he was around Ken, he was motivated to do more, even at his age.

Their partnership brought both Ken and Norman a world of **opportunity.** After meeting him through Norman, Ken coauthored a book with Truett Cathy called *The Generosity Factor: Discover the Joy* *of Giving Your Time, Talent, and Treasure*. With Ken, Norman got to participate in stimulating new seminars across the country.

By the time Norman and Ken's book was published, they had developed a friendship/mentorship that they would **review and renew** regularly. Over the years, they continued to encourage and support each other. Norman suggested that Ken write a book about his spiritual journey, which Ken dedicated to Norman.[4]

Creating a Mentoring Program in Your Organization

Many companies have discovered that formal mentoring programs are one of the best ways to groom newly hired people to become successful. These internal mentoring programs have many benefits for the organization as well: more highly trained employees, increased engagement, decreased turnover, and leadership development, to name just a few. As a result, corporate mentoring programs are popping up everywhere.

At Chick-fil-A, all executive officers are asked to mentor others. The pairings are made by the company's executive committee. Other leaders can "nominate" people to be mentored. Some mentor more than one person per year, based on their availability and interest.

Intel runs a long-standing program that matches employees with mentors based on the skills and interests of the mentee. These mentorships can be in-person or virtual. Potential mentees are asked to fill out a questionnaire, which is used to match them with people who can teach them the skills they're interested in mastering.

If you are interested in helping your organization set up a mentoring program, here are a few things to keep in mind:

Start with your Human Resources department. If you work at an organization large enough to have an HR department, it should be your first stop in discussing the idea. Has the idea been considered before? Is the HR team amenable to spearheading the effort? What support can you provide as the program develops? If you can get your HR department people excited about the idea, you'll be able to rely on their expertise in setting up the program. This usually entails finding employees who are interested in a mentoring partnership and then matching people up.

Teach mentors and mentees The MENTOR model. Many times, potential mentors are scared of mentoring because they think they don't know enough, when in reality the opposite is likely true. Life experience is one of the greatest predictors of a successful mentoring partnership, and most people find they have that in spades. By following the six steps in The MENTOR model, you will be well on your way to having a dynamic and powerful mentoring relationship.

Establish essential guidelines. Mentoring can only reach its maximum potential if a regular system of checks and balances is in place. Within a company environment, it's a good idea for all mentoring partnerships to follow some general guidelines. Set parameters around such items as these:

- Frequency of meetings between mentor and mentee
- Timelines of the overall mentoring partnership
- Dates of reviews between mentor and mentee

Putting in the work to create a formal mentoring program is one of the smartest investments an organization can make. Not only does mentoring educate and revitalize people within the organization, it also preserves and expands critical corporate knowledge. With approximately ten thousand people turning sixty-five every day, a formal mentoring program can also be a good strategy for transferring older employees' knowledge and skills to the younger members of the workforce.

Tailoring Mentoring to Career Stages

In establishing an in-house mentoring program, it is important to match mentees and mentors on where they are in their careers. For example, the food services company, Sodexo, offers three types of mentoring programs to help employees at different stages of their careers: their Bridge program, where new hires are paired with seasoned managers; the IMPACT program, which forms 100 formal partnerships over the course of a year to employees at any level; and a less formal Peer-to-Peer program, which employees can choose to participate in at any stage of their career.

Early or Entry Level

For early- or entry-level employees, it's beneficial to offer on-the-job training. Even better is offering a new hire mentoring program. This can pair a new hire with a seasoned employee to help the new hire understand the basics of the job and how they might chart a career path from their starting point.

Remember that entry level doesn't necessarily mean youth. In today's workplace, more and more Baby Boomers are beginning second careers. This trend was dramatized in the 2015 film, *The Intern*, where a 70-year-old widower (Robert De Niro), hoping to update his skills, accepts a job as an intern for an online retailer and becomes the mentee of its 30-something founder and CEO, Jules (Anne Hathaway). The film not only highlights a classic case of reverse mentoring, but also shows how mutually beneficial entry-level mentoring can be.

Mid-Career or Management Level

For employees who have learned the basics of their job, the emphasis will shift from technical, job-related skills toward people and relationship skills. Their best mentor at this middle stage may be a peer— someone at their same skill and career level—because these people will be familiar with the kinds of challenges mid-career employees face each day.

Executive or Master Level

For those who have reached the C suite or attained a secure spot at the top of their chosen profession, it's time to suggest they move from success to significance by becoming a mentor. This is an excellent way for people to experience the truth of the old adage, "It is better to give than to receive." The rewards of passing along knowledge and wisdom may not be measured by promotions and increased earnings, but people will be enriched by a deep sense of purpose and joy.

Again, the executive or master stage is defined more by competence than age. People have reached this stage when they have valuable wisdom and experience that can benefit others. For example, you may be a 28-year-old tech master, ready to mentor middle-aged but less experienced people in your field. The point is that you've become a leader and now it's your turn to cultivate future leaders.

Being an executive or master mentor means that you are a role model; therefore, you will be guiding your mentee as much by what you do as by what you say. In fact, the best senior-level mentors employ top-notch listening and questioning skills to draw out the concerns and aspirations of their mentees. When you do speak, be candid. Let your mentee learn from your failures so they don't have to make the same mistakes.

It's true that mentoring will take some time and intention. It also takes time and intention to learn to drive—but once you know how, you can really go places! The same is true with mentoring. We all have 168 hours each week. Investing a few of those hours in a mentoring relationship will energize you in a way that web surfing and TV watching never will. When a mentorship is done well, both mentor and mentee can look to the relationship as a major factor in a successful, fulfilling life.

*****

We've explored the many ways leaders can achieve results through one-on-one relationships. In the next chapter, we'll learn how leaders can move beyond the one-on-one relationship to build high performing teams.

11

Team Leadership

Don Carew, Eunice Parisi-Carew,
Lael Good, and Ken Blanchard

Teams have become a major strategy for getting work done. We live in teams. Our organizations are made up of teams. We move from one team to another without giving it a thought. The percentage of time we spend in team settings—project teams, work groups, cross-functional teams, virtual teams, and management teams—is ever-increasing.

In our latest Blanchard research involving 1,300 people—in partnership with *Training* magazine in 2017[1]—we learned that people spend more than half their work time in teams, and the more senior the respondent in terms of organizational level, the more that time increases.

Yet only 27 percent of the respondents felt that their teams were high performing. And these views on performance differ within age groups. The most important takeaway from these findings, however, is that regardless of age, people did not perceive the majority of their teams as high performing.

What is happening in today's teams that is contributing to this performance gap?

When asked about the areas that have the greatest impact on improved team performance, the following were identified:

- Establishing team purpose, goals, and expectations from the start
- Regular communication regarding team progress and achievement

- Regular feedback discussions
- Recognizing and celebrating team achievements

The most important skill for a team leader at the team's beginning is to ensure that the team has a clear purpose, as well as clear goals, roles, strategies, and expectations.

Our research confirms that being effective in today's organizations is a team game, and without the right team leadership approach, a team is unlikely to be successful.

Why Teams?

In "HR Technology Disruptions for 2018," Josh Bersin of Deloitte Consulting LLP identifies three microtrends that are driving a reinvention of the HR marketplace:

- Changes in the overall technology landscape
- Changes in the way we work
- Changes in the way we manage organizations

Teams are at the heart of these changes. The article reinforces our findings that leading with teams is the best approach in today's business environment. Bersin points out that "companies are increasingly operating as networks of teams" and that "team-centric tools, platforms, coaching, analytics, monitoring, and assessment tools are red hot—because they are needed."

The days of top-down management are over. "As companies replace hierarchical management with a networked team structure, we are going to be using new tools purpose-built for teams," Bersin notes. "Companies want management tools that help enable and empower teams, drive team-centric engagement and performance, and support agile, network-focused HR practices."[2]

Teams have the power to increase productivity and morale—or destroy it. Working effectively, a team can make better decisions, solve more complex problems, and do more to enhance creativity and build skills than individuals working alone. The team is the only unit that has the flexibility and resources to respond quickly to changes that have become commonplace in today's world.

People no longer have the luxury of going it alone. Technology change is occurring so quickly that it is impossible for one person to be able to accomplish goals on his or her own.

No one of us is as smart as all of us.

At the same time, the business environment itself has become increasingly competitive, and the issues it faces are increasingly complex. This challenging environment has caused organizations to realize that they can no longer depend on hierarchical structures and a few peak performers to maintain a competitive advantage.

The demand is for collaboration and teamwork in all parts of the organization. Success today comes from using the collective knowledge and richness of diverse perspectives. There is a conscious movement toward teams as the strategic vehicle for getting work accomplished and moving organizations into the future.

Fast-paced, agile work environments require teams to operate virtually around the world. These geographically dispersed teams face special challenges in building trust, developing effective communication, and managing attentiveness.[3] However, with the proper leadership and technology, virtual teams are every bit as productive and rewarding as face-to-face teams.

Teams are not just nice to have. They are hard-core units of production.

It's a fact that people's health and well-being are directly affected by the amount of involvement they have in the workplace. Twelve thousand male Swedish workers were studied over a 14-year period. Workers who felt isolated and had little influence over their jobs were 162 percent more likely to have a fatal heart attack than were those who had greater influence in decisions at work and who worked in teams.[4] Data like this—combined with the fact that teams can be far more productive than individuals functioning alone—provides a compelling argument for creating high-involvement workplaces and using teams as the central vehicle for getting work done.

Obstacles to High Performance

Teams are a major investment of time, money, and resources. The cost of allowing them to falter or underproduce is staggering. Even worse, a team meeting that is considered a waste of time has wide-ranging effects. The energy does not dissipate when the meeting is over but spills into every aspect of organizational life. If people leave a meeting feeling unheard—or if they disagree with a decision made in the team—they leave angry and frustrated. This impacts the next event. The opposite happens when meetings feel productive and empowering—the positive energy spreads.

Teams are not able to achieve high performance for many reasons, from lack of a clear purpose to lack of training. These obstacles keep a team from reaching its potential.

Our survey of 1,300 respondents found that the top obstacles to team performance were these:

- Lack of accountability
- Unclear decision making
- Poor leadership

followed by these:

- Poor or no planning
- Disorganization or unclear roles
- Lack of clear purpose or goals

An awareness of the obstacles to optimal team performance can prepare team leaders and members to proactively address these issues.

An Effective Team Leadership Approach

High performance teams can be vehicles for getting the job done and increasing engagement throughout your organization. Yet understanding the dynamics of teamwork has never been easy. Working in a team is both an art and a science, and leaders must systematically develop an effective team leadership approach.

In our team leadership approach, it is important to first understand the characteristics that make a high performance team. Knowing what a high performance team looks like will provide a benchmark for team success.

Next, leaders need to identify the team's stage of development, ensure that the team gets off to a good start by creating a team charter, and then provide a set of leadership behaviors that will keep the team moving through the stages of development to ultimately reach and sustain high performance.

This approach to team leadership can be adapted to any team, regardless of its purpose, pursuit, type, or size.

Understanding the Characteristics That Make a High Performance Team

We define a team as *two or more persons who come together for a common purpose and who are mutually accountable for results*. This is the difference between a team and a group. Often, work groups are called teams without developing a common purpose and shared accountability. This can lead to disappointing results and a belief that teams do not work well. A collection of individuals working on the same task are not necessarily a team. They have the potential to become a high performance team once they clarify their purpose, strategies, and accountabilities.

Some teams achieve outstanding results no matter how difficult the objective. They are at the top of their class. What makes these teams different? What sets them apart and makes them capable of outperforming their peers? Although each team is unique, each has characteristics that are shared by all outstanding teams regardless of their purpose or goals.

Building highly effective teams, like building a great organization, begins with a picture of what you are aiming for—a target. It is imperative to know what a high performance team looks like. That is why the journey to high performance begins with understanding the characteristics that make up a high performance team (see Figure 11.1).

These characteristics represent the gold standard for teams committed to excellence. By benchmarking your team in each of these areas, you can identify where you need to focus team development.

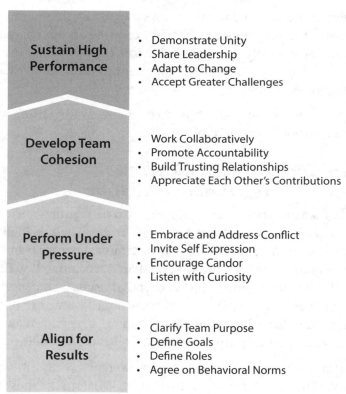

Characteristics of High Performance Teams

Sustain High Performance
- Demonstrate Unity
- Share Leadership
- Adapt to Change
- Accept Greater Challenges

Develop Team Cohesion
- Work Collaboratively
- Promote Accountability
- Build Trusting Relationships
- Appreciate Each Other's Contributions

Perform Under Pressure
- Embrace and Address Conflict
- Invite Self Expression
- Encourage Candor
- Listen with Curiosity

Align for Results
- Clarify Team Purpose
- Define Goals
- Define Roles
- Agree on Behavioral Norms

Figure 11.1 Characteristics of a High Performance Teams

As you read from the bottom to the top about the characteristics of high performance teams, it's probably no surprise that teams like these are effective.

For example, Ken was invited to a Boston Celtics practice during the heyday of Larry Bird, Robert Parish, and Kevin McHale. Standing on the sidelines with Coach KC Jones, Ken asked, "How do you lead a group of superstars like this?" KC smiled and said, "I throw the ball out and every once in a while, shout 'Shoot!'" In observing Jones as a leader, Ken noticed he didn't follow any of the stereotypes of a strong leader. During time-outs, the players talked more than KC did. He didn't run up and down the sidelines yelling things at the players during the game; most of the coaching was done by the team members. They encouraged, supported, and directed each other.

This team exhibited the characteristics of a high performance team. They were aligned for results, knew how to perform under pressure, had built team cohesion, and had reached a level of sustained high performance that did not rely on the coach for direction to get the job done.

When this low-key leader, KC Jones, retired, all the players essentially said he was the best coach they'd ever had. Why? Because he permitted everyone to lead, and that's what a team is all about.

Don Carew observed an extraordinary example of team leadership while working with Caterpillar's Track Type Tractors (TTT) division in Illinois.[5] The TTT division was in deep trouble. The lowest-performing division of the company, it was losing millions of dollars a year and had been involved in a bitter strike. The Blanchard team worked with TTT to implement a new set of values and behaviors based on trust, mutual respect, teamwork, empowerment, risk taking, and a sense of urgency. In less than three years, the company realized a $250 million turnaround. Quality as measured by customers improved by 16 times. Employee satisfaction moved from being the lowest in Caterpillar to being the highest. All of this was achieved by people at all levels working together in teams and by the organization creating the conditions that supported teamwork, mutual respect, and trust.

Identifying the Team's Stage of Development

Building a high performance team is a journey—a predictable progression from a collection of individuals to a well-oiled system where all the characteristics of a high performance team are evident.

Knowing the characteristics and needs of a high performance team is critical. It gives you a target to shoot for. Obviously, teams don't start with all the characteristics of a high performance team in place. All teams are unique and complex living systems. The whole of a team is different from the sum of its members.

Research over the past seventy years has consistently demonstrated that, regardless of their purpose, teams, like individuals, go through a series of developmental stages as they grow.

All these comprehensive research efforts were surprisingly consistent in their conclusions.[6] They all identified either four or five stages of development and were very similar in their descriptions of the characteristics of each stage. After a comprehensive review of more than 200 studies on group development, Roy Lacoursiere identified five stages of team development:

1. Orientation
2. Dissatisfaction
3. Integration
4. Production
5. Termination

We will focus in detail on the first four team development stages (see Figure 11.2), and will discuss the Termination stage later in the chapter. Understanding these development stages and a team's characteristics and needs at each stage is essential for team leaders and team members if they are to be effective in building successful, productive teams.

That's what *diagnosing* is all about. The ability to determine a team's stage of development and assess its needs requires stepping back and looking at the team as a whole, rather than focusing on individual behaviors and needs.

The Stages of Team Development

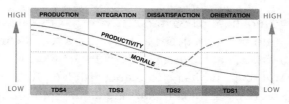

Figure 11.2 The Stages of Team Development[7]

Productivity and Morale

Two variables determine the team development stage: productivity and morale.

Productivity is the amount and quality of the work accomplished in relation to the team's purpose and goals. Productivity is dependent on team members' ability to collaborate, their knowledge and skills, clear goals, and access to needed resources. *Morale* is the sense of pride and satisfaction that comes from belonging to the team and accomplishing its work.

Productivity often starts out low. When a group first comes together, its members can't accomplish very much. Often, they don't even know each other. Over time, as they learn to work together, their performance should gradually increase. If that is not the case, something is seriously wrong. Either they have a leadership problem, or the skills necessary to perform well are not present in the group.

Morale, on the other hand, starts out high and takes a sudden dip. People are usually enthusiastic about being on a new team unless they've been forced to join. The initial euphoria dissipates quickly when the reality of the difficulty of working on a team comes into play. Now you might hear people say, "Why did I agree to be on that team?" As differences are explored and people begin to break through initial frustrations and working together becomes easier, the team begins to achieve results, and morale begins to rise again. Ultimately, both morale and productivity are high as a group becomes a high performance team.

Why are high morale and high productivity the ultimate goals? High morale with no performance is a party, not a team. On the other hand, a team that is achieving good results yet has low morale will eventually stumble, and its performance will fade. The bottom line is that *both* productivity *and* morale are required to produce a high performance team with sustainable results.

Diagnosing the level of productivity and morale is a clear way to determine a team's development stage and understand team needs at any point in time.

Team Development Stage 1 (TDS1)—Orientation

Most team members, unless coerced, are eager to be on the team. However, they often come with high, unrealistic expectations. These expectations are accompanied by some anxiety about how they will fit in, how much they can trust others, and what demands will be placed on them. Team members are also unclear about the team's purpose, goals, roles, and how the team will work together.

In this stage, team members depend strongly on the leader for purpose and direction. Some testing of boundaries occurs, and the central leader's behavior is usually tentative and polite. Morale is moderately high and productivity is low during this stage.

Two of us were asked to serve on a project team to study and modify the compensation system for our consulting partners. At the first meeting, we were excited and eager to see who else was a part of the project team. Many complaints about the system had been registered, and we were eager to make positive changes. We were apprehensive about whether "they" would really listen. We also wondered how much time this would take, who would be in charge of the team, and how we would fit in with the other members. We had no idea how to proceed or even what our goals should be. We looked to the team leader to steer us in the right direction. These feelings of excitement, anxiety, and dependence on the leader are normal for team members at Stage 1.

The challenge at the Orientation stage is to get the team off to a good start by identifying a purpose and structure for the team, as well as beginning to build relationships and trust.

The duration of this stage depends on the clarity and difficulty of the team purpose, as well as clarity about how the team will work together. With simple, easily defined goals, the Orientation stage may be relatively short—5 to 10 percent of the team's life. On the other hand, with complex goals, the team may spend 30 to 60 percent of its time in this stage.

Team Development Stage 2 (TDS2)—Dissatisfaction

As the team gets some experience under its belt, morale may dip as team members experience a discrepancy between their initial expectations and reality. Reluctant team members start out in Stage 2. If purpose, goal, roles, and behavioral norms were not established or agreed upon in Stage 1, the difficulties in accomplishing the goal and in working together lead to confusion and frustration, as well as a growing dissatisfaction with dependence on the leader. Negative reactions to each other develop, team members may avoid expressing their opinions, and subgroups form that can polarize the team. The breakdown of communication and the inability to solve problems or constructively address conflict result in lowered trust. Productivity increases somewhat but may be hampered by low morale.

Back to that compensation project team we just mentioned: While we started off with enthusiasm, we quickly realized how much hard work would be involved, the goal's controversial nature, and the possibility that recommendations we would make might not be accepted. We began to experience some strong negative feelings among members, and subgroups began to form. Frustration with the team leader began to develop. We started to wonder whether this was worth our time. These feelings of questioning, doubt, and frustration are typical of team members during Stage 2.

The challenge in the Dissatisfaction stage is helping the team manage issues of power, control, and conflict and begin to work together effectively.

The amount of time spent in this stage depends on how quickly issues can be resolved. It is possible for the team to get stuck at the

Dissatisfaction stage and to continue being both demoralized and relatively unproductive.

Team Development Stage 3 (TDS3)—Integration

Moderate to high productivity and variable or improving morale characterize a team at the Integration stage. As issues encountered in the Dissatisfaction stage are addressed and resolved, morale begins to rise. The team embrace practices that allow members to work together more easily. Goal accomplishment and technical skills increase, which contribute to positive feelings. Increased commitment to the team's purpose and goals occurs. Different viewpoints are viewed as the heart of creativity. Trust and cohesion grow as communication becomes more open and goal oriented. Team members are willing to hold each other accountable.

> *You will never, never, never have a high performance team unless leadership and control are shared.*

Team members learn to appreciate the differences among themselves. Team members begin to see the team as a whole and start thinking in terms of "we" rather than "I." Although the team understands the importance of addressing and embracing conflict in order to move forward, the newly developed feelings of trust and cohesion are fragile, and team members may tend to avoid conflict for fear of losing the positive climate. This reluctance to deal with conflict can slow progress and lead to less effective decisions.

Back to our project team: As we began resolving the frustrations we experienced in Stage 2, we began listening more carefully and came to appreciate different points of view. We developed some initial strategies for accomplishing our team purpose and clarified our goal and roles. In spite of the difficulty of achieving our goal, working with the team now became more fun. People were getting along, and at every meeting we were more clearly seeing what needed to be done. We even began to see the possibility of some success down the road. These feelings of increasing satisfaction and commitment, and the development of skills and practices to make working together easier, are typical of Stage 3.

Learning to build team cohesion and getting past the tendency to agree in order to avoid conflict are the challenges at the Integration stage.

The Integration stage can be quite short, depending on the ease of resolving feelings of dissatisfaction and integrating new skills. If members prolong conflict avoidance, there is a possibility that the team could return to the Dissatisfaction stage.

Team Development Stage 4 (TDS4)—Production

At this stage, both productivity and morale are high and reinforce one another. This is high performance in action. There is a sense of pride and excitement in being part of a high performance team. The primary focus is on performance. Standards are high, and team members are committed not only to meeting standards, but also to continuous improvement. Team members are confident in their ability to perform and overcome obstacles. They are proud of their work and enjoy working together. Communication is open, and leadership is shared. Mutual respect and trust are the norm. The team is agile and handles new challenges as it continues to grow.

Our project team really started to hum, and the completion of the job became a reality in our minds after many meetings and a careful study of alternatives. It finally began to feel as if the effort was worth it, and we were optimistic that the outcomes would be positive for both the company and the consulting partners. We all shared the responsibility for team leadership. We felt this had become a really great team to be on, and we were proud to be part of it. These feelings of accomplishment, pride, confidence, and a sense of unity are typical of teams who have reached Stage 4.

The challenge in the Production stage is sustaining the team's high performance through new challenges and continued growth. This stage is likely to continue—with moderate fluctuations in feelings of satisfaction—throughout the team's life.

While the stages of team development are described as separate and distinct, they share considerable overlap. Some elements of each stage can be found in every other stage. However, the team's dominant characteristics and needs determine its development stage at any given time. A change in these characteristics and needs signals a change in the team's stage of development.

Why is understanding your team's stage of development and corresponding needs such an important step in the process? Because it allows team leaders or members to accomplish the next key step: providing leadership behaviors that respond to those needs.

Providing Leadership Behaviors That Match the Team's Needs

As it moves through the different development stages, a team requires leadership that is responsive to its needs at each stage. SLII®, used extensively in self and one-on-one leadership, works equally well when applied to team leadership.

Directing behavior structures and guides team outcomes. Behaviors that provide direction include organizing, structuring, educating, and focusing the team. For example, when you first join the team, you want to know how it will be organized. What do you need to learn to be a good team member? Where will the team focus its efforts? What's the structure? Does anybody report to anybody? Who does what? When? And how?

Supporting behavior develops mutual trust and respect within the team. Behaviors that provide support include involving, encouraging, listening to, and collaborating with team members. For example, in developing team harmony and cohesion, people want to be involved in decision making, be encouraged to participate, be acknowledged and praised for their efforts, be valued for their differences, and able to share leadership when appropriate.

Without team leadership training, people who are called to lead a team are usually clueless about what to do. They often operate on instinct. For example, suppose an inexperienced team leader thinks that the only way to lead a team is to use a participative leadership style. From Day 1, she asks everybody for suggestions about how the team should operate. The team members think the leader should answer that question. "After all," they say, "she's the one who called the meeting." They begin to question why they joined this team. The leader, getting little response from her team, becomes frustrated and wonders why she agreed to lead the team in the first place. Everyone is confused.

Without understanding the framework of team development stages, it is only by chance that a leader's behavior matches the team's needs. The Team Leadership model (see Figure 11.3) creates a framework for matching each stage of team development with appropriate leadership behaviors.

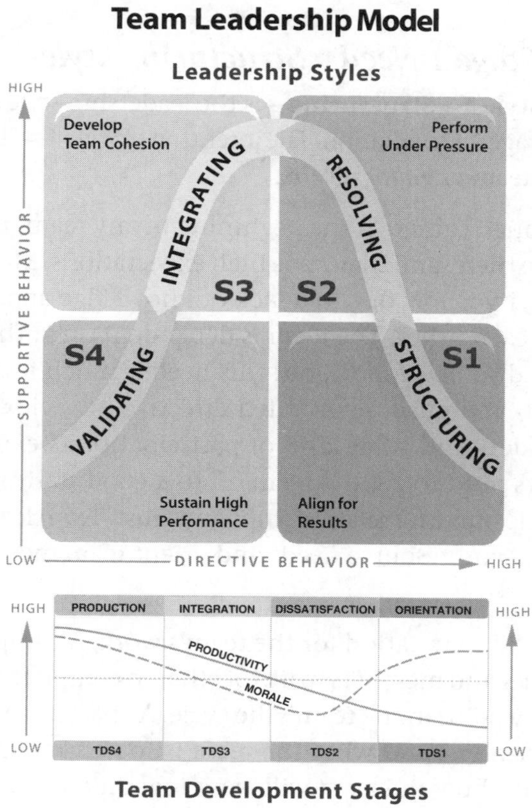

Figure 11.3 Team Leadership Model

For team leaders and members to determine the appropriate leadership style, first diagnose the team's stage of development in relation to its purpose, considering both productivity and morale. Then locate the team's present stage of development on the continuum and follow a vertical line up to the curve on the leadership style quadrant in the model. The point of intersection indicates the appropriate leadership style for the team.

Intervening with the appropriate leadership style that is responsive to the needs of the team at each stage of development will help the team progress to and sustain high performance. Matching leadership style to the stage of team development, similar to one-on-one leadership, works best when the team leader(s) and team members all know and agree on the team's purpose and are doing the diagnosis together.

Teams at Stage 1 Need a Structuring Style

Leadership Style 1—Structuring—is the leadership style appropriate for a team at Stage 1, Orientation. The intention of Style 1—Structuring—is to help the team *align for results*.

As we mentioned earlier, at the beginning of any team, most people are eager to be there, and they have high expectations. Morale is high, but productivity is low due to a lack of knowledge about the team purpose and each other. The team is dependent on authority. Team members need some support, but this need is much less than their need for goal- and purpose-oriented directive behavior. They need to clearly understand what kind of participation is expected from them. Leaders need to get the team off to a good start by providing structure while building relationships and trust. Team leaders should assess training and resource needs and orient team members to one another.

To create a solid foundation for the team's work, it's important that the team leader and members work together to complete a team charter at this early point in the team's life cycle. A charter is a set of agreements that clearly states what the team is to accomplish, why it is important, and how the team will work together to achieve results. The charter aligns the team for results, but it is also a dynamic document that can be modified as team needs change.

The team charter agreements directly link the team's purpose to the organizational vision and purpose. Team values and norms should reflect the organization's values, as well as provide guidelines for appropriate behavior within the team. Identifying team initiatives sets the foundation for determining goals and roles. This is when the team establishes strategies for communication, decision making, and accountability. Once completed, the charter provides a touchstone for making sure the team is on track. The team is now ready to move from planning to doing, and it will keep the charter visible and available to navigate the stages ahead.

Teams at Stage 2 Need a Resolving Style

Leadership Style 2—Resolving—is the appropriate leadership style for a team at Stage 2, Dissatisfaction. The intention of Style 2—Resolving— is to help the team *perform under pressure*.

At this point the team could be experiencing confusion and frustration and needs to learn how to manage conflict and work together more effectively. Now is when the leader should reconfirm or clarify the team's purpose, goals, roles, and norms; develop team skills necessary for the team to perform under pressure; address difficult issues; and recognize helpful behaviors and small accomplishments.

The Dissatisfaction stage is characterized by a gradual increase in performance and a decrease in morale. Anger, frustration, confusion, and discouragement can arise due to the discrepancy between initial expectations and reality.

The Dissatisfaction stage calls for continued high direction and an increase in support. Team members need encouragement and reassurance as well as skill development and strategies for working together and toward goal achievement. At this stage, it is important to clarify the big picture and reconfirm the team's purpose and goals. It is also important to give the team more input into decision making. Recognizing team members' accomplishments and giving feedback on progress reassures people, encourages progress, and boosts morale. Help team members adopt a learning attitude where there are no failures—only learning opportunities. This is a critical time to encourage active and open listening and reaffirm that the team values differences of opinion and invites self-expression. It is also helpful at this stage to have open and honest discussions about issues such as emotional blocks and coalitions and to resolve any personality conflicts.

Teams at Stage 3 Need an Integrating Style

Leadership Style 3—Integrating—is the appropriate style for a team at Stage 3, Integration. The intention of Style 3—Integrating—is to help the team *develop team cohesion*.

The team, now working together more effectively but cautiously, must learn to work collaboratively and hold each other accountable.

Goals and strategies are becoming clearer or have been redefined. Negative feelings are being resolved. Confidence, cohesion, and trust are increasing but are potentially still fragile. The team must build a trust-based environment. Trust is built by sharing information, ideas, and skills. Building trust requires that team members cooperate rather than compete, judge, or blame. Trust is also built when team members follow through on their commitments. It is critical that team members communicate openly and honestly and demonstrate respect for others. Team members are more willing and able to assume leadership functions.

Support and collaboration are needed in the Integration stage to help team members develop confidence in their ability to work together. The team needs less direction around the goal and more support focused on building confidence, trust, cohesion, involvement, and shared leadership. This is a time to encourage people to voice different perspectives, show appreciation for each other's contributions, share responsibility for leadership, and examine team functioning. Now the focus should be on increasing productivity and developing problem-solving and decision-making skills.

Teams at Stage 4 Need a Validating Style

Leadership Style 4—Validating—is the appropriate style for a team at Stage 4, Production. The intention of Style 4—Validating—is to help the team *sustain high performance*.

Now operating with high productivity and high morale, the team is challenged by the need to sustain its high performance.

At this stage, the team members have positive feelings about each other and their accomplishments. The quality and amount of work produced are high. Teams at this stage often need new challenges to keep morale and team focus high.

The team generally provides its own direction and support at this point and needs to be validated for that accomplishment. Team members demonstrate unity and are fully participating in achieving the team's goals. If an outsider were to come in and attempt to determine who the leader was, it would be a challenge because all the team members are participating in leadership. Continued recognition and celebration of the team's accomplishments are needed at this time, as well as the creation of new challenges and higher standards. Because the team is functioning at a high level, at this stage it is appropriate to foster decision-making autonomy within established boundaries.

Strategies for Higher Team Performance

The leader's major role is to guide the team members through the stages of development so they can achieve team and organizational goals. This means letting go of control and sharing leadership as the team develops. Teams aren't static. They are unique and complex living systems. By observing the balance of productivity and morale, one can apply the appropriate leadership style to meet the needs of the team at each stage. This matching behavior is the key to success.

Keep the Team Moving Forward

We refer to matching as staying on the railroad track; however, that is not to say that a team won't regress for a whole variety of reasons. If this happens, it is important to change leadership style based on the needs of the team at any point in time. In other words, stay alert to shifts in development level, and change leadership behaviors as

---

needed to keep the team moving forward. Additionally, at all stages of development, the team leader needs to do the following:

- Keep the team aligned to the team's purpose and agreements

- Monitor progress and provide feedback

- Create a safe environment with opportunities to be heard and a respect for differences

- Hold team members accountable for behavior and commitments

- Be aware of ongoing team dynamics

Observe Team Dynamics

Team Dynamics are the patterns of behaviors that occur within a team at any given time. They include the overt interactions between members as well as the more subtle verbal and nonverbal clues to feelings that may go on beneath the surface. Observing dynamics provides information as to how the team is functioning. It is the key to diagnosing the stage of development and the interventions that are needed at that time.

The most basic, critical skill in understanding team dynamics is that of being a participant observer. This means being totally involved in *what* the team is doing while simultaneously observing *how* the team is functioning (see Figure 11.4).

The first step in developing this skill of being a participant observer is to distinguish between *content* and *process*. The content is what the team is doing—developing the budget, creating a new strategic plan, or working on a specific goal. The process is how the team is functioning while doing its work—how it is communicating, how decisions are being made, how conflict is being managed, and what behaviors are disrupting the team or helping the team to move forward.

Often, little attention is paid to the process, which results in ineffective team action. In other words, "We know what we did but have no clue on how we got there." The reality is that outcome depends on process. So attention to both is a must.

Focus of a Participant Observer

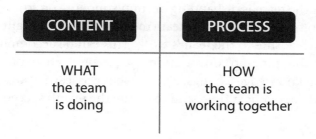

Figure 11.4 Focus of a Participant Observer

There are several ways to build this skill in team members. You might consider spending the last ten minutes of your team meeting discussing what went well, what improvements are needed, whether people were involved and heard, and how decisions were made. Another way to build this skill is by rotating responsibility among team members to take the role of being a participant observer during meetings and reporting results. The point is for the team to examine itself and be conscious of how it is functioning, and that is the role of all members.

Paying attention to the dynamics is the way to understand and make sense of these complex systems called teams and the interventions needed to help them grow.

Manage Closure

Although we do not include it in our Team Development Stages model, there is often a Stage 5—Termination—when a team will conclude its work. This occurs when a goal has been achieved, a milestone has been reached, or a project has been completed. At this point the team may disband altogether. This stage may vary in duration from a small part of the last meeting to a significant portion of the last several meetings, depending on the length and quality of the team experience. For some teams with a distinct ending point, productivity can continue to increase as they rush for the finish line, or it may go down as the end is in sight. It's the same for morale: The team may experience real celebration in the last stages of the project or a feeling of sadness as they know their time is coming to the end.

Whether the team is disbanding or simply moving on to a new challenge or project with the same team members, it is important to bring honorable closure to the team's work. This can be accomplished by having a wrapping-up conversation with the team to express appreciation, acknowledge feelings, discuss what was learned and identify what to do better next time, and celebrate the team's success.

The Power of Teams

When faced with pressure or complexity, leaders must acknowledge that it is often the actions and skills of many, as opposed to those of one person, that make a complicated procedure successful. Today's complex work can no longer be left to a lone hero's expertise; we need high performance teams working together to bring the results and passion that are foundational to the world in which we live.

And when teams function well, miracles can happen. A thrilling and inspiring example of a high performance team is the 1980 United States Olympic hockey team.[7] Twenty young men—many of whom had never played together before—came from colleges all over the country. Six months later they won the Olympic gold medal, defeating the best teams in the world—including the Soviet Union, a team that had been playing together for years. No one expected this to happen. It is considered one of the greatest upsets in sports history and is labeled a miracle. Thirty-eight years to the day later, the American women's hockey team pulled off a similar miracle.

When members from both teams were interviewed, all without exception attributed their success to teamwork. The drive, commitment, cohesiveness, cooperation, trust, team effort, and a passionate belief in a common purpose—"Go for the gold"—were the reason for their success.

Teams are especially essential when dealing with emergencies and critical situations. Think about the Hudson River plane crash in 2009, when Captain Sullenberger, First Officer Jeffrey Skiles, and the rest of the flight crew worked together to land the plane safely under dire circumstances, saving all the lives aboard.

Whether it's a medical team of surgeons, anesthetists, and nurses all working together and using their individual specialties as a team to save lives, or a team of tech wizards collaborating on a new software that changes the world we live in, we know that humans can achieve great things when they work effectively as teams.

Individually, we are one drop.
Together, we are an ocean.

—Ryunosuke Satoro

But these high performance teams don't just happen. They take practice, discipline, and hard work. Moving a team from a group of individuals to a highly interdependent and productive team with a shared purpose requires an effective team leadership approach. You can make the most of teamwork by building teams that are diverse, connected, motivated, and high performing. This will give your business the edge when solving new problems and embarking on complex projects.

In the next chapter you'll learn about the role collaboration plays in building high performance teams.

12

Collaboration: Fuel for High Performance

Jane Ripley, Eunice Parisi-Carew, and Ken Blanchard

Collaboration creates high performing teams and organizations. And with today's diverse, globalized workforce, it's crucial. Organizations that embrace a collaborative culture benefit internally from increased sales, improved innovation, and better business processes. The external benefits can include new products and services and a smoother running business that delivers higher client satisfaction and increased revenues and profitability. Additional, less tangible benefits include knowledge sharing and competence building of employees and contractors.

Collaboration Is Not Coordination, Cooperation, or Teamwork

Many people think of collaboration as being the same as coordination, cooperation, or teamwork. However, these words are not interchangeable.

- *Coordination* is when one department or function independently completes a specific task before handing off to another department, which is then able to complete its own specific task. Neither needs the other to complete its own goal, and the outcome of the two efforts is the completion of the final goal.

- *Cooperation* is when one party benefits from the help of another. For example, a salesman needs a product to be delivered to a client in three days to meet his sales goals and earn commission. Regular delivery takes ten days. The salesman asks the fulfillment department to expedite delivery, and the fulfillment department complies with his request.

- The most common confusion is between collaboration and teamwork. *Teamwork* is defined as two or more people working toward the same goal. This structure is considered to be a static team; in other words, the team members are permanent. While goals may change on a weekly, monthly, or quarterly basis, the team in essence remains the same. It is important to understand the difference between teamwork and collaboration, as teams can collaborate with one another.

Collaboration involves bringing resources from various areas together to create something better or to solve a complex problem. These resources may come from different departments, teams, or locations and may even include people from other organizations.

This kind of collaboration can save lives. For example, during the wildfires of 2003 in San Diego, the efforts of police, firefighters, and first responders were fragmented due to unaligned communication systems. In 2003, as firefighters flocked to the county from all over the west, some had only 800-megahertz radios rather than the traditional VHF radios—meaning they couldn't talk to each other. By 2007, when the Cedar Fire hit, all the police, fire, and emergency responder agencies were equipped with VHF radios.[1]

Collaboration can happen even between organizations that traditionally might be thought of as competitors. In 2011, the Nature Conservancy and Dow Chemical Company partnered to demonstrate that integrating the value of nature into business decisions can lead to better business and conservation outcomes. Projects such as constructing a wetland for water recycling have proven beneficial for both nature and Dow's bottom line.[2]

Creating a Collaborative Framework

Organizations that successfully collaborate focus on four key areas, which we call the Four Key Predictors of Success:

- **Mission, Goals, and Results:** Collaboration should not be treated as something that is nice to have, something to implement only when there are no other ideas, or as a fallback position in the event of a crisis. It should be perceived as a way to ensure the organization achieves its goals and results. In other words, the organization's mission, goals, and results are key to its enduring success—and collaboration should be deployed only when it can help meet these elements.

- **Culture and Values:** Values shape the behaviors of an organization's people and support the achievement of the vision and mission. If collaboration is viewed as key to an organization's success, somewhere in the values there needs to be a reference to collaborative behaviors. If this is not explicit, they may get lost in the priorities of the organization, may not be lived, and leaders could be forgiven for not modeling them. Once leaders fail to demonstrate collaborative behaviors, others will lose their collaborative compass and will fulfill the prophecy that collaboration is time consuming and expensive.

- **Leadership and Empowerment:** Leaders who value collaboration will generally model it and encourage their staff to build their collaboration skills. However, middle managers can struggle to encourage and embrace the value of leadership— often because they are more focused on delivering results than on the bigger picture. They might espouse the importance of mission, vision, and values but fail to model them, thus discouraging collaborative efforts of their staff. The managers' failure to acknowledge the value of collaboration will ensure that few if any collaborative efforts will succeed—again fulfilling the prophecy that collaboration is inefficient and not cost effective. Leaders who fail to empower their staff make the lives of their people difficult. The unintended consequence of a lack of empowerment is eventually business failure on many levels: It stifles creativity and innovation and makes the delivery of customer service difficult. This can lead to poor results, which is the focus of the middle manager. Middle managers have no idea their actions are actually holding themselves and their organization back.

Empowerment of direct reports is easier said than done. In fact, we have found that empowerment is the hardest skill for leaders to adopt and for individuals to truly understand and apply appropriately. Over-supervision and under-supervision of staff by leaders are barriers that lead to inefficient collaboration. Therefore, it is incumbent on leaders to not only learn how to empower their people but ensure their staff has the appropriate training and the opportunity to use the newly acquired skills.

- **Systems, Structures, and Policies:** Finally, systems, structures, and policies need to be formally aligned to ensure that leaders model collaboration. Those who don't collaborate don't get promoted. As a last resort, anyone failing to model the company culture may be "shared with the competition."[3] Senior leaders need to declare and demonstrate, not just declare and hope, turning a blind eye because middle managers are getting short-term results.

While technology has increased communication and collaboration, outdated IT systems can sometimes erect barriers to the sharing of information. As costly as upgraded IT systems can be, they need to be a top priority now more than even a few years ago. While time and budget are spent on updating crucial data systems, an extra step is needed to ensure that everyone who needs the information can access it and communicate it efficiently. Open and transparent communication between all parties helps build an agile and intelligent organization that allows people to cross boundaries, discourages silos, and builds in flexibility to enable appropriate collaboration.

Collaboration Versus Competition

Collaboration has been around since the beginning of mankind—an instinctive behavior to protect against attack, hunt and gather food, and share resources for the good of all.

Instinctive collaborative behaviors can be observed at an early age. A small group of children aged two to four playing together in a sandpit, when asked to build the biggest sandcastle, will naturally organize themselves into a collaborative group often without any formal leader. After the initial buzz about the project, they will move into excited action. One will heap sand for others to fill buckets, some will level the building ground, while others will simply sit on the sidelines and encourage the group. That's not to say there won't be disagreements or even a brief withdrawal by an individual from the project. As these instances occur, others will act as peace makers and bring the group back together until they congratulate themselves on their achievement.

Now contrast that lovely scene with the behaviors of many coworkers today. How is it that collaborative behaviors have all but disappeared?

The fading of these skills starts in school, when resources or prizes require competition. Competition to be in the top ten or top three in various subjects sparks competitive behaviors. And as children start to realize that not everyone can be number one, they learn they can improve their chances of succeeding by hoarding knowledge and resources and withdrawing support from fellow competitors. Innate collaborative skills grow dimmer as young adults compete for acceptance at top universities. Competitive skills have become instinct by the time the four-year-old has matured to work age and vies for the best job or better pay and again for scarce promotions or specialist roles.

Team experts Don Carew and Eunice Parisi-Carew observe when teaching team skills that the problem for western cultures is the inability of workers to move from *me* to *we*. This is at the root of understanding when and how to collaborate effectively. Organizations who wish to reap the benefits of collaboration must not only create a collaborative framework but also reacquaint their staff with the skills of collaboration. It is important to make collaboration a key competence and to promote only those who collaborate effectively: people who collaborate get promoted and get the best jobs. Those who don't wish to collaborate should find organizations that better suit their individualist, competitive natures.

Reciprocity is a behavior that should be encouraged because it is at the heart of collaboration. Information, data, experiences, people, and resources should all be shared freely without expectation of getting something back from the other party.

What It Takes to Be Collaborative

Most people believe they collaborate well and that it is "the other guy" who doesn't. Of course, at some point you may find that you are "the other guy." Our attitude can color our view on the importance of collaboration and our willingness to be collaborative as well as our ability to collaborate well. To improve this attitude, let's split skills and behaviors into three domains: the heart, hands, and head.

The *heart*. The heart is the first of the domains because collaboration is an inside-out mind-set. It has to start on the inside, with the heart. If you don't get the heart part right, you'll never be effective as a collaborative leader. The heart is really who you are as a collaborator—your character and intentions.

The *head*. The second domain is the head, which is about what you know—your beliefs and attitudes about collaboration. These beliefs and attitudes drive your behavior. For example, leaders who are competitively focused on the achievement of short-term goals are less likely to collaborate. Their attitude is that the goal is more important than collaborating to achieve the goal.

The *hands*. The final domain, the hands, is about your actions and behaviors. When your heart and head are right, your behaviors and actions align to support collaboration.

The UNITE Model

The UNITE model shown in Figure 12.1 was developed to identify within each domain—the heart, the head, and the hands—best practices for developing collaborative competence.

The UNITE Model

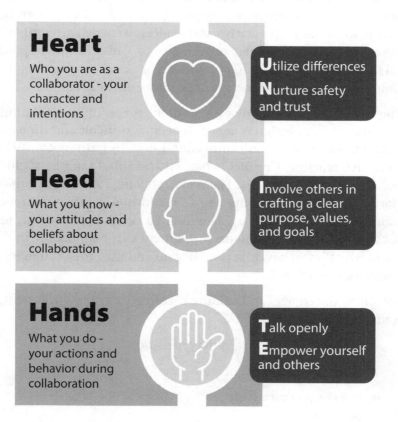

Heart
Who you are as a collaborator - your character and intentions

Utilize differences
Nurture safety and trust

Head
What you know - your attitudes and beliefs about collaboration

Involve others in crafting a clear purpose, values, and goals

Hands
What you do - your actions and behavior during collaboration

Talk openly
Empower yourself and others

Figure 12.1 The UNITE Model

The Heart: Utilize Differences

Leaders who have a heart for collaboration instinctively utilize differences. Utilizing differences is especially important if organizations want to innovate or to recombine existing resources to deliver better customer service or products. Diversity has long been recognized as a source of creativity and innovation. Yet, within many organizations, when a new project team is put together, the same people tend to be included—often because they have learned to work together and have a proven track record.

The problem with always returning to the same people is that there are no new ideas. The workgroup should be encouraged to seek out new members who might hold opposing views. An ideal opportunity that helps build collaborative and leadership bench strength is to have new hires be members of such groups. This gives them practical field experience prior to promotions or career assignments. This simple action demonstrates the importance of collaboration.

The key to encouraging diverse opinions is the ability to skillfully manage conflict, which is generally seen as difficult and time consuming. But people don't understand how to harness conflict as a creative crucible. Conflict is natural and should not be avoided, nor should it be intense and personal. Sticking to the issue and the clarity around the outcome helps. In addition, conflict awareness training can go a long way. The use of a conflict assessment tool such as the Thomas Kilmann Instrument can help people understand why they behave the way they do and how they can manage their emotions.[4]

To utilize differences in building a collaborative environment, a leader must:

- Seek opinions from a variety of sources
- Value diverse points of view
- Use conflict creatively

The Heart: Nurture Safety and Trust

Leaders who have a heart for collaboration intuitively nurture safety and trust. This is one of the most important behaviors leaders and their organizations need to master. People need to feel safe to be who they are—to speak up when they have an idea, or to speak out when they feel something isn't right. They also need to trust that they won't be punished if something goes wrong. View mistakes as learning opportunities.

The biggest barrier to people wanting to share their perspective is fear. Fear is a big inhibitor. Besides keeping people from speaking up, it also stops them from experimenting with an idea—and that's exactly what you need for innovation.

It is impossible to create a collaborative environment without safety and trust. Where trust exists, silos are minimized because people feel safe to help others, inside or outside their department.

To nurture safety and trust, leaders should:

- Encourage people to share their perspectives

- Encourage people to experiment with ideas

- View mistakes as learning opportunities

The Head: Involve Others in Crafting a Clear Purpose, Values, and Goals

Leaders with collaborative attitudes and beliefs realize how important it is that all members of an organization or workgroup create together a collaborative vision with a clear purpose, shared values, and established goals. A clear purpose unites everyone around a common objective, values guide behavior, and goals provoke action—but only when everyone has the chance to contribute.

The accountability of each person to the vision and to the achievement of the established goals is crucial. Without everyone's commitment to the vision, collaboration will break down and silos will be the norm. That is why it is essential that everyone participates in creating the vision.

To involve others in crafting a clear purpose, values, and goals, leaders should:

- Create a collaborative vision

- Ensure everyone is clear about the purpose and goals of the group

- Hold each other accountable for the jointly created and agreed-upon values

The Hands: Talk Openly

Leaders who demonstrate collaborative actions and behavior model open and transparent communication. When people talk to them, they listen to understand, not to argue. They are candid, and respectfully tell the truth. Sometimes this is counterintuitive. As humans, our competitive nature predisposes us to withhold information and resources that may give us an advantage over another.

To be a leader who talks openly:

- Share relevant information. Failing to inform others of a failure or missed deadline can create distrust.

- Give constructive feedback. Not holding each other accountable can lead to a lack of safety and thereby undermine the whole project.

- Master the art of candor; share information in a straightforward and easy-to-understand way.

If you model open communication, those who receive the information will learn to listen to understand, not criticize or undermine, and ask questions.

Respect for each other is essential in creating an environment where people feel they can talk openly. To summarize, leaders should:

- Listen to understand

- Encourage candor with respect

- Share relevant information and give constructive feedback

The Hands: Empower Yourself and Others

Leaders who demonstrate collaborative actions and behavior master the skills of empowerment, either as leaders empowering others or as individual contributors empowering themselves. To empower yourself and others, become interested in your own and others' growth. Practice knowledge sharing, networking, and continual learning.

In a culture of collaboration, individual contributors see themselves as self leaders. Leaders empower these individuals by building trust and coaching them to become competent in their jobs. Individuals also empower and inspire each other when they share ideas and deliver on their agreed-upon tasks and goals.

Empowered people feel more trusted and competent, and therefore feel more of an individual responsibility to contribute and become a more integral part of the organization.

Leaders seeking to empower themselves and others should:

- Share knowledge and experiences with a view to individual growth
- Build and share their own networks
- Participate in and encourage lifelong learning

Collaboration: Fuel for High Performance

Effective collaboration is the key to organizational effectiveness. It requires commitment from the top as well as buy-in from throughout the organization. If collaboration is a nice thing to do and not the norm, the organization will miss out on the power of synergy and the realization that "None of us is as smart as all of us."

*****

In the next chapter, we'll see how to make leadership come alive and be effective at the organizational level.

13

Organizational Leadership

Ken Blanchard, Jesse Stoner, Don Carew,
Eunice Parisi-Carew, and Fay Kandarian

J ust as team leadership is more complicated than one-on-one leadership, leading an entire organization is more complicated than leading a single team. As is true with building a high performing team, building a high performing organization is a journey. The quality of a leader's influence at the organizational level is built upon the perspective, trust, and community the leader attains while mastering self, one-on-one, and team leadership.

An effective leader's influence on an organization can create a culture that brings together people and systems in a harmonious whole.

Real Life Examples of HPO SCORES®

In Chapter 1, we introduced the HPO SCORES® model to provide an overview of high performing organizations—organizations that over time continue to produce outstanding results with the highest level of human satisfaction and commitment to success.

In this chapter we will use the HPO SCORES® model to describe what leaders believe and do to produce high performing organizations— and what that looks like in real life. Our research at Blanchard reveals that these six elements are distinct, yet interdependent. For example, empowerment without a shared vision is a recipe for chaos. However, empowerment with a shared vision becomes a competitive advantage as it frees up leaders to focus on strategy and growth opportunities.

S—Shared Information and Open Communication

Leaders in high performing organizations (HPOs) lean toward transparency, both internally with employees and externally with stakeholders, in contrast to the old-school approach, where information is only available on a need-to-know basis.

Leaders understand that information is power, and the more readily available information is to employees, the more empowered and able people are to make solid decisions aligned with the organization's vision, values, and goals.

This philosophy is a key strength at Google, both internally with employees and throughout its products and services, as its mission is "to organize the world's information and make it universally accessible and useful."

Patagonia provides transparency throughout its supply chain. To avoid being caught off guard by information about environmentally unfriendly habits of its manufacturers or distributors, Patagonia has established "Footprint Chronicles" to ensure no harm is being caused in the making of its products.[1]

Buffer's policy of "Default to Transparency" is integrated into every aspect of its business. For example, the salaries of all employees throughout the organization are publicly available, from co-founder and CEO Joel Gascoigne to managers to engineers.

Leaders of HPOs understand that open communication is the lifeblood of the organization. Their encouragement of dialogue lessens the danger of territoriality and keeps the organization healthy, agile, flexible, and fluid.

In their eight-point plan[2], Google outlines that, as a manager, you are expected to "be a good communicator and listen to your team." The three points that focus on communication are

- Communication is two-way. Both listen and share information.
- Hold all-hands meetings, and be straightforward about the messages and the goals of the team.
- Encourage open dialogue.

C—Compelling Vision

As we've emphasized throughout this book, in high performing organizations everyone is energized by, excited about, and dedicated to a compelling vision. They can clearly describe the vision, are deeply committed to it, and clearly see what their role is in supporting it. People are energized and excited by a noble purpose that creates and focuses energy. Their personal values are aligned with the values of the organization. They can describe a clear picture of the future—what they intend to create. Everyone is in the same boat moving "full steam ahead."

Patagonia's vision is "to build the best product, cause no unnecessary harm, and use business to inspire and implement solutions to the environmental crisis." The company is known for integrating this vision both in terms of how employees are treated as well as how it produces and markets its products. Recently Patagonia took its vision a step further by being one of the first businesses to take a public stand on environmental issues not directly tied to its bottom line. It filed a suit to block federal plans to chop up two large national parks in Utah. Yet results didn't suffer—under CEO Rose Marcario, profits have tripled since 2008.[3]

A shared vision is the glue that holds an organization together and guides it successfully into the future. Southwest has been in operation for over 50 years and has continued to communicate its vision— "to democratize the airways"—to employees in a way that makes them part of a unified team. For the 24th year in a row, Southwest has been ranked as one of the world's most-respected companies in *Fortune* magazine's survey of the Top 50 Most Admired Companies.[4]

High performing organizations with a compelling vision have a strong and distinct culture. Zappos ensures culture fit starting with its recruitment process. Prospective new employees are interviewed for culture fit, which carries half the weight on whether the candidate is hired. And new employees are offered $2,000 to quit after the first week of training if they decide the job isn't for them.[5]

O—Ongoing Learning

Leaders in high performing organizations are committed to learning—both individual learning and incorporating learning to continually improve ways of doing business.

Learning processes involve gathering information from feedback; experimenting and developing new products and services; tracking competitive, customer, and technological trends; taking disciplined approaches to solving problems; and training to develop employee capabilities.

The U.S. Army's After Action Review (AAR) process, which involves a systematic debriefing after every mission, project, or critical activity, is now widely used by many companies. This process involves four questions:

1. What did we set out to do?
2. What actually happened?
3. Why did it happen?
4. What do we do the next time?[6]

Toyota Motor Company uses lean manufacturing and continuous improvement to make small but never-ending improvements in products and processes.

Leaders in high performing organizations understand that knowledge exists in knowledgeable people. Unless the individual learns, the organization cannot. Therefore, development of people is a given in a high performing organization. Ongoing learning is part of the culture of a high performing organization and is viewed as an investment in the organization's knowledge capital.

Steve McCarty, vice president of training and talent development for Enterprise Rent-A-Car says, "Focusing on employee development and promoting from within drive profit. And we have an engagement culture to make sure that happens."[7]

At Google, managers are expected to "help employees with career development."

R—Relentless Focus on Customer Results

Leaders in high performing organizations are result-driven, and they measure results in terms of the customer experience. Customer needs and trends drive innovation, new products, and services. In other words, new products and services are developed in anticipation of customer needs. Next, work processes are designed starting with the customer experience. Internal cross-functional relationships and structures are organized around customer needs. Empowered employees respond quickly to customer needs and concerns.

High performing organizations watch customers to discern unmet needs. They also survey their customers to get feedback.

Trader Joe's provides outstanding customer service by acquiring customer intelligence and acting on it. It uses this data to gain insight into the customer's overall experience, develop better products, and provide customers with the services they desire.[8]

Customer-centricity is embedded into the DNA of Amazon. CEO Jeff Bezos leaves one seat open at the conference table, stating that the seat is occupied by the "the most important person in the room—the customer." He believes that, "Everyone has to be able to work in a call center" so that they have insight into the customer's perspective. So, each year he and thousands of Amazon managers attend two days of call center training and field calls periodically.[9]

People used to believe they would get better service if they went to a brick and mortar store. But many of these stores show up on lists of companies with the worst customer service.[10] And today more people purchase electronics from Amazon, not only because of convenience but because Amazon stands behind its products.

E—Energizing Systems and Structures

In high performing organizations, the systems, structures, processes, and practices make it easy for people to take action aligned with the vision and strategies.

Because creativity is so important to the success of Adobe, it has created an environment that supports risk taking without fear of penalty. Adobe is known for giving employees challenging projects and providing the support needed to help them meet those challenges successfully through ongoing training. Because the company believes rating employees inhibits creativity and harms teamwork, employees meet with managers to determine how they should be assessed. Adobe's managers avoid micromanaging in favor of trusting employees to do their best. Adobe's managers act more like coaches.[11]

Chevron doesn't just say it cares about the well-being of employees; it provides programs that prove it with health and fitness centers onsite or health-club memberships, health-oriented programs such as massages and personal training, and an insistence that employees take regular breaks.[12]

Google found that women were leaving the company at twice the rate of everyone else, particularly new mothers. While he was senior vice president of people operations, Laszlo Bock changed the maternity leave plan so new mothers could get 5 months paid time off with full pay and benefits. This resulted in a 50 percent reduction in attrition for new mothers.[13]

Netflix believes in hiring outstanding people and giving them freedom and responsibility to do their job. That might sound like the rhetoric of many companies, but Netflix's policies radically reflect this stance.[14] The company rewards high performance, not hard work—sustained B-level performance, despite "A for effort," gets a generous severance package, with respect. Sustained "A"-level performance, despite minimal effort, gets more responsibility and great pay.

The Netflix Vacation and Tracking Policy reads: "There is no policy or tracking. There is also no clothing policy at Netflix, but no one comes to work naked. Lesson: you don't need policies for everything."

Netflix's travel policy is simply: "Act in Netflix's best interest."

S—Shared Power and High Involvement

In high performing organizations, leaders share power instead of guarding it closely. They seek others' opinions and encourage collaboration and teamwork. They understand that involvement in decision making increases employee engagement and ownership as well as effectiveness. So day-to-day decision making occurs closest to the action and on the front line by those directly involved with the customer. These decisions are often made in a team environment where everyone can respond to each other and arrive at "collective wisdom."

Participative practices strongly impact financial results through productivity, retention, and employee satisfaction. Using U.S. Department of Labor data and surveys of over 1,500 firms from various industries, Huselid and Becker found that participative practices significantly improved employee retention, increased productivity, and improved financial performance. In fact, they were able to quantify financial impact of participative practices with enough confidence to say that each standard deviation in the use of participative practices increased a company's market value between $35,000 and $78,000 per employee.[15]

Southwest employees are encouraged to make the customer happy and are empowered to use their own judgment in how they do that. It sometimes results in flight attendants singing songs or tossing peanuts around the cabin, but when there is a shared vision, like at Southwest, empowerment pays off—their customers are among the most loyal.[16]

United Parcel Service (UPS) has been a leader in employee engagement, with an overall 73 percent engagement rate. Seeking to increase that, vice president of global employee relations Joe Finamore instituted a program to encourage employees to suggest and spread innovations in best practices. UPS found that bottom-up suggestions from those on the job were effective in saving time, and therefore money, and even further increased engagement.[17]

The coaching-style management approach of other companies like Google, Netflix, and Adobe, where employees are encouraged to use their own judgment and not be afraid of risks, not only leads to increased creativity, but also increased engagement.

Determining the Appropriate Leadership Style for Your Organization

As we mentioned in Chapter 4, "SLII®: The Integrating Concept," SLII® applies whether you are leading yourself, another individual, a team, or an organization. In the self and one-on-one context, the leader diagnoses the competence and commitment of a direct report on a specific task. In the team context, a leader diagnoses the team's productivity and morale. In the organizational context, the focus is on diagnosing results and relationships.

Diagnosing Your Organization's Development Level

Let's look at the two key variables that determine an organization's stage of development: results and relationships.

Results can be defined as the amount and quality of the work accomplished in relation to the organization's purpose and goals.

Relationships can be defined as the quality of interaction people have with the organization, their leaders, their coworkers, their customers, and the environment.

If an organization is to become high performing, results and relationships both must be high.

Results and Relationships: The Determinants of a High Performing Organization

Great relationships with no performance might be fun, but they will not create a long-lasting organization. On the other hand, an organization with great results and poor relationships will also be short-lived. Without good relationships, the organization will begin to lose its best people, and the results will decline. The bottom line is that *both* results *and* relationships are required for high performing organizations.

Diagnosing an organization's results and relationships is key to determining an organization's development level and understanding its needs.

Organizational Development Stage 1: Start-Up

Low Results/High Relationships

In a start-up organization, results are typically low because the goals are new and most people have never worked together before. However, relationships tend to be high because when people first come together to create a new venture, they are enthusiastic.

This certainly described the early days of The Ken Blanchard Companies®, initially known as Blanchard Training and Development. In the winter of 1977, Ken Blanchard had the opportunity to speak at a Young President's Organization (YPO) international university event. At that time, the requirement for membership of YPO was to be president of a business before the age of 40, with at least 50 employees and $5 million in sales. Having made a big hit giving speeches on leadership, motivation, and managing change, Ken was asked by several YPO members about his plans.

"I plan to return to teaching at the university level after my sabbatical," Ken replied.

"No, you're not," they said. "You're going to start your own company!"

Ken and his wife Margie laughed, saying, "We can't even balance our own checkbook. How are we going to do that?"

Five YPO presidents promised to help them and agreed to be part of an advisory board to assist the Blanchard company in getting started.

While the Blanchards were excited, they also were apprehensive about how to build a business that would make a difference for their customers and sustain a full staff—typical concerns at this stage of organizational development.

Organizational Development Stage 2: Improving

Improving Results/Declining Relationships

At this stage, results are beginning to show. However, while relationships are typically high at Stage 1—during the beginning of creating a new organization—they often dip at Stage 2, when the difficulty of building a new business sets in. This is when issues around systems and structures and dissatisfaction with leadership may arise.

It didn't take long for Ken and Margie to realize that it's easier to talk about running a business than to actually do it. It became obvious that sales had to exceed expenses. Yet most of the people who initially joined the company were teachers and trainers, not salespeople or accountants. At this stage, it's important to find ways to balance your organization's purpose and passion with the realities of doing and staying in business. Strategies must be in place to sustain ongoing business.

While Blanchard Training & Development was getting some results at this stage, the long hours and constant pressure to learn were taking an emotional and physical toll on the founders and their early associates and putting a strain on some relationships. As a result, Margie—who'd had little experience running a business—decided to step down as president. To replace her, the company hired an outside consultant with business experience. Rather than helping, this new president—who knew how to get results but not how to motivate people—made the situation worse, lowering morale.

Organizational Development Stage 3: Developing

Increasing Results/Variable Relationships

At Stage 3, results continue to improve as skills within an organization are strengthened and effective strategies are put into place. People are working hard, and the organization is becoming more creative and nimble. Relationships are variable in this stage because new challenges arise almost daily. People need positive reinforcement for relationships to continue to improve.

Blanchard Training & Development moved into this stage with the publication of Ken's bestselling book *The One Minute Manager* and the national recognition that it brought. Now, rather than worrying about seeking sales, the company had to manage a deluge of requests.

Given the problems with the appointed president, Margie—who had maintained her good relationship with the people—stepped back into her old role. With a more energized and skilled team of leaders, she began to restore morale and implemented important structural changes.

Organizational Development Stage 4: High Performing

High Relationships/High Results

In this stage both results and relationships are robust, organizational goals are being met, and morale is high. In an organization at Stage 4, people are working together with enthusiasm, leaders are emerging when and where they're needed, and customers are raving fans. The quadruple bottom line—employer, provider, investment, and corporate citizen of choice—is healthy.

After the success of *The One Minute Manager*, the Blanchard company's speaking and consulting skills were in demand. Newly published books by Ken and his coauthors opened more doors. Results and relationships reached a new high.

Yet this stage is not the end of the game. Becoming a high performing organization is something leaders need to keep working on, always striving to actualize the vision and live by the values.

Matching Leadership Style to Your Organization's Development Stage

As we stressed earlier, building a high performing organization is a journey from start-up to high performing—and then working to sustain that high performance.

In Chapter 1, "Is Your Organization High Performing?" you filled out the HPO SCORES® Quiz to help you determine your reading strategy for this book. In this chapter we'd like to use the elements of the quiz to describe what leaders using each of the four leadership styles—*directing, coaching, supporting,* and *delegating*—should focus on at each stage of organizational development.

When we combine the four SLII® leadership styles with the four stages of organizational development—*start-up, improving, developing,* and *high performing*—we have a framework for matching each stage with an appropriate leadership style (see Figure 13.1).

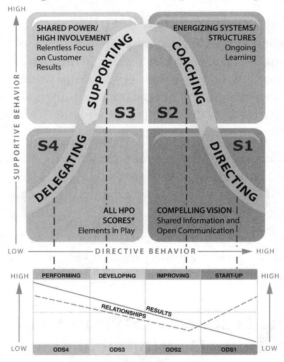

Figure 13.1 Matching Leadership Style to Organizational Development Stage

For leaders to determine the appropriate leadership style to use at a given time, they must first diagnose the organization's stage of development, keeping both results and relationships in mind. Next, they should locate the organization's present stage of development on the Organizational Development continuum of the SLII® model and match the appropriate style by following a vertical line up to the curve running through the four styles. The point of intersection indicates the leadership style the organization needs.

Applying the Appropriate Leadership Style at Each Development Level

Understanding the four stages of organizational development and applying the appropriate style at each stage is essential for creating a high performing organization.

Stage 1: Start-Up

Compelling Vision/Shared Information and Open Communication

At the *start-up* stage (ODS1)—when results are low and relationships are high—a *directing* (S1) style is appropriate. People look to the leaders to provide direction to get the organization moving. Leaders need to focus on establishing a clear purpose, vision, and values.

To make this happen, the HPO SCORES® element that needs to be emphasized at this stage is C—Compelling Vision.

- Is your organization aligned around a shared vision and values?

- Do the people in your organization have passion around that vision and those values?

If the organization is to begin to thrive, people need an inspiring picture of the future to work toward.

The S in the HPO SCORES® model—Shared Information and Open Communication—must come into play as well.

- Do people have easy access to the information they need to do their jobs effectively?

- Are plans and decisions communicated so that they are clearly understood?

These two elements will build trust and encourage people to act like owners. They are essential to ensuring everyone is aligned and going in the same direction.

Stage 2: Improving

Energizing Systems and Structures/Ongoing Learning

At the *improving* stage (ODS2)—when results are improving but relationships are declining—a *coaching* (S2) leadership style is appropriate. People need leaders to provide direction and support to keep results moving in a positive direction, as well as deal with the frustrations and growing pains that are typical at this stage.

What can help with these Stage 2 issues is to focus on the E— Energizing Systems and Structures—element of the HPO SCORES® model.

- Are systems, structures, and formal and informal practices integrated and aligned?

- Do they make it easy for people in the organization to get their jobs done?

When people feel supported by integrated and aligned systems and structures, results and relationships improve.

The other HPO element important for this stage is O—Ongoing Learning.

- Are people in your organization actively supported in the development of new skills and competencies?

- Does your organization continually incorporate new learning into standard ways of doing business?

Organizational learning is different from individual learning. High performing organizations encourage both. Leaders at this stage needs to support Ongoing Learning, both individually and as an organization.

Stage 3: Developing

Shared Power and High Involvement/Relentless Focus on Customer Results

At the *developing* stage (ODS3)—when results are increasing and relationships are variable—a *supporting* (S3)leadership style is appropriate. People are working together more effectively but are not yet fully confident. They need encouragement from their leaders to take initiative, develop new ideas, and forge new relationships—all elements that will lead to a high performing organization.

The HPO SCORES® element that drives this development stage is S—Shared Power and High Involvement.

- Do people have an opportunity to influence decisions that affect them?

- Are teams used as a vehicle for accomplishing work and influencing decisions?

At this stage, power and decision making are shared and distributed throughout the organization, not guarded at the top of the hierarchy. Participation, collaboration, and teamwork are a way of life. This sets up a focus on R—Relentless Focus on Customer Results—in the HPO SCORES® model.

- Is everyone in the organization maintaining the highest standards of quality and service?

- Are morale and satisfaction high, and are organizational values being lived by?

- Are all work processes designed to make it easier for your customers to do business with you?

It's now clear to everyone who their customers are—both internally and externally—and people focus their energies accordingly.

Stage 4: High Performing

All HPO SCORES® Elements

At the *high performing* (ODS4) stage—when both results and relationships are high—a *delegating* (S4) leadership style is appropriate. This does not mean that there is no direction or support, but it is now coming from individuals and teams throughout the organization. People are acting like owners and taking responsibility for both results and relationships. What people need from their leaders at this stage is encouragement to engage in autonomous decision-making within established boundaries. The focus for leaders at this stage is to cultivate new strategic challenges and opportunities.

At the high performing stage, all six elements of the HPO SCORES® model are regularly in play.

Once Stage 4 is reached, it is important that the O in the HPO SCORES® model—Ongoing Learning—remains central; otherwise, complacency could set in, and progress will come to a halt. Worse yet, the organization could begin to decline. For example, Kodak, the camera film company established in 1880, ignored the digital innovations that transformed its industry and in 2012 filed Chapter 11, nearly going out of business. In the worst-case scenario, companies that don't participate in Ongoing Learning go completely out of business.

The Importance of Diagnosis and Matching

It is important to diagnose an organization's development level and match leadership style to that level. That way, as a leader, you don't cause the organization to move backward rather than forward in the quality of results and relationships. New leaders coming into an organization need to be conscious of the leadership style of the leader who preceded them. Was the previous leader's style a match for the organization's stage of development?

We've seen too many situations where new CEOs—wanting to make a quick impact—enter organizations and immediately go to their favorite leadership style rather than to the one that is needed. A good example is how Carly Fiorina entered Hewlett Packard—a high performing organization—with a "my way or the highway" leadership style.

Looking to increase revenue and patents, in 2002 Fiorina led the acquisition of PC competitor Compaq. It was the biggest technology merger in history at the time, and as a result, HP became the world's biggest PC manufacturer. While results initially looked impressive, relationships under Fiorina took a beating. As part of a reorganization, she oversaw the elimination of a whopping 30,000 U.S. employees. As a result, the company lost several of its most talented, high performing people. In time, the results suffered and investors were left with falling stock values and disappointing earnings. Rather than involve people in leading the change, Fiorina refused to delegate authority to division heads. In 2005, she was asked by her board to resign.[18]

This can happen in any organization, whether it's a business, government, or nonprofit. Applying the appropriate leadership style at each stage will ensure that the organization progresses to or maintains high performance.

If leaders enter organizations where performance is declining, they might have to move back through the SLII® curve to provide more direction and support. But before doing that, it would be best to visit every department in the organization and discover what is working and what is not, using the HPO SCORES® elements as a guide. Leaders should survey and talk to people. This not only gives them vital information, but also makes people feel important and heard. Leaders should gather information about what's going right in the organization and build on that. This will make it much easier to implement a strategy to improve the organization's performance.

A History-Making Organizational Turnaround

There is perhaps no better example of a CEO who entered an organization and adopted the right leadership style than Alan Mulally. When Mulally joined Ford Motor Company in 2006, the organization was in deep trouble. That year it reported a $12.7 billion loss for 2006—the biggest in its 103-year history. The company's debt was rated seven levels below investment grade, and all its assets were mortgaged. To the consumer, Ford had become synonymous with "Fix Or Repair Daily."

Mulally began the tough climb back to profitability with a strong vision:

> *People working together as a lean, global enterprise for automotive leadership... measured by the satisfaction of our customers, employees, investors, dealers, suppliers, and communities.*

Mulally understood the importance of creating a compelling vision. "All of us want to know that we are doing great things, that we are touching a lot of people, and that what we are doing is something bigger than ourselves."

Understanding that Ford's people would be the key to a turnaround, Mulally lived collaboratively—he ate with employees in the cafeteria and regularly conversed with secretaries and assembly line workers. Upholding the value of transparency, Mulally and the company's CFO and operations executives sat down with union officials and shared the books. "Utter transparency of data" convinced labor that if the company was going to "save the place, we'd save it together." The leadership team and union collaborated to reduce Ford's employees from 100,000 to 45,000 through retirements and voluntary buyouts instead of involuntary reduction.

The results—and relationships—flourished under Mulally. By the time Mulally retired in 2014, Ford had posted 19 consecutive profitable quarters. Under Mulally's leadership, one of America's iconic 20th century companies had weathered the tumultuous changes of the early 21st century.[19]

*****

Driven by technology, business today is more complex, global, and fast-changing than ever before. In the next chapter, we'll drill down into leading change.

14

Organizational Change: Why People Resist It

Pat Zigarmi, Judd Hoekstra, and Ken Blanchard

ne of the reasons organizational leadership is more complicated than one-on-one or team leadership is that it often involves leading change. This can be chaotic and messy.

The Importance of Leading Change

Once there was a time when you could experience change and then return to a period of relative stability. In that era, as things settled down, you could thoughtfully plan and get ready for another change. Kurt Lewin described these phases as unfreezing, changing, and refreezing. The reality today is that there is no refreezing. There's no rest and no getting ready.

Today we live in "permanent whitewater." What do we know about whitewater? It's exhilarating and scary! You often have to go sideways or upside down to go forward. The flow is controlled by the environment, and there are unseen obstacles. Occasionally it's wise to use an eddy to regroup and reflect, but eddies are often missed because whitewater seems to create its own momentum.

Sometimes in the midst of change, it's hard for people to maintain perspective. This reminds us of the story about the little girl who comes home from school one day and asks her mother—although today it certainly could be her father—"Why does Daddy work so late every night?" The mother gives a sympathetic smile and replies,

"Well, honey, Daddy just doesn't have time to finish all his work during the day." In her infinite wisdom the little girl says, "Then why don't they put him in a slower group?" Alas, there are no slower groups. Constant change is a way of life.

Mark Twain once said, "The only person who likes change is a baby with a wet diaper." Like it or not, in the dynamic society surrounding today's organizations, the question of whether change will occur is no longer relevant. Change will occur. That is no longer a probability; it is a certainty.

The issue is, how do managers and leaders cope with the barrage of changes that confront them daily as they attempt to keep their organizations adaptive and viable?

Why Is Organizational Change So Complicated?

Consider what happens when someone takes a golf lesson. The instructor changes the golfer's swing to improve his score. However, golfers' scores typically get worse while they are learning a new swing. It takes time for golfers to master a new swing and for their scores to improve. Now think about what happens when you ask each member of a team of golfers to change their respective swings at the same time. The cumulative performance drop is larger for the team than it is for any one golfer.

The same performance drop occurs in organizations where large numbers of people are asked to make behavior changes at the same time. When one person on a team is learning a new skill, the rest of the team can often pick up the slack and keep the team on track. However, when everyone is learning new skills, who can pick up the slack?

When a change is introduced in an organization, an initial drop in organizational performance typically occurs before performance rises to a level above the prechange level. Effective change leaders, being aware of this and understanding the process of change, can minimize the drop in performance caused by large numbers of people learning new behaviors at the same time. They can also minimize the amount of time to achieve desired future performance. Furthermore, they can improve an organization's capacity to initiate, implement, and sustain successful changes. That's exactly what we hope you will be able to learn from this chapter and Chapter 15, "Leading People Through Change."

When Is Change Necessary?

Change is necessary when a discrepancy occurs between an actual set of events—something that is happening right now—and a desired set of events—what you would like to happen. To better understand where your organization might be in relation to needed change, consider the following questions:

- Is your organization on track to achieve its vision?

- Are your organization's initiatives delivering the desired outcomes?

- Is your organization delivering those outcomes on time?

- Is your organization delivering those outcomes on budget?

- Is your organization maintaining high levels of productivity and morale?

- Are your people energized, committed, and passionate?

- Are your customers excited about your organization?

If you find it difficult to say yes to these questions, your focus on leading change should be more intense.

Most managers report that leading change is not their forte. In a survey of 350 senior executives across 14 industries, 68 percent confirmed that their companies had experienced unanticipated problems in the change process.[1] Furthermore, research indicates that 70 percent of organizational changes fail, and these failures can often be traced to ineffective leadership.

Why Change Gets Derailed or Fails

Our research and real-world experience have shown that most change efforts get derailed or fail for predictable reasons. Many leaders don't recognize or account for these reasons. As a result, they make the same mistakes repeatedly. As is often said:

Insanity is doing the same things over and over and expecting different results.

Fortunately, there is hope. If you recognize the reasons change typically gets derailed or fails, leadership can be proactive, thereby increasing the probability of success when initiating, implementing, and sustaining change. On the following page is a list of reasons why change fails.

When most people see this list, their reaction depends on whether they have usually been the target of change or the change agent. Targets of change frequently feel as though we have been studying their organization for years because they have seen these reasons why change fails in action, up close and personal. The reality is that while every organization is unique in some ways, organizations often struggle with change for the same reasons.

When change agents look at this list, they get discouraged because they realize how complicated implementing change can be and how many different things can go wrong. Where should they start? Which of the fifteen reasons why change fails should they concentrate on?

Over the years it has been our experience that if leaders can understand and overcome the first three reasons why change typically fails, they are on the road to being effective leaders of change.

Predictable Reasons Why Change Efforts Typically Fail

1. People leading the change think that announcing the change is the same as implementing it.

2. People's concerns with change are not surfaced or addressed.

3. Those being asked to change are not involved in planning the change.

4. There is no compelling reason to change. The business case is not communicated.

5. A compelling vision that excites people about the future has not been developed and communicated.

6. The change leadership team does not include early adopters, resisters, or informal leaders.

7. The change is not piloted, so the organization does not learn what is needed to support the change.

8. Organizational systems and other initiatives are not aligned with the change.

9. Leaders lose focus or fail to prioritize, causing "death by 1,000 initiatives."

10. People are not enabled or encouraged to build new skills.

11. Those leading the change are not credible. They undercommunicate, give mixed messages, and do not model the behaviors the change requires.

12. Progress is not measured, or no one recognizes the changes that people have worked hard to make.

13. People are not held accountable for implementing the change.

14. People leading the change fail to respect the power of the culture to kill the change.

15. Possibilities and options are not explored before a specific change is chosen.

Focus on Leading the Journey

In working with organizations for four decades, we have observed a leadership pattern that sabotages change. Leaders who have been thinking about a change for a while know why the change needs to be implemented. In their minds, the business case and need to change are clear. They are so convinced that the change must occur that, in their minds, no discussion is needed. So they put all their energy into announcing the change and very little effort into involving others and leading the journey of change. They forget this:

> *Managing change is more about leading the journey of change than announcing the destination.*

In SLII® terms, leaders who announce the change use a directing style. They tell everybody what they want to have happen, and then they disappear. Using an inappropriate delegating style, they expect the change to be automatically implemented. Unfortunately, that never happens. They are not managing the journey. As a result, the change gets derailed. Why?

Change gets derailed because people know they can outlast the announcement, or at least the person making the announcement. Because they haven't been involved up to this point, they sense that the organization is concerned only with its own self-interests, not with the interests of everyone in the organization.

Change that is done to people creates more resistance. The moment vocal resistance occurs, the people leading the change break ranks. The minute they do, their lack of alignment signals that there's no need for others to align to the change because it's going nowhere.

A poor use of directing style, followed by an inappropriate delegating style—announcing the change and then abdicating responsibility for the change—means that the change will never be successfully implemented. To assure success, leaders should involve those impacted by the change in every phase of the change process.

Surfacing and Addressing People's Concerns

A U.S. Department of Education project originally conducted by Gene Hall and his colleagues at the University of Texas[2] suggests that people who are faced with change express six predictable and sequential concerns (see Figure 14.1):

1. Information concerns

2. Personal concerns

3. Implementation concerns

4. Impact concerns

5. Collaboration concerns

6. Refinement concerns

Stages of Concern

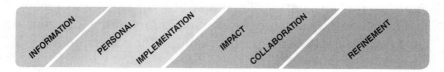

Figure 14.1 The Stages of Concern Model

People going through a change often ask questions that give leaders clues about which stage of concern they are in. Most of the time, the people leading a change don't hear these questions because there are no forums for people to express them. Or, if there are forums, the communication is one way. Those impacted by the change have little to no opportunity to question the reasons for the change or what the change will look like when it's implemented. So instead of becoming advocates for the change because their concerns are surfaced and addressed, those impacted by the change become resistant to it.

Let's look at each stage of concern and the questions people are asking themselves and their peers.

Stage 1: Information Concerns

At this stage, people ask questions to get information about the change. For example: What is the change? Why is it needed? What's wrong with how things are now? How much and how fast does the organization need to change?

People with information concerns need the same information used by those who decided to move forward with the change. They don't want to know if the change is good or bad until they understand it. Assuming that the rationale for change is based on solid information, share this information with people, and help them see what you see. Remember, in the absence of clear, factual communication, people tend to create their own information about the change, and rumors become facts.

In a SAP[3] implementation where the change leadership team had done a good job explaining the business case, people said: "Fewer errors will occur with a single data entry. It will save money because we will eliminate double entries. Fewer steps will be needed, and more functionality and collaboration will occur across work groups. It will be ten times easier to access information. In the long run, it will save time because things will be done in the background. It will eliminate redundancy."

Their information concerns were largely answered by the data the leadership team provided them through multiple vehicles.

Stage 2: Personal Concerns

At this stage, people ask questions about how the change will affect them personally. For example: Why should I change? Will I win or lose? Will I look good? How will I find the time to implement this change? Will I have to learn new skills? Can I do it?

People with personal concerns want to know how the change will play out for them. They wonder if they have the skills and resources to implement the change. As the organization changes, existing personal and organizational commitments are threatened. People are focused on what they are going to lose, not gain.

These personal concerns must be addressed in such a way that people feel they have been heard. As Werner Erhard often said, "What you resist, persists." If you don't permit people to deal with their feelings about what's happening, these feelings stay around. The corollary to this principle is that *if you permit people to deal with what is bothering them, in the very process of dealing with their feelings, the concerns often go away*. Have you ever said to yourself, "I'm glad I got that off my chest"? If so, you know the relief that comes from sharing your feelings with someone. Just having a chance to talk about your concerns during change clears your mind and stimulates creativity that can be used to help rather than hinder change efforts. This is where listening comes in. Executives and managers must permit people to express their personal concerns openly, without fear of evaluation, judgment, or retribution.

> *Personal concerns are the most often ignored stage of concern during a change process.*

In some cases, personal concerns are not resolved to an individual's satisfaction, but the act of listening to these concerns typically goes a long way toward reducing resistance to the change effort.

If you don't take time to address individual needs and fears, you won't get people beyond this basic level of concern. For that reason, let's look at some of the key personal concerns people often have about change.

People are at different levels of readiness for change. Although almost everyone experiences some resistance to change, some individuals may quickly get excited by an opportunity to implement new ideas; others need some time to warm up to new challenges. This doesn't mean there's any one "right" place to be on the readiness continuum; it just means that people have different outlooks and degrees of flexibility about what they've been asked to do. Awareness that people are at different levels of readiness for change can be extremely helpful in effectively implementing any change effort. It helps you identify "early adopters" or change advocates who can be part of your change leadership team. This awareness will help you reach out to those who appear to be resisting the change. Their reasons for resisting may represent caution, or they could be clues to problems that must be resolved if the change is to be successfully implemented.

People initially focus on what they have to give up. People's first reaction to a suggested change often tends to be a personal sense of loss. What do we mean by "a loss"? A loss includes, among other things, the loss of control, time, order, resources, coworkers, competency, and prestige. To keep people moving forward, leaders need to help them deal with this sense of loss. It may seem silly, but people need to be given a chance to mourn their feelings of loss, perhaps just by having time to talk with others about how they feel. Remember, what you resist persists. Helping people get in touch with what they think they will be losing from the change will help them accept some of the benefits.

Ken Blanchard and John Jones, cofounder of University Associates, worked with several divisions of AT&T during the breakup of the corporation into seven separate companies.[4] When they announced it, the leaders of this change started out by talking about the benefits. Ken and John realized that nobody could hear these benefits at the time because people's personal concerns had not been dealt with. To resolve this, they set up "mourning sessions" throughout these divisions where people could talk openly about what they thought they would have to give up with this change. The following were the biggest issues that surfaced:

Loss of status. When you asked people at that time who they worked for, their chests would puff out as they said, "AT&T." It just had a much better ring to it than "Jersey Bell" or "Bell South."

Loss of lifetime employment. A classmate of Ken's, after he graduated from Cornell, got a job with AT&T. When he called home to tell his mother, she cried with joy. "You're set for life," she said. In those days, if you got a job with AT&T, the expectation was that you would work for them for thirty or thirty-five years, have a wonderful retirement party, and then ride off into the sunset. In these days of constant change, people have personal concerns about long-term employment, knowing it's a rarity.

Ken and John found that after people had expressed their feelings about these kinds of losses, they were much more willing and able to hear about the benefits of divestiture.

People feel alone even if everyone else is going through the same change. When change hits, even if everyone around us is facing the same situation, most of us tend to take it personally: "Why me?" The irony is that for the change to be successful, we need the support of others. In fact, we need to ask for such support. People are apt to feel punished when they have to learn new ways of working. If change is to be successful, people need to recruit the help of those around them. We need each other. This is why support groups work when people are facing changes or times of stress in their lives. They need to feel that their leaders, partners, co-workers, and families are on their side in supporting the changes they need to make. Remember, you can't create a world-class organization by yourself. You need the support of others, and they need your support, too.

People are concerned that they will have insufficient resources. When people are asked to change, they often think they need additional time, money, facilities, and personnel. But the reality today is that we will have to do more with less. Organizations that have downsized have fewer people around, and those that *are* around are being asked to accept new responsibilities. They need to work smarter, not harder. Rather than providing these resources directly, leaders must help people discover their own ability to generate them.

People can handle only so much change. Beyond a few changes—or even only one, if the change is significant—people tend to get overwhelmed and become immobilized. That's why it's probably not best to change everything all at once. Choose the key areas that will make the biggest difference.

Whatever you do, make sure people have some success experiences to build on before implementing more change.

In the SAP implementation mentioned earlier, what personal concerns were expressed, and how were they addressed? In interviews, people said: "I saw the databases yesterday and realize I don't have to do anything right now. It's less intimidating now that I've been able to play with it a little. I'm worried about the timing—the 'go live' date is in the middle of everything else. It will take more time. I'm concerned that it will be hard to learn and use. I don't think my team leader can speak for us. She doesn't have a good enough view of our day-to-day work. I hope there will be one-on-one support because the training won't create the sense of security I'll need to be able to use the system confidently. If things run smoother, what will we do with our time? We have to answer the question 'What does this mean for me?' now. I can't do this and my real job at the same time. When this project is over, I'll have to go back and fix everything else."

The SAP change leadership team in this company set up forums for people to express their personal concerns and then systematically worked at providing responses to questions about timing, involvement, support systems, and managing multiple priorities.

Once people feel that their personal concerns have been heard, they tend to turn their attention to how the change will really shake out. These are called implementation concerns.

Stage 3: Implementation Concerns

At this stage, people ask questions about how the change will be implemented. For example: What do I do first, second, third? How do I manage all the details? What happens if it doesn't work as planned? Where do I go for help? How long will this take? Is what we are experiencing typical? How will the organization's structure and systems change?

People with implementation concerns are focused on the nitty-gritty—the details involved in implementing the change. They want to know if the change has been piloted. They know the change won't go exactly as planned, so they want to know, "Where do we go for technical assistance and solutions to problems that arise as the change is being implemented?" People with implementation concerns want to know how to make the best use of information and resources. They also want to know how the organization's infrastructure will support the change effort (the performance management system, recognition and rewards, career development).

In the SAP example mentioned earlier, implementation concerns such as these were voiced: "I'm concerned that people will hold onto their pet systems. Some other applications may survive, and we'll end up with redundant systems. We don't have the hardware to run the software. I'm concerned there won't be enough time to clean up the data or verify the new business processes we've designed. I want to touch it now, sooner rather than later. We need more information about what we can expect and when we can give suggestions. I could really use a timeline—what I've seen has been too detailed or too sparse. I need to know when I'll be involved/crunched. Will people really be held accountable for using the new system?"

These concerns were best addressed when the people closest to the challenges of implementing the change were involved in planning the solutions to the problems that were surfaced.

Stage 4: Impact Concerns

Once people's anxiety about the first three stages of concern is lowered, people tend to raise impact concerns. For example: Is the effort worth it? Is the change making a difference? Are we making progress? Are things getting better? How?

People with impact concerns are interested in the change's relevance and payoff. Now that the change has gone "live," the focus is on evaluation. This is the stage where people sell themselves on the benefits of the change based on the results being achieved. This is also the stage where leaders lose or build credibility for future change initiatives. If the change doesn't positively impact results—or if people don't know how to measure success—it will be more difficult to initiate and implement change in the future. Conversely, this is the stage where you can build change leaders for the future if you identify the early adopters and recognize their successes with the change.

Stage 5: Collaboration Concerns

People at this stage ask questions about collaboration during the change. For example: Who else should be involved? How can we work with others to get them involved in what we are doing? How do we spread the word?

People with collaboration concerns are focused on coordination and cooperation with others. They want to get everyone on board because they are convinced the change is making a positive difference. During this stage, get the early adopters to champion the change, and influence those who are still undecided.

Stage 6: Refinement Concerns

People at this stage ask questions about how the change can be refined. For example: How can we improve on our original idea? How can we make the change even better?

People with refinement concerns are focused on continuous improvement. During an organizational change journey, a number of learnings usually occur. As a result, new opportunities for improvement often come to the surface at this stage.

When SAP got to the refinement stage, we heard the following: "We expect a drop in productivity when we go live. We have to begin to define who owns which work processes and who upstream/downstream needs to change when we go live. SAP isn't just the implementation of new technology; it is business process redesign. We have to build the linkages and do the data conversions now. The experienced SAP users in the company haven't been tapped. I'm concerned we'll ship late when we make the conversion. Exceptions to usual flows are not being anticipated. Old-timers won't be able to take the shortcuts they are used to. Real-time processing will help us eventually, but at first it will add time. It's important to be thinking about integration across all processes now. I'm sure things will get worse in the first few weeks."

We've learned that when people have refinement concerns with one change, they often are hatching the next change. The more you involve others in looking at options and in suggesting ways to do things differently, the easier it will be to build the business case for the next round of change.

Different People Are at Different Stages of Concern

While dealing with people's concerns about change may seem like a lot of hand-holding, each stage of concern can be a major roadblock to the change's success. Since the stages of concern are predictable and sequential, it is important to realize that, at any given time, different people are at different stages of concern.

For example, before a change is announced, the leaders of the change often have information that others in the organization don't. In addition, these change leaders typically have figured out how the change will affect them personally and even have gone so far as to formulate an implementation plan before others in the organization are even aware of the proposed change. As a result, the change leaders have often addressed and resolved information, personal, and implementation concerns; now they are ready to address impact concerns by communicating the change's benefits to the organization. The rest of the organization, however, still has not had a chance to voice their concerns. As a result, they will not be ready to hear about the change's benefits until their information, personal, and implementation concerns have been addressed.

The Importance of Involving Those Who Are Being Asked to Change

When leaders don't involve people by surfacing and diagnosing their stage of concern, resistance to the change increases and the change process delays or stops.

In contrast, when leaders involve people by surfacing, accurately diagnosing, and responding appropriately to the specific concerns people have in each stage of organizational change, the result is less resistance, greater buy-in, and faster change adoption.

Furthermore, resolving concerns throughout the change process builds trust in the change leadership team, puts challenges on the table, gives people an opportunity to influence the change process, and allows people to refocus their energy on the change.

The lesson: When it comes to leading people through change, what you are changing is important, but *how* you involve people in the change is the difference between failure and success.

People often resent change when they have no involvement in how it should be implemented. So, contrary to popular belief, people don't resist change—they resist being controlled.

*****

In this chapter, we focused on change at the organizational level and why people resist it. In the next chapter, we share five specific change leadership strategies to lead people through change. These strategies provide details on how leaders can proactively respond to each stage of concern and overcome the Predictable Reasons Why Change Efforts Typically Fail.

15

Leading People Through Change

Pat Zigarmi and Judd Hoekstra

A s we discussed in the last chapter, leaders often get overwhelmed when they implement change. In many ways, they feel trapped in a lose-lose situation. If they try to launch a disruptive change effort, they risk unleashing all kinds of pent-up negative feelings in people. On the other hand, if leaders don't constantly drive change, their organizations will be displaced by organizations committed to innovation. It's been said that if you don't change, you're dying. Add to that the fifteen Predictable Reasons Why Change Efforts Typically Fail, and it's easy to see why leaders become immobilized around change. That's why Pat Zigarmi and Judd Hoekstra developed a Leading People Through Change model—to make the seemingly complicated simple (see Figure 15.1.)[1]

Five Change Leadership Strategies

The Leading People Through Change model defines five change leadership strategies and their respective outcomes. These change leadership strategies are a response to the six stages of concern and serve as the antidote to the fifteen Predictable Reasons Why Change Efforts Typically Fail. They also describe a process for leading people through change that differs dramatically from how change is introduced in most organizations.

Leading People Through Change®

Figure 15.1 Leading People Through Change Model

Change Strategy 1: Expand Involvement and Influence

Outcome: Buy-In

The first change leadership strategy, *Expand Involvement and Influence*, is at the heart of the Leading People Through Change model and must be used consistently throughout the change process to gain the cooperation and buy-in of others. This change strategy addresses four of the fifteen predictable reasons why change efforts fail:

1. People leading the change think that announcing the change is the same as implementing it.

2. People's concerns with change are not surfaced or addressed.

3. Those being asked to change are not involved in planning the change.

4. The change leadership team does not include early adopters, resisters, or informal leaders.

The core belief of our approach to leading organizational change is that the best way to initiate, implement, and sustain change is to increase the level of influence and involvement from the people being asked to change, surfacing and resolving their concerns along the way. This was a key strategy in the preceding chapter.

Which of the following are you more likely to commit to: a decision made by others that is being imposed on you, or a decision you've had a chance to provide input into?

What may seem obvious to you isn't obvious to many leaders trying to implement organizational changes. They believe change will be implemented much faster if they make quick decisions, and it is quicker to make decisions with fewer people providing input into the decision-making process. *While it is true that decisions can be made faster when fewer people are involved, faster decisions may not translate into faster and better implementation.* These change leaders believe that they can announce the change and it's done! The "top-down, minimal involvement" leadership approach ignores the critical difference between compliance and commitment. People may comply with the new directive for a short time until the pressure is off, and then they typically return to old behavior because their concerns are not surfaced or addressed and they believe the change is being done to them, not with them.

Keep Figure 15.2 in mind as you think about how much you want to involve people in the change process. Resistance increases the more people sense that they cannot influence what is happening to them.

If people aren't treated as if they are smart and would reach the same conclusion about the need to change as the change leadership team, they perceive a loss of control. Their world is about to change, but they have not been asked to talk about "what is" or "what could be." Without involvement, there isn't a vehicle for them to express and resolve their information concerns. Similarly, if personal concerns

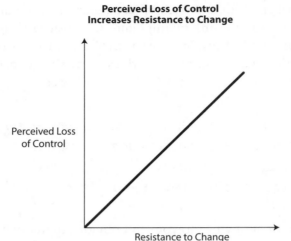

**Perceived Loss of Control
Increases Resistance to Change**

Perceived Loss
of Control

Resistance to Change

Figure 15.2 Perceived Loss of Control Increases Resistance to Change

are not surfaced and acknowledged, people lose a sense of autonomy. They collude with others and become anxious, and their resistance increases. Then, when T-shirts with a slogan are given out and everyone is sent to "one size fits all" training, people begin to believe that the leadership really is out of touch with what is really happening in the organization. This puts their sense of control in jeopardy, which again increases resistance. The bottom line is that people have to influence the change they are expected to make, or, as Robert Lee said:

> *"People who are left out of shaping
> change have a way of reminding us that
> they are really important."*

There are lots of ways to involve people in the change process. They can be scouts for solutions that other organizations who are facing the same challenges have implemented. They can be asked to pilot the change. They can be brought onto the change leadership team optimally as members, minimally as advisors. Although it may feel uncomfortable at first, it is helpful to include at least one or two people who would be considered "resistant" and who can articulate the concerns of those who share that perspective on the change leadership team. When resisters have a forum to surface and address their concerns, they often become the most effective problem solvers and spokespeople for the change.

Ultimately, you want to engage the early adopters of the change as peer advocates. Peer advocates can often influence the people who are neutral to the change before they become resistant by helping build the business case for the change and by sharing their personal success with the change. You want to enlist them in training others and modeling the behaviors expected of others who are being asked to change.

The goal of a high involvement change strategy is to build a broad-based coalition of leaders at all levels who support the change and can advocate for the change with one voice to multiple stakeholders. If a diverse group of leaders from across the organization is aligned on the need for the change and how it will positively impact the organization, there is less resistance, less passivity, and less blaming. When people see a lack of alignment at the top, they know they don't have to align. In addition, they know that because there is low alignment, the change will stall or derail and that they can outlast it. Remember: Sustainable organizational change happens through conversation and collaboration, not by unilateral action by a few.

High involvement also gets concerns and challenges on the table sooner. As a result, there is increased alignment and clarity about what and how things have to change, a better change implementation plan, and a higher probability of success. A favorite guideline we share with change leaders is this:

> *Those who plan the battle rarely battle the plan!*

Flexibility: Using Several Different Change Leadership Strategies to Successfully Lead Change

The other four organizational change leadership strategies on the perimeter of the model proactively address the other Predictable Reasons Why Change Efforts Typically Fail.

When these change leadership strategies are thoughtfully used during a change process, a compelling case for the change and inspiring vision are created. The right resources and infrastructure are put in place to ensure successful implementation. Sustainable results are achieved. And options for ongoing innovation and change are explored.

To help make these change leadership strategies come alive, we offer the following case study involving a problem that has plagued millions of people in America. If you live outside the United States, you can probably come up with a similar "systems" change.

Case Study: Non-Support-Paying Parents

As many as 20 million children in America may have noncustodial parents who avoid child support obligations. According to the Federal Office of Child Support, the total unpaid child support in the United States is close to $100 billion, and 68 percent of child support cases are in arrears. An overwhelming majority of children—particularly minorities—residing in single-parent homes, where child support is not paid, live in poverty.

In the United States, child support enforcement is a loose confederation of state and local agencies all operating with different guidelines, all accountable to the Federal Office of Child Support Enforcement. Getting agencies to work together is the greatest challenge. While legislation exists to enforce child support payments, there is too much bureaucracy and not enough manpower to pursue non-support-paying parents across state lines and take them into custody. As a result, many of these parents beat the system.

Up until recently, information on these parents was stored in paper files in clerks' offices in the county where the parent resided. County clerks were responsible for using this information to try to enforce the collection of child support payments. Often, as a county clerk got close to tracking down a parent not paying court-ordered child support payments, the parent would move to a different county or even a different state.

Without a system for sharing information stored in paper files across county lines or even state lines, it became nearly impossible to catch the non-support-paying parents. As a result, custodial parents and kids who were due to receive child support ended up losing the support they needed.

As frustration grew over this situation, the federal government decided to take on the challenge. Federal legislation was passed that mandated that each state implement an electronic tracking system that facilitated the sharing of current information across county and state lines to better enable the tracking of these parents. This may sound like a relatively simple change to make, considering computer use today. However, when the legislation was passed, many county clerks were in their fifties and sixties, lived in rural areas, had never used a computer, and had been trying to track non-support-paying parents with a notepad, pencil, and telephone for decades.

Do you think the county clerks being asked to change had concerns about the proposed change? Of course they did. Many of these county clerks had *information concerns,* such as how having an electronic tracking system would improve enforcement in their county. In counties that were already doing a good job of collecting child support, clerks wondered if they could continue using their paper files as long as they were successful. Counties that had been using a computer system for years to track cases wondered if they needed to use the new mandated system, or if they could keep using their current system. People wondered how long it would take to move the information from their paper files to the computer.

Many of the county clerks had *personal concerns* as well. People said things like, "How can I learn to use this new system? If I can't learn to use the new tracking system and software, will I still have a job? Besides being told to use the new electronic tracking system, how else is my job changing? This sounds like a lot of extra work. I'm not ready for this." These questions are typical at this stage of the change process and reflective of fears that the change would probably make their work harder.

In addition, the clerks had *implementation concerns.* They wanted to know when they would be trained on the new electronic tracking system. They wanted to know who to contact if they needed help after training. Many wondered if any counties were "going live" before they were and if they could talk with people in those counties. They also wondered when the whole state would be up and running on the new system. Finally, they wondered what would happen if the electronic tracking system went down or was unavailable.

Once the change was in motion, some of the clerks brought forward *impact concerns*. For example, they wanted to know if they were catching any non-support-paying parents they wouldn't have caught without the new system. They wanted to know how much more money they were collecting compared to when they were doing things the old way. Many were curious to know if custodial parents who began receiving payments saw positive changes in how they worked with the clerks and in the amount of money they were collecting. They wanted to know how much more money they were collecting compared to when they were doing things the old way. Many were curious to know if their customers (custodial parents) saw a positive change in how they were working with them and the results they were achieving.

In time, the clerks' *collaboration concerns* began to surface. Here are some of their comments: "I've seen the success of this new system firsthand. Is there anybody who is not yet convinced that this is a good idea? It will only work if we do it across the state and across the country."

"I'm so glad I got to be part of the pilot. I can't wait to go back to my county and share the results we've achieved. There are a lot of people who are currently pretty skeptical about this new system."

"The system is working pretty well within the counties around us that have 'gone live.' But we need to broaden the implementation and connect every county in the country to a common database."

Once the new system was up and running, the clerks brought forward their *refinement concerns*. While they acknowledged that the new system was an improvement over how things used to be, they suggested areas that might be improved. For example, a question came up about how they could connect their system to other systems (other county and state child support systems, the Department of Motor Vehicles, the new-hire database, the IRS) so that they could better track people and enforce the collection of child support. So, how did those responsible for this massive systems change decrease information, personal, and implementation concerns and create buy-in for the proposed change?

Change Strategy 2: Explain Why the Change Is Needed

Outcome: A Compelling Business Case and Inspiring Vision for the Change

The second change leadership strategy is Explain Why the Change Is Needed. This strategy addresses the following two reasons why change efforts fail:

5. There is no compelling reason to change. The business case is not communicated.

6. A compelling vision that excites people about the future has not been developed and communicated.

This second change leadership strategy addresses *information concerns* and, to some extent, personal concerns.

When leaders explain why the change is needed, the outcome is a compelling case that helps people understand the change being proposed, the rationale for the change, and why the status quo is no longer a viable option.

When you lead a change initiative, expect that many people in the organization will not understand the need for a change; they will feel good about the work they are currently doing. As a result, they will have information concerns and likely will ask questions such as, "What is the change? Why is it needed? What's wrong with the way things are now? How much and how fast does the organization need to change?"

Most likely, those initiating the change were frustrated by something that was wrong with the status quo or were anxious about an opportunity that would be lost by continuing with business as usual. This spirit of discontent with the status quo needs to be shared and felt by those being asked to change.

You need to create enough disequilibrium to create change, but not so much that others fight, flee, or freeze.

Suppose a leader mistakenly attempts to create and communicate a change-specific vision to the organization before demonstrating that the status quo is no longer a viable option. The inertia of the status quo will likely prove too strong, and the very people whose cooperation the leader needs will be much less likely to embrace the picture of the future the leader intends to create. As John Maynard Keynes[2] said:

"The difficulty lies not so much in developing new ideas as in escaping from old ones."

In the child support example described earlier, it was critical to have custodial parents and county clerks share their stories about the frustration and hopelessness they felt in trying to track down and enforce the collection of child support from non-support-paying parents with only pen-and-paper support from government agents. Without county clerks feeling this frustration, it was very unlikely that they would be willing to learn a new electronic tracking system and adopt new ways of working just because it was mandated by federal legislators.

As you build the case for change, one of the best ways to get buy-in from employees is to share information broadly and then ask people at all levels in the organization to tell you why they believe the organization needs to change.

To do that, bring people face to face with the reality of what is prompting the need for change. Think of it as turning up the thermostat to create discomfort and a sense of urgency that the change is needed. Ask people for their reasons why the organization needs to change even if you already think you know the answers. When they respond, don't respond with certainty. It will lead to overselling what you know and discounting what you don't know.

Go toward resisters, and learn why they are resisting. By doing so, your case for change will be more compelling in people's eyes because they came up with it. As a result of their ownership in making the case for change, people are much more likely to leave the status quo behind.

Returning to the example we cited in Chapter 3, "Empowerment Is the Key," The Ken Blanchard Companies® needed to make several changes as a result of the economic downturn following the terrorist attacks on September 11, 2001. The leaders shared information broadly with the organization regarding projected revenue, current expenses, and break-even figures. This brought people face to face with the reality of the situation and ensured that everyone in the organization understood that "business as usual" was no longer a viable option. Then the leaders asked associates what would happen if the status quo were maintained. The associates clearly stated that the company's survival was at stake. As a result of their involvement in building the case for change, associates bought into a number of cost-cutting initiatives, even when the initiatives weren't in their own best interest.

Once a gap between what is and what could be is identified, an inspiring vision of the future needs to be shared. An inspiring vision is what creates a commitment to change.

The process used to create a vision, whether it is for an entire organization or for a specific change initiative, is the same. This process is described in detail in Chapter 2, "The Power of Vision." As Ken Blanchard and Jesse Stoner point out in *Full Steam Ahead! Unleash the Power of Vision in Your Company and Your Life*, the process you use to develop a vision is as important as the vision itself. In other words, if people are involved in the process and feel the vision is theirs— as opposed to some words on a poster from an executive retreat— they are more likely to see themselves as part of the future when the change is implemented. When they are involved in creating the picture of the future, they begin to believe they will adapt, and they will be much more likely to show the tenacity needed during the challenging times that inevitably accompany change.

Getting people involved in the visioning process is also a key way to help them resolve the *personal concerns* they experience during a change. The more you can get people involved in the visioning process, the more likely it is they will want to be part of the future organization. They need to be able to see themselves *in* the picture of the future for it to inspire them. This is why it is so important for leaders to understand the fears, aspirations, and loyalties of the people being asked to change.

In our earlier child support example, the change leadership team was responsible for drafting the initial vision. Because there was no existing vision for the state's Child Support Program to compare it to, they needed to create a brand new vision for the entire program, not just for the implementation of the new electronic tracking system. Next, they took the draft vision to the county clerks across the state and asked them for input. The result was the creation of a shared vision that was compelling for the majority of those being asked to change. It read:

Our state's Child Support Program helps children thrive by providing financial stability to their families and offering the highest-quality service as a nationally recognized model of excellence for child support enforcement.

While a small group of leaders could have come up with these words, giving the county clerks who were being asked to change an opportunity to provide input ensured that the vision was understood and embraced.

Change Strategy 3: Collaborate on Implementation

Outcome: The Right Resources and Infrastructure

The third change leadership strategy, Collaborate on Implementation, is designed to create the right conditions for the successful implementation of the change and to surface and address *personal and implementation concerns.*

When leaders engage others in planning and piloting the change, they encourage collaborative effort in identifying the right resources and building the infrastructure needed to support the change. This change leadership strategy addresses the following reasons why change efforts fail:

7. The change is not piloted, so the organization does not learn what is needed to support the change.

8. Organizational systems and other initiatives are not aligned with the change.

9. Leaders lose focus or fail to prioritize, causing "death by 1,000 initiatives."

There are lots of ways organizations can involve others in crafting successful change implementation plans. They include:

Involve others in planning and pilots. We've all seen or been part of changes that have not gone well. In most of these cases, the implementation plan was not developed by people anywhere near the front line. As a result, the plan did not account for some real-world realities and was shrugged off as flawed, unrealistic, and lacking the details required for action—or, worse yet, flat-out wrong.

As with the earlier change leadership strategies we described, when you involve people and give them a chance to influence, you get not only their buy-in, but a better outcome. Your planning process needs to account for the fact that you won't have it all figured out ahead of time. Run some experiments or pilots with early adopters to work out the kinks and learn more about the best way to implement the change with the larger organization. Ensure that your change implementation plan is dynamic.

By getting others involved in the planning process, you can surface and resolve many lingering *personal and implementation concerns*.

Here's an old adage we love:

"Listen to the whispers to avoid the screams."

Test drives, pilots, and experiments can also teach you what else needs to change in terms of policies, procedures, systems, and structures so that the probability of successful implementation across the larger organization improves. The positive outcomes of engaging others at this stage of the change process are collaborative effort, a high degree of alignment on the best way to implement the change, a realistic assessment of the resources needed, and the right infrastructure.

Many change plans underestimate the momentum generated by short-term wins that can be realized when the change is piloted. Short-term wins are improvements that can be implemented within a short time frame—typically three months—with minimal resources, at minimal cost, and at minimal risk.

Pilots that result in short-term wins have several benefits. First, they address implementation concerns around the mechanics of the change, priorities, and obstacles to the efficient implementation of the change. Second, they proactively address *impact concerns* (such as "Is the change working?"). Third, pilots get more people involved with influencing the change, generating more buy-in. Fourth, they provide good news early in the change effort, when good news is hard to come by. Fifth, they reinforce behavior changes made by early adopters. Sixth, they help sway those who are "on the fence" toward action. Remember, motion creates emotion.

In the child support case study pilot described earlier, it was critical to select counties that had the greatest probability of seeing significant short-term results from implementing the new electronic tracking system. This would help surface and address implementation concerns and build momentum for post-pilot implementations with other counties where the impact was more in question.

Avoid death by 1,000 initiatives. With limited resources, it is critical to make choices about what change initiatives will allow your organization to achieve its vision most effectively and efficiently. Individual change initiatives need to be scheduled and implemented in light of other activities and initiatives competing for people's time, energy, and mindshare.

During times of change, it is critical to provide people with direction on priorities. Like a sponge, after a certain amount of change, people cannot absorb any more, no matter how resilient and adaptive they are. Another way to involve others in the implementation of change is to ask those impacted by the change about what work processes, systems, and policies need to change to ensure successful implementation.

Decide what not to do. While it is important to provide direction on what to do, it is just as important to provide direction on what *not* to do. Ask the following questions: What project or initiative will have the greatest impact on your vision? What provides the greatest value for resources expended (money, people, time)? Can the people responsible for working on the project handle it with all the other things they have been assigned to do? Are there enough qualified people who can dedicate time to work on the project? Are there any synergies between this project and other critical projects?

Once you have prioritized and sequenced a list of possible change projects, recognize that, because we live in a dynamic environment, priorities can shift and resources can become more abundant or scarce. This may shift the type and number of projects an organization undertakes at any point in time as well. Prioritizing change initiatives and steps within a single change initiative is a key tactic for lowering implementation concerns.

Decide how and when to measure and assess progress. The adage is true: What gets measured gets done. Because it is difficult to predict human behavior with absolute certainty—especially in the face of major change—assess the progress being made on a number of fronts in an effort to identify potential risks to the change's success. These areas include sponsor commitment, employee commitment and behavior change, the achievement of project milestones, and progress toward the accomplishment of business results.

The measurement plan crafted at this step needs to describe what will be measured, how it will be measured, and how frequently it will be measured. To increase the probability of successful change, consider using Blanchard's Change Readiness Survey[3] to determine what's working well and what requires additional work. And constantly ask the early adopters of the change how they think it's going.

Communicate, communicate, communicate. Much has been written about the importance of communication during times of change. Why is it so important? A significant amount of resistance encountered during organizational change is caused by a lack of information, especially details about the what, why, and how. In the absence of honest, passionate, and empathetic communication, people create their own information about the change, and rumors begin to serve as facts.

For example, we worked with an organization going through a tremendous amount of change. As we started our work, we quickly realized that little or no rationale was being provided for key decisions that affected a large number of people. Without supporting rationale, the facts appeared harsh to team members:

- The development project I was working on was stopped.

- My budget was cut.

Based on these facts alone, many people assumed that the company's future was bleak. As a result, tremendous effort was required to overcome the rumor mill that led to drops in productivity and morale and caused some people to begin looking for other jobs.

Let's consider these same facts, only this time with supporting rationale. Can you see how providing this rationale could have prevented the rumors and resistance that occurred?

- The project I was working on was stopped because we found that customer safety was at risk. Customer safety is our highest-priority value, so we made a decision in line with our values.

- My budget was cut because the organization is reallocating these funds toward another drug development project based on a recent licensing agreement we signed.

Some of the strongest resistance to change occurs when reality differs from expectations. Therefore, understanding the current expectations of those affected by the change is critical if leaders are to manage and shape or transform those expectations effectively.

Recognize that covert resistance kills change. Effective leaders not only tolerate the open expression of concerns, they actually reward their people for sharing their concerns in an open, honest, and constructive manner. It is critical that leaders provide opportunities for two-way communication because concerns cannot be surfaced and resolved without give-and-take dialogue.

It is also important to recognize that communicating your message once is not enough for most people to act on it. People in organizations are so bombarded with information that one of the best ways to sort out what requires action versus what does not is to listen for the messages that are communicated repeatedly over time. These can be distinguished from the flavor-of-the-month messages that come and go. Communicate your key messages at least seven times in seven different ways. Better yet, communicate them at least ten times in ten different ways.

Change Strategy 4: Make the Change Sustainable

Outcome: Sustainable Results

The fourth change leadership strategy, Make the Change Sustainable, addresses both *implementation and impact concerns*. When leaders make the change sustainable, they set the stage for sustainable results. This encourages people to embrace the change, develop new skills, and make a deeper commitment to the organization. This change leadership strategy addresses the following reasons why change efforts fail.

10. People are not enabled or encouraged to build new skills.

11. Those leading the change are not credible; they undercommunicate, give mixed messages, and do not model the behaviors the change requires.

12. Progress is not measured, or no one recognizes the changes that people have worked hard to make.

13. People are not held accountable for implementing the change.

Our experience has shown that most organizations jump into this change leadership strategy—Make the Change Sustainable—much too soon. In many cases, executives announce the change and try to get people into training as soon as possible. Unfortunately, people's *information and personal concerns* have not yet been addressed, so the results of the training are less than optimal. Also, training often is delivered before all the kinks are worked out, contingencies are planned for, help desks are created, or systems are aligned. Finally, early training usually fails because it's "one size fits all." After the learnings from pilots and experiments are culled and the right infra-structure is in place, training for the change should be done in as individualized a way as possible. Ideally, a training strategy for each individual should be delivered at just the right time.

Notice how three other change leadership strategies come before the Make Change Sustainable strategy. There is a reason for this—namely, because most organizations don't do a good job on the early work that needs to be done to set up a successful change. The rallying cry we often hear in our work with organizations going through change is, "We're raising the bar!" This rallying cry is not bad in and of itself. However, nothing kills motivation faster than telling people to raise their performance but failing to provide them with the new skills, tools, and resources required to leap over the height of the recently raised bar. As a result, people's reaction to leadership's statement that "We're raising the bar!" is often along the lines of "Do you mean that I'm not doing a good job now?"

After the roles, responsibilities, and competencies required for lasting change are determined, skill gaps need to be closed. As SLII® would suggest, leaders need to use a directing style 1 (with high direction and low support) or, more likely, a coaching style 2 (with high direc-tion and high support) to build people's competence and commit-ment. Leaders need to use mistakes as opportunities for further learning, and they need to praise progress.

In the child support case study we described earlier, a group of county clerks involved in the pilots were chosen to train other county clerks on the new electronic tracking system and new work processes. This brought county clerk trainees face to face with others in similar posi-tions who had gone down the path before them. Because the trainers were speaking from a position of experience, they were credible and could set realistic expectations for what other county clerks could expect when their county "went live."

In addition, the county clerks facilitating the training used the sessions as opportunities to gather additional input and ensure that the implementation plan was as strong as it could be.

When leaders pay attention to the change effort at this phase—rather than announcing the next change!—they create conditions for accountability and early results. Some tactics for Making Change Sustainable are:

- **Walking the talk.** Although it is critical for the change leadership team to communicate with one voice, it is even more important that the change leaders walk their talk and model the behaviors they expect of others at this phase of the change cycle.

  It is estimated that a leader's actions are at least three times as important as what he or she says. Leaders need to display as much or more commitment to the change as the people they lead. People will assess what the leader does and doesn't do to assess the commitment to the change. The minute that associates or colleagues sense that their leader is not committed or is acting inconsistently with the desired behaviors of the change, they will no longer commit themselves to the effort.

- **Measure, praise progress, and redirect when necessary.** As stated earlier, what gets measured gets done. Keep in mind that people's thoughts and actions are leading indicators of business and financial performance. Leading indicators allow you to drive by "looking through the windshield" rather than by relying solely on lagging indicators such as financial performance, which is akin to driving while looking in the rearview mirror.

  Once measurement occurs, praise the progress that is being made. Don't wait for perfect performance. If you do, you'll be waiting a long time. This concept has been key to our teachings for decades:

  The key to developing people and creating great organizations is to catch people doing things right and to accentuate the positive.

Because you've planned for short-term wins, you should be able to find and share success stories as a means of influencing people who remain on the fence. Follow through on your promise to recognize and reward the behavior you expect, and follow through on your promise to impose consequences for anyone attempting to derail the change program. This is the stage where you either redirect people's efforts or let go of the people who continue to resist.

In our child support case study, the state government called monthly meetings for county clerks across the state with similar "go live" dates. During these meetings, each county was asked to share a success story as well as any challenges it was having. The idea of holding each county accountable for sharing a success story in front of its peers created some healthy competition to make the new tracking system work. It allowed early-adopting counties to sway those that were on the fence. Discussing the challenges also provided opportunities for learning that could be fed back into the design of the tracking system, the planning process, and the training of the next group of county clerks.

In another example, a change leadership team we worked with instituted the use of a "performance dashboard" to continually measure progress against a set of key performance indicators. The change leadership team met twice a month to discuss the plan's progress, as seen by green, yellow, and red indicators on the performance dashboard. If a key performance indicator was green, this was praised and celebrated. If a key performance indicator was yellow or red, the team would discuss how best to redirect efforts to get that indicator back on track. This process held people accountable for performance and ensured that people got the direction and support they needed.

- *Kill bureaucracy.* Bureaucracy kills change. At this phase of the change process it's important again to involve others in identifying work processes, policies, and procedures that get in the way of the successful implementation of the change.

Change Strategy 5: Explore Possibilities

Outcome: Options

The fifth change leadership strategy, Explore Possibilities, addresses *collaboration and refinement concerns*.

This strategy addresses the final two reasons why change efforts typically fail.

14. People leading the change fail to respect the power of the culture to kill the change.

15. Possibilities and options are not explored before a specific change is chosen.

While a high performing change leadership team can generate enthusiasm and short-term success during times of change, it is critical that the change be embedded in the organization's culture—its attitudes, beliefs, and behavior patterns—if it is to be sustainable.

If a change is introduced that is not aligned with the current culture, you must alter the existing culture to support the new initiative or accept that the change may not be sustainable. The best way to alter the culture is to go back to the organization's vision and examine its values. Identify which values support the new culture and which don't. Then define the behaviors that are consistent with the values, and create acknowledgment and accountability for behaving consistently with the values. It is energizing for an organization to do this in the context of implementing change.

In many cases, a change is implemented within some business units before other business units are engaged. The change process defined by the Leading People Through Change model needs to be repeated for each new business unit as it launches the change.

Citing our child support case study again, it was critical to ensure that all obstacles to using the new tracking system were removed. While there were some common obstacles to overcome for most counties, many obstacles differed by county. As a result, embedding the change on a local level required attention at the local level. Because ongoing support was provided, obstacles were removed, and the counties themselves sold each other on the benefits of implementing the new tracking system. Doing so allowed the initiative to be extended across an entire state and eventually the entire country.

Ideally, those who are closest to the problems and opportunities in an organization are the ones who come up with the options to be considered by the change leadership team. To ensure face validity and inclusion of the best options, the options identified should be reviewed by a representative sample of those being asked to change.

In our child support case study, custodial parents and county clerks across the country expressed frustration with the fact that non-support-paying parents were getting harder to track and more elusive than ever. As a result, the federal government took this input, explored the root causes of the problem, and identified several possible responses. Several change projects were chosen as part of an integrated strategy to enforce the collection of child support payments. These projects included but were not limited to withholding income from the noncustodial parent's employer and intercepting income tax refunds, unemployment compensation benefits, and lottery winnings. The projects also included reporting to the credit bureau, suspending driver's and professional licenses, locating bank assets, cross-matching new-hire reporting, suspending hunting and fishing licenses, denying passports, assigning liens, matching federal loan data, and automating child support operations, including interfaces with numerous other state agency systems.

Some of these options were potentially more feasible and would have more impact than others. By simply having options, people felt they had choices and could influence what changed.

Since the electronic enforcement tracking system was implemented, annual child support collections have increased from $177 million to more than $460 million. Increased collections mean that more children are receiving the child support they deserve, and fewer families have to resort to public assistance to survive.[4]

The Importance of Reinforcing the Change

It is our hope that instructing leaders how to implement each change strategy and overcome the 15 reasons why change typically fails has taken much of the mystique out of the change process. Responding to others' concerns and paying attention to how you increase involvement and influence at each step in the change process is the best way we know to build future change receptivity, capability, and leadership.

To summarize, here's a good rule of thumb:

> *Organizations should spend ten times more energy reinforcing the change they just made than looking for the next great change to try.*

*****

It's worth repeating that if the change you're introducing is not aligned with the current culture, you must re-create the existing culture to support the new change initiative. Given the importance of culture, in the next chapter we will discuss in detail how to build or transform an organizational culture.

16

Managing a Successful Cultural Transformation

Garry Demarest, Chris Edmonds, and Bob Glaser

Look closely at the operations of any high performing organization, and you are bound to find a strong and distinct culture. While most people have heard the term and it has been written about widely, culture can be a slippery concept to describe.[1] As we indicated in Chapter 2, "The Power of Vision," we define culture as the context in which all practices exist. It is the organization's personality; it's "how things are done around here." When we talk about an organization's culture, we are referring to the values, attitudes, beliefs, behaviors, and practices of the organizational members.

In our experience, most members of an organization find it difficult to describe their company's culture, often because they are so immersed in it. They have not thought about the unique elements, symbols, rituals, stories, events, and demonstrated behaviors that make their organization's culture what it is.

New members of an organization often learn about the culture the hard way, by bumping into it as they attempt to navigate their way through it. Experienced members are quick to correct the newcomers and educate them about the "expected behavior." For example, when teaching a class at one of American Honda's manufacturing plants several years ago, one of our consulting partners was reprimanded by a manager for bringing food into the classroom. He was told that associates were not allowed to eat in the classrooms, and he was expected to follow the same rule.

Every organization has a culture; it can be formally defined or evolve entirely by default. The company's culture will enhance organizational performance and employee passion—or erode it. Culture can be complex. Within an organization, different divisions, regions, or departments can have slightly—or hugely—different cultures. Those intact cultures may, as with the broad organization, help, hinder, or hurt organizational performance and employee passion.

Culture not only underlies all that an organization does. As we learned in the preceding chapter, it also determines the organization's readiness for change. When organizations seek greatness, they often find aspects of their organizational culture that need change.

Leaders begin to consider a culture change when they know something in their organization is not working or is broken. It may be a single incident that raises eyebrows—or requires a costly recovery—or patterns of behavior that demonstrate a low threshold of trust, respect, and confidence across the organization. Perhaps a series of low scores on employee morale surveys tells leaders the organization is less than healthy.

Gung Ho!: A Starting Point

We have recognized for a long time that culture has a profound effect on the behavior of organizational members, the trust and respect that exist between them, and ultimately the organization's success. However, we hadn't spent much time studying culture until after the publication of Ken Blanchard and Sheldon Bowles's book *Gung Ho!: Turn On the People in Any Organization*. It was the story of two unlikely characters—Peggy Sinclair, a new top manager, and Andy Longclaw, an often-criticized manager. They went on an unconventional journey to successfully change the culture in their manufacturing plant.[2]

We received many calls and emails from organizational leaders about their efforts and hopes for putting the *Gung Ho!* story into practice. Some had attempted to implement the key principles based on the book—needing worthwhile work (the Spirit of the Squirrel), being in control of achieving the goal (the Way of the Beaver), and cheering each other on (the Gift of the Goose). But they found that their changes were not sustainable or didn't produce the anticipated results. Some who focused on the Gift of the Goose "Cheering Each Other On" principle found that the positive feelings generated were short-lived and didn't change people's behavior in the long term.

Interacting with these leaders, we realized that while all three principles are part of any great culture, we had to get smarter about how to create a strong and distinct culture and how to change a culture that was hindering the implementation of a major initiative. Early on, we learned four things. First, there is no one "right" culture. Second, most organizations do not consciously create their culture. Third, senior leaders often don't understand the impact of culture on performance. Finally, a strong, focused culture starts with a compelling vision.

One "Right" Culture?

There is no "right" or "correct" organizational culture. We've seen high performing organizations in a variety of industries around the world. They have slightly different value descriptions, and different behaviors that are expected, but one thing is true among all of them— the culture serves their people, customers, and stakeholders equally.

The biggest question everyone faces is, "What is the right culture for our organization?" The answer depends on several factors. What values do you want demonstrated, day in and day out, in your organization? What behaviors will consistently create the desired high performance while enabling strong trust and respect across all employees and customers? What behaviors do star performers consistently demonstrate? How do you want managers and employees to treat each other? What would you like customers to consistently say about your products and services and about their interactions with your staff?

Culture by Design, Not by Default

Our extensive experience with a wide variety of organizations has led us to conclude that most organizations do not consciously create their culture. Their company's culture simply emerged as the organization's products and services were developed, purchased by customers, and delivered. Culture, therefore, typically happens by default, not by design.

If your current organizational culture does not serve customers well, maintain passionate employees, and create profits for your enterprise to continue growing and serving, you must consider revising the organization's way of operating by embracing cultural transformation.

The key question for senior leaders is:

Does your culture serve your organization?

If it doesn't, it is time to become proactive about building a culture that serves the needs of the entire organization, not just the leaders.

Skepticism about Culture from Senior Leaders

Very often leaders cannot diagnose a sick culture. For example, they attribute low morale or poor performance to poor management skills, inconsistent teamwork, or outside influences. They don't see that these issues may be a result of a culture that needs attention.

One reason that culture is not at the top of leaders' minds is the prevailing notion that culture is not relevant to bottom-line business—not linked to an organization's performance. This belief has been reinforced by the fact that much of the business press continually focuses on increasing organizational performance. Very few books—and even fewer consultants—have focused on the power of culture to positively impact both performance and employee passion. Yet we believe culture drives organizational performance as much as it drives employee passion.

The reason business writers have focused primarily on organizational performance is rational. Most senior leaders will tell you their primary performance metric is organizational performance—sales, productivity, and profits. Financial performance is of critical importance to senior leaders because *that's how they get evaluated and rewarded.* Unfortunately, this situation produces a single-minded focus on short-term results at the expense of longer-term outcomes that contribute to and drive performance, such as employee passion, customer service, and consistent quality. These are all things that a high performing culture can impact.

For example, Merck, one of the world's most successful pharmaceutical companies, experienced a remarkable turnaround in a sales division that embraced the culture change process. The division was one of the poorest performers at the time, and the division vice president had left for another opportunity in the company. This transition presented a "great opportunity to think about the culture we wanted" in the division, related Tim Schmidt, then director of sales training and professional development. The management team internalized, applied, and modeled the culture change process, with emphasis on teamwork, responsibility, and accountability for everyone in the division. Within a year, and still without a vice president at the helm, the division rose to the number-two performer in the country. Senior business director of the division at the time, Janet Crawford, stated that the culture change process had "a direct link to our success."

A culture change can improve the bottom line—and quickly. Under the guidance of president Mark Deterding and his senior leadership team, Banta Catalog Group's transformed culture increased employee engagement by 20 percent, increased employee retention by 17 percent, and improved profitability by 36 percent—all within eighteen months.

Bowater Pulp and Paper in Gatineau, Ontario, Canada attributed over $50 million in cost reductions to the culture change process. It noted, among other positive changes, a 40 percent improvement in clarity of work objectives and responsibilities, a 44 percent improvement in managerial follow-up to employee suggestions, and a 24 percent improvement in interdepartmental relations.

The culture change process of Minera El Tesoro, a copper mining operation in Chile, helped the mine generate production levels 29 percent over design capacity by the fourth year. After the culture change, accidents were reduced by 40 percent, and the company was recognized as one of the ten best places to work in Chile.

The Importance of a Compelling Vision

As we discussed in Chapter 2, a strong, focused organizational culture starts with a compelling vision that tells everyone who you are (your purpose), where you're going (your picture of the future), and what will guide your journey (your values).

Of these three key elements, the most impactful one for a high performing culture is values because they should guide behavior and decisions on a daily basis. Most senior leadership teams are not clear about the values and behaviors that are expected of their members. In fact, most organizations have not even defined values, such as "what a good citizen looks like around here." Yet understanding an organization's core values is vital to decoding an organization's culture. Corporate values, if they exist, typically are communicated during a new member's orientation to the company. Those values may be described in the annual report, posted in the lobby or on hallway walls, or even printed on the backs of business cards. But these espoused or stated values may not be well communicated or understood by employees or visible to customers, as they are in organizations like Southwest Airlines, Disney, and Nordstrom.

Try this test: Ask a few frontline employees if they can recite your company's values. In many organizations around the globe, you won't get a confident, clear answer. You'll get a blank look!

Even if an organization's desired values are clear, senior leaders typically are not as disciplined in examining the extent to which members of their organization are living these espoused organizational values. If the lived values are not aligned with the espoused values, you will not see desired behaviors demonstrated in the organization. In fact, you'll see undesirable behaviors that cause you to cringe and undermine your organization's success and integrity. Enron is an example of an organization whose lived values were inconsistent with its espoused values. Enron's "integrity" value was displayed for all to see and was even behaviorally defined. However, it was not a lived value—at least in the executive suites—as we so sadly learned.

Managing a Successful Cultural Transformation

If senior leaders are to effectively transform their organization's culture, they need to create a foundation of clear performance expectations, behaviorally defined values, and accountability for demonstrating both. To make that happen, senior leaders *must* be the champions of the culture change. They alone have the power to define the desired culture and create or refine systems, policies, and procedures to reinforce that desired culture. They must "walk the talk," modeling the behavior expected of all organization members.

A training program or quick fix alone will not generate the traction needed to make long-term culture change happen. True change requires a deeper commitment.

It takes years for any organizational culture to reach its current stage. With consistent, focused effort, leaders can expect to spend two to five years successfully transforming their organization's culture. It took Jack Welch nearly ten years to turn around General Electric in the mid-1980s.

As we discussed in the previous chapter, people resist change. Keep this in mind. Even if the present isn't fun, people prefer the known to the unknown. Patience and persistence will pay off. Senior leaders need to continually communicate the need for change, celebrate progress, and reinforce the desired behaviors.

If cultural change is to be successful, everyone—senior leaders, managers, supervisors, team leads, frontline staff—should be held accountable for achieving performance and living the organizational values. Remember, organizational culture will change when individuals change their behavior.

Don't embark on this cultural transformation journey casually. The promise of culture change raises hopes in the hearts and minds of staff members that department silos, unethical behavior, and inconsistent policies will go away. If the senior leadership team does not follow through on declared commitments for transforming the culture, credibility and trust will be eroded. If you're not certain that this is the right path for your organization, and you're unwilling to commit to a multiyear initiative, *don't start.*

A culture change process has four distinct phases: *discovery, immersion, alignment,* and *refinement.* These usually occur in chronological order. However, some overlap occurs as an organization moves into the later phases. This process has been proven over many years. We've seen consistent successes when organizations create a culture change team and follow these steps.

As we discuss these four phases below, we'll use the WD-40 Company as an example. In Chapter 7, "Essential Skills for One-on-One Leadership," we covered how CEO/President Garry Ridge implemented a major change in his company's performance review system. However, Garry relates, "To make a significant change in something as important as an organization's performance review system, [we] first had to focus on the culture.... Impacting the WD-40 Company culture I inherited was not a quick fix."

Phase One: Discovery

This initial phase allows the culture change team to learn about the current organizational culture and understand the issues and opportunities senior leaders are concerned about. During this phase the culture change team focuses on the present reality. They find out from senior leaders and selected frontline staff what performance outcomes are expected. The team discovers what values, if any, are defined, known, or acted on. They talk to frontline staff and sometimes even customers to assess the degree of employee passion that exists. Finally, they determine what accountability systems are in place to ensure that people's behavior matches the organization's values.

At the end of the discovery phase the culture change team makes specific recommendations that address the organization's issues and gaps.

WD-40 Company wasn't broken when Garry stepped into the role of CEO in 1997. It was a brand leader that had produced consistent profits for more than forty years. WD-40 Company's philosophy and culture were conservative, and that cautious approach had served the company well. Yet that wasn't good enough for Garry, who sensed greater potential in the organization.

Garry had been in international marketing with WD-40 Company for almost ten years before being named CEO. Coming from inside the company was an advantage to Garry during the discovery phase. Being familiar with the existing culture, he knew where the trouble spots were. He also knew the key people who would be needed to get behind any culture change effort.

Phase Two: Immersion

The immersion phase focuses on giving senior leaders, managers, and supervisors thorough exposure to the best practices of high performing, values-aligned organizational cultures. Because senior leaders are the key players in this initiative and will be the champions and banner carriers throughout, it is important that they immerse themselves in the culture change process. They should conduct an assessment that compares best practices of high performing, values-aligned organizations to the practices of their organization. The results of that assessment can serve as the basis for identifying key issues and culture gaps.

The next step is action planning to formalize the organization's new vision, purpose, and values. Senior leaders must develop a communication plan that clearly describes the reasons for the culture change and that fully explains the desired values and behaviors. As we discussed in Chapter 2, it is imperative that senior leaders invite everyone to provide thoughts and insights as the new organizational vision, purpose, and values are developed.

As the senior leadership team focuses on these action steps, the culture change process should be cascaded throughout the management hierarchy. In these sessions, managers get feedback about how their teams are functioning compared to best practices. They also get to give feedback on the initial work done by the senior leadership team. The managers' action plans typically are more tactical and day-to-day in nature than the action plans of the senior leaders, which are usually more strategic and across-the-organization in nature.

During the immersion phase—as the company was formulating WD-40 Company's new vision, purpose, and values—Garry Ridge encouraged everyone to go beyond a mere business case statement. The company eventually created an inspiring vision that was easy to grasp:

"Our products fix squeaks and get rid of smells and dirt. In essence, we are in the quality-of-life business. By fixing squeaks and getting rid of smells and dirt in an almost magical way, we create positive, lasting memories by solving problems in workshops, factories, and homes around the world."

Once the vision was set, Garry and his team developed a set of values that would guide the WD-40 Company journey:

- Doing the right thing
- Creating positive, lasting memories in all our relationships
- Making it better than it is today
- Succeeding as a team while excelling as individuals
- Owning it and passionately acting on it
- Sustaining the WD-40 Company economy

Phase Three: Alignment

Alignment is the phase in which structures and systems are reengineered to be consistent with the desired culture expressed by the new vision, purpose, and values. During the alignment phase, people learn to walk the talk and be accountable for the new vision and desired changes. Accountability can happen only when expectations are clear. Everyone must understand what's expected of them in terms of performance and values. Only after these expectations have been defined and agreed on can coaching, celebrating, or redirecting occur.

During the alignment phase, the senior leadership team must identify key metrics for the culture change initiative, such as performance gains, efficiency, growth, and employee engagement or passion. These metrics need to be measured regularly, with the results published throughout the organization. This will ensure that people know what the targets are and how well they are meeting them.

Leaders need to assess the organization's systems to ensure that they support performance expectations *and* desired values. If systems are not aligned, people get confused. Systems that compete with the stated vision, purpose, and values frustrate staff and reduce employee passion.

Senior leaders must be democratic about the alignment process, inviting thoughts, ideas, and insights from people across the organization. Inviting everyone to chime in creates buy-in. It usually takes two to three months to finalize the initial draft of the values and behaviors on which the values survey will be based.[3]

When Garry Ridge stepped into his leadership role at WD-40 Company, he knew that people hoarded knowledge, knowing that it gave them power. This competed with the new stated value of "succeeding as a team while excelling as individuals." During the alignment phase of the culture change process, Garry led the charge in breaking up the knowledge silos into what he called "fields of learning." People were incentivized to share knowledge and encourage ongoing learning. Mistakes were reframed as "Learning Moments," so knowledge hoarding lost its power.

To support the new culture, people throughout the organization were asked to think of WD-40 Company as a tribe rather than a team to open their minds to the new "Don't Mark My Paper, Help Me Get an A" performance review philosophy and to open up communication in general.

The Employee Survey

To ensure that the culture stays aligned with the vision, purpose, and values, the employee survey is an invaluable tool. These surveys can be customized to each organization's unique culture.

Once survey responses have been received, senior leadership team members must analyze the results for gaps in values alignment and develop tactical plans for quickly addressing the gaps. It is of the utmost importance that leaders share the resulting data, refine their behavior, and fix broken systems as soon as possible.

After each round, a summary of successes and gaps should be published, and staff members should be made aware of what is being done to address those gaps.

WD-40 Company surveys its global employees annually and publishes the results on its public website. Responses to statements such as "I feel I am a valued member of WD-40 Company" and "I would recommend WD-40 Company to my friends as a good place to work" are tallied. At the time of this printing, every measure of employee engagement was above the 92nd percentile.

Phase Four: Refinement

The refinement phase is an ongoing project. To reinforce the desired behavior and values, senior leaders must continue to refine systems and policies—and at times even "refine" staff members, or as Garry Ridge says, "share them with the competition." During refinement, leaders should continue to monitor key metrics through surveys and provide feedback, ideally featuring grand celebrations of accomplishments. Additional leadership training should be scheduled to refine the skills needed to keep the cultural change alive. The organization should create a new employee orientation process to include the newly clarified purpose, values, and performance expectations.

At WD-40 Company, "constantly evolving" was identified as a key aspect of the new tribal culture. Tribe members didn't want to stagnate. In their terms:

"If our lake is drying up—a product's sales are going south because of new technology or innovative, competitive products—our roles as tribe members are to make sure we're moving on to another pond."

Since implementing the new culture, WD-40 Company has grown from $100 million—with only 30 percent coming from domestic sales—to more than $380 million in 2017—with a more balanced 53 percent coming from sales outside the United States. It is notable that the company was able to achieve these results while maintaining an outstanding employee engagement metric.

Critical Success Factors for Cultural Transformation

As was revealed in our discussion of the four phases of an effective cultural change process—and highlighted by the WD-40 Company case study—high performing, values-aligned cultures share five critical success factors:

- **The senior leadership team demonstrates commitment to the long-term process.** The culture change process must be embraced and championed by the senior leadership team. They will be held to high standards as the values are defined and communicated. Cultural transformation is an ongoing project that will never go away.

- **Values are defined in behavioral terms.** This is the only approach that makes your desired behaviors observable, tangible, and measurable.

- **Accountability for delivering promised performance and demonstrating valued behaviors is paramount.** Consequences must be swift and consistent. Positive consequences for meeting performance and values expectations must be described and demonstrated, and agreed-upon negative consequences must be applied when performance is below standards or valued behaviors are not demonstrated.

- **All staff members are involved in and buy into the culture transformation at every phase.** This process is not about "managing by announcements," where leaders tell everyone what the new expectations are but don't invite thoughts or hold people—including themselves—consistently accountable. For everyone to embrace the desired culture, they must be included in the process. They must help define and commit to what the new culture will demand of them in their roles.

- **The elephant is eaten one bite at a time.** Find a manageable scope for the change initiative. Don't try to change everything at once. Start with one aspect of the culture change at a time and see how it goes. Then, with learnings clearly in mind, select another aspect of the culture change, and continue the process until you've digested the entire elephant.

*****

A happy organizational culture produces happy people, and happy people treat customers right—which leads to happy customers and a healthy bottom line. In the next chapter we'll drill down into how to treat customers right by delivering legendary service.

SECTION III

Treat your Customers Right

Chapter 17 Serving Customers at a Higher Level 265

17

Serving Customers
at a Higher Level

Ken Blanchard, Kathy Cuff,
Vicki Halsey, and Jesse Stoner

The third step in leading at a higher level is to treat your customers right. While everybody seems to know that, organizations with exceptional service are rare. People seem to forget that customers fuel business! When an organization delivers with such excellence and consistency that its service reputation becomes a competitive edge, that's Legendary Service.

Getting Legendary SCORES from Your Customers

In Chapter 1, "Is Your Organization High Performing?," we discussed HPO SCORES®; one of the key elements was *relentless focus on customer results*. In high performing organizations, everyone passionately holds and maintains the highest standards for quality and service from the customers' perspective. These organizations use the customer experience to evaluate how well they are doing in every aspect of the organization. Processes are designed with the customer in mind.

In high performing organizations, the people in contact with the customers are empowered and can make decisions. This is a radical shift from organizations whose business design puts the customer at the end of the chain. For example, at the renowned Golden Door Spa, all systems are set up to wow the customer. Everyone knows their job is to exceed expectations and to back up the key frontline person.

As we pointed out in Chapter 13, "Organizational Leadership," in high performing organizations, customer needs and trends drive innovation, new products, and services. These organizations design work processes from the customer backward to ensure a flow that makes sense from a customer's perspective. Internal cross-functional relationships and structures are organized around customer needs. High performing organizations ensure that they can respond quickly to customer needs and adapt to changes in the marketplace. They anticipate trends and get in front of them. Innovations in processes are developed to make it easier for customers to do business with them. This creates constant innovation in operating practices, market strategies, products, and services.

In high performing organizations, management has regular face-to-face contact with customers—not only with devoted customers, but also with those who are frustrated, angry, or not using the organization's products and services. Leaders are passionate about developing sophisticated knowledge of customers and sharing the information broadly throughout the organization. Working with the people they serve and listening intently allows high performing organizations to respond rapidly and flexibly to changing conditions.

Connecticut's Trader Joe's grocery exceeds expectations by making sure customers get the best of what they want. One of the HPO SCORES® researchers, Fay Kandarian, had an experience with this when she brought red tulips to the checkout line. The associate checked the tulips before ringing them up and suggested looking for a fresher bunch. Together they went to look at other tulips, and after checking for color preference, the associate picked out the freshest-looking tulips, which were pink and white. After ringing up the new tulips, the associate said, "Since I need to throw away these red tulips, I'll give them to you to enjoy for the few days they will last." This is another example of how high performing organizations encourage those who touch the customer to create the best possible customer experience and act on their ideas.

Nordstrom's core ideology, "service to the customer above all else," was a way of life for the company long before customer service programs became stylish.[1] Planning starts with the customer, and execution focuses on the customer. For example, planning the sale environment exceeds the effort put into planning sale advertising. To ensure customer comfort, sale planning may involve valet parking, extra fitting rooms, and additional sales staff. A key aspect of the orientation of new associates is teaching them how to say "no problem" and mean it. To ensure that their frontline people put all their initiative into serving customers, Nordstrom's rule of thumb and main guideline for employees is that they should always use their best judgment. In fact, that is the only rule that is really enforced. Combining the service ethic with best judgment has resulted in legendary tales of clothes being pressed, Macy's packages being wrapped, outfits being personally delivered, and two different-sized shoes being sold as a pair to fit a customer's different-sized feet. The result? Customers are dedicated to Nordstrom with almost as much passion as Nordstrom's long-term associates, who also enjoy profit sharing year after year.

Creating Legendary Service

High performing organizations that have relentless focus on customer results deliver the kind of service that becomes legendary. As Ken Blanchard, Kathy Cuff, and Vicki Halsey discuss in their book *Legendary Service*, this goes beyond delivering merely good customer service—and it doesn't happen by accident. It begins with leaders who believe that outstanding service is a top priority. We call them service champions—inspirational leaders who create passion and momentum in others to better serve their customers. These leaders follow up their inspiring words with actions, creating systems and processes that support their belief that service is vitally important.

According to Kathy Cuff and Vicki Halsey, the designers of Blanchard's Legendary Service program, exceptional service starts with leaders serving their people at the highest level so that people on the front line can in turn serve their customers at the highest level. Creating Legendary Service is everyone's job—not just the people standing at the cash register or dealing directly with customers.

Legendary Service consists of four basic elements, as shown in Figure 17.1:

C **Committed:** Creating an environment that focuses on serving customers—both internal and external—so you can live the customer service vision.

A **Attentive:** Listening in a way that allows you to identify your customers' needs and wants.

R **Responsive:** Demonstrating a genuine willingness to serve others by taking action that shows you care.

E **Empowered:** Sharing information and tools to unleash the full extent of your power to meet customer needs.

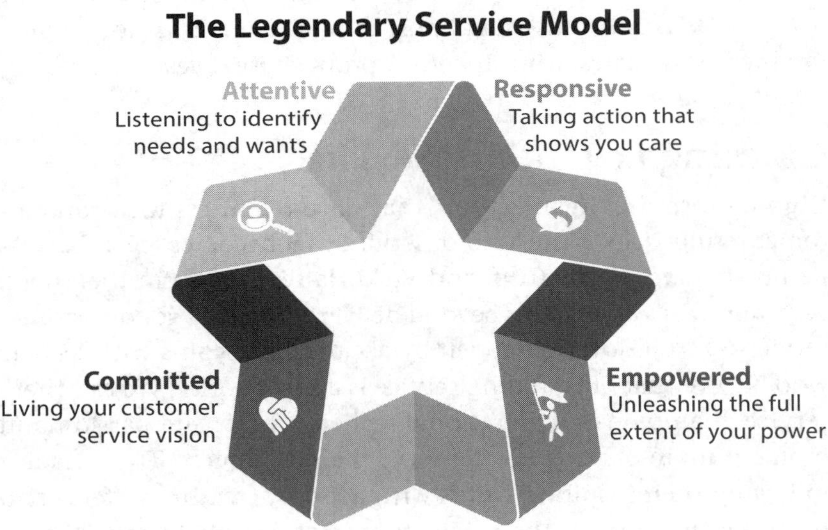

The Legendary Service Model

Attentive
Listening to identify needs and wants

Responsive
Taking action that shows you care

Committed
Living your customer service vision

Empowered
Unleashing the full extent of your power

Figure 17.1 The Legendary Service Model

Together, these elements spell CARE, which is fitting, because great customer service hits people at an emotional level and creates a connection. We've all experienced the counter clerk who takes our money and bags our goods but leaves us feeling cold. One of our consulting partners describes it this way:

"I was at this little family-owned pet store, buying a collar for my puppy. You'd never know the lady behind the counter was trying to build business. Her face and mood were as flat as a pancake. I said, 'I wanted to support my community pet store instead of going to the chain store.' Instead of smiling, she frowned and said, 'They'll reel you in based on cheap food, but they won't keep you.' And I thought, *Hey, you're not keeping me either, lady.*"

Compare that experience with the Legendary Service received by Milt Garrett, a resource trainer who has worked with us over the years. At the end of a week of training, Milt and his wife Jane took a walk on Friday night. Jane said to him, "Milt, you missed my anniversary this week."

Surprised, Milt said, "What anniversary?"

"Five years cancer-free," said Jane. Five years ago, Jane had had a mastectomy. She and Milt celebrated every year that she was cancer-free.

Milt felt awful. He couldn't believe he had forgotten. The week before, when he and Jane had been talking one night, they'd decided that she needed a new car. Since their son was still in college in Australia, they'd decided to wait a year until he graduated. That night, Milt said to himself, "Why am I waiting? I am so lucky that Jane is still in my life."

The next morning, he called the Saturn dealership in Albuquerque and talked to one of their salespeople, whose name was Billy Graham. (No, we're not kidding.) Milt explained the situation to Billy, saying that his kids had told him Jane really wanted a white car. "Could you get me a white Saturn by next Saturday when I get back home from training?" Milt asked.

Billy told Milt that white Saturns were hard to get. "But if you'll come in next Saturday, I'll have one ready," he said.

The next Saturday morning Milt told Jane that he was running a bunch of errands, but he invited her to come with him so that they could go out to lunch. During their drive, they passed the Saturn dealership. Milt told Jane he had to stop in for some materials because he was giving a speech about Saturn to the Chamber of Commerce. When they entered the dealership, they saw only one car: a white Saturn in the center of the showroom.

"Milt, that's the kind of car I'd love to have!" Jane said. She ran over to the Saturn and, with a big grin on her face, got in. When she got out of the car and walked around to the front of it, she let out a scream and began to cry. Milt had no idea what had happened. When he got to the front of the car, he saw a beautiful sign on the hood of the car that read:

> Yes, Jane, this is your car!
>
> Congratulations on five years cancer-free.
>
> Love,
>
> Milt, Billy, and the whole Saturn staff

When Billy saw them coming, he got everyone out of the showroom and into the parking lot so that Milt and Jane could be alone. As they were crying in each other's arms, all of a sudden they heard applause. They looked up to see everyone giving them a hand.

The people at the Saturn dealership in Albuquerque took Legendary Service seriously and lived it on an ongoing basis. Saturn became known for these kinds of stories. For example, a pregnant woman bought a Saturn from a dealership in San Diego. She loved the car, but three months later, she learned she was expecting twins. The car wasn't big enough, so she called the dealership and told them about her situation. They told her that they would give her money back and help her find another car that better met her needs.

Legendary Service inspires customers to tell stories about your company. When customers tell positive stories about you and your level of service, you cannot ask for better publicity.

Recovering quickly from your mistakes will also make your customers want to brag about your service. If you make a mistake with a customer, do whatever you need to fix the problem and create or win back a devoted customer. Legendary Service is not about arguing over who is right or finding someone else to blame—it's about fixing the problem for the customer. Research has shown that 95 percent of the time customers will continue to do business with you if you can solve their concern on the spot.[2]

For example, a hotel in Southern California had a history of poor guest ratings. When foreign owners took over the hotel, they felt the poor ratings were mainly because of the aging, dilapidated condition of the property. They decided to put millions of dollars into refurbishing the hotel. Management decided not to tell the customers about the renovations, which would take nine months to a year. They felt that if the customers knew the extent of the renovations, they would move their meetings to other locations. Given that strategy, the general manager brought all the hotel workers together and told them this:

> "It will be tough sledding around here for the next twelve months or so. The noise and inconvenience may not be popular with our guests. Do whatever it takes to recover from any inconvenience caused by our remodeling. If you want to send someone a bottle of champagne, do so. If you want to hire a babysitter for them, do it. Do whatever it takes to recover from this trying situation."

With that recovery strategy in place, the hotel entered the remodeling phase. To the amazement of management, during the renovations, their guest ratings were the highest they had ever received. Even though things were bad for the guests, their memories of their experience with the hotel were formed by the customer-oriented staff who recovered quickly when things went wrong for guests. Management had empowered their frontline people to be all-out recovery experts. The results showed in highly satisfied customers.

If you empower people to do what's necessary to serve the customers' best interests to begin with, you are more likely to exceed customer expectations and minimize the need to recover. Most businesses believe that only a small percentage of customers are out to take advantage of them, while the vast majority are basically honest and loyal. That's why Nordstrom decided to train its customer contact people to use the phrase "no problem" as their first response to customer concerns. Yet because many businesses set policies, procedures, and practices to try to catch the small percentage of unethical customers, they miss servicing the honest majority. Have you ever attempted to try on clothes that have so many safety gadgets that it's almost impossible? There are risks to providing Legendary Service, but the gains can far outweigh the drawbacks, particularly when your customers start acting like part of your sales force. That's when you know you're treating your customers right. As Sheldon Bowles and Ken Blanchard contend, your customers are now raving fans.

Serving Customers at a Higher Level

In their book *Raving Fans*, Sheldon and Ken write that there are three secrets to treating your customers right and turning them into raving fans: Decide, Discover, and Deliver Plus One Percent.[3]

Decide What You Want Your Customer Experience to Be

If you want Legendary Service, you don't just announce it. You have to plan for it. You have to decide what you want to do. What kind of experience do you want your customers to have as they interact with every aspect of your organization? Some people would argue that you should ask your customers first. While you do want input from your customers, they often are limited to certain things they like and don't like. They don't know what the possibilities are beyond their own experience. They don't have the big picture. It's important that *you* determine from the beginning what you want your customers' experience to be. This doesn't mean that customers' opinions aren't important. In *Full Steam Ahead!*, Ken Blanchard and Jesse Stoner describe how the needs of your customers should determine the Law of the Situation—what business you are really in. Understanding what your customers really want when they come to you helps you determine what you should offer them.

A good example of how this works is Domo Gas, a full-service gasoline chain in Western Canada cofounded by Sheldon Bowles. The customer service vision that Sheldon and his cofounders imagined was an Indianapolis 500 pit stop. They dressed all their attendants in red jumpsuits. When a customer drove into one of Sheldon's stations, two or three people ran out of the hut and raced toward the car. As quickly as possible, they looked under the hood, cleaned the windshield, and pumped the gas. A California station that got excited about the concept gave customers a cup of coffee and a newspaper and asked them to step out of their cars while the interior was vacuumed. As customers pulled away, they were given flyers that said, "P.S. We also sell gas."

In deciding what experience you want your customers to have, you are creating a picture of what things would look like if everything were running as planned. World-class athletes often picture themselves breaking a world record, pitching a perfect game, or making a 99-yard punt return. They know that power comes from having a clear mental image of their best potential performance. Developing a clear picture of how you want to serve your customers is almost like producing a movie in your mind.

We had a chance to work with the top management and heads of dealerships for Freightliner, a leading manufacturer of large trucks. Jim Hibe, the president at the time, spearheaded the creation of a new picture of service for their dealerships—one that permitted them to go way beyond their competition. In preparation for their key annual conference, Freightliner produced a 30-minute video that illustrated two hypothetical dealerships. The first, called Great Scott Trucking, typified the present mode of operating for many of the dealerships: limited hours (8 to 5 Monday through Friday and 9 to 12 on Saturday); uncommitted employees; few, if any, extras (like donuts and coffee for truckers waiting for their vehicles); and so on. When you entered the dealership, everything seemed to be organized to serve the policies, rules, and regulations and not the customers. For example, suppose the manager comes in about 11:45 on Saturday. Seeing a long line in the parts department, he says, "Make sure you shut her down at 12. The line will make for a good Monday."

The other hypothetical dealership, called Daley Freightliner, was a customer-centered operation with 24-hour service. Seven days a week, committed and trained employees were willing to go the extra mile and provide all kinds of services for the truckers. They had a lounge with recliners and a huge TV showing movies. There was a quiet, dark room with bunk beds in case the truckers wanted to sleep. Employees drove repaired trucks to the front rather than making the drivers retrieve them from the back lot.

Many of the dealerships were closer to Great Scott Trucking than they were to Daley Freightliner. So when the conference opened with the video, it made some people squirm. But it beautifully depicted the new service vision for all to see and experience. Throughout the conference, dealers who were closest to the positive image shared their success stories. That program was an excellent way to convey a customer service vision.

The Moments of Truth concept that Jan Carlzon used to create a customer-focused culture when he was president of the Scandinavian Airlines System (SAS) is most helpful in deciding what you want your customer experience to be. A Moment of Truth can be described as follows:

> Any time a customer comes in contact with anyone in our organization in a way that they can get an impression. How do we answer the phone? How do we check people in? How do we greet them on our planes? How do we interact with them during flights? How do we handle baggage claim? What happens when a problem occurs?

For Carlzon and other great service providers, Moments of Truth could cover every detail, including coffee stains. When he was chairman of People Express Airlines, Donald Burr contended that if the flip-down trays were dirty, customers would assume that the plane's engines were not well maintained either.[4] When looking for a place to stay after a long day's drive, how many people would choose a motel with a sign having some burned-out lights?

While most of our examples have focused on external customers, it is important to recognize that everyone has a customer. An external customer is someone outside your organization who you serve or provide with a service. A person who takes orders at a quick-service restaurant is a good example of someone who serves external customers. An internal customer is someone within your organization who may or may not serve external customers.

For example, people who work in the human resources field have mainly internal customers. And some people, like those in the accounting department, have both external and internal customers.

They send bills and invoices to external customers, and they provide reports and information to internal customers. The point is, everyone has a customer.

Great customer service organizations analyze every key interaction they have with customers, whether they are external or internal, and they determine how they would like that scenario to play out. One of the ways to think about that is to suppose that word has gotten out about how fabulously you are serving customers. Ecstatic customers are running all over the place, bragging about you. A well-known television station gets word of this and decides to send a crew in to film what is going on in your organization. Who would you want them to talk to? What would your people tell them? What would these folks see?

Creating raving fans starts with a picture—an image of what kind of experience you want your customers to have. Analyzing your Moments of Truth for each department and deciding how you want them played out is a good start. This will serve as your guide as you target new customers and adjust to changing conditions.

Discover What Your Customers Want

After you decide what you want to happen, it's important to discover any suggestions your customers may have that will improve their experience with your organization. What would make their experience with you better? Ask them! But ask them in a way that stimulates an answer. For example, how many times have you been eating at a restaurant when the restaurant manager comes over and says, "How is everything tonight?" Isn't your usual response, "Fine"? That gives the restaurant manager no information. A better conversation would be, "Excuse me. I'm the restaurant manager. I wonder if I could ask you a question. Is there anything that we could have done differently tonight that would have made your experience with us better?" That question invites an answer. If the customer says "No," you can follow it up with a sincere "Are you sure?"

> *High performing organizations regularly solicit customer and market feedback.*

Organizations that provide Legendary Service are masters of listening to their customers. When a customer tells you something, you have to listen *without being defensive*. One reason people get uptight when they listen to customers is because they think they always have to do what the customer wants them to do. They don't understand that listening has two parts. As Steve Covey says, "Seek first to understand." In other words, listen for understanding. Try saying, "That's interesting. Tell me more. Could you be more specific?"

The second aspect of listening is deciding if you want to do anything about what you heard. You have to separate that from the understanding aspect of listening. And it is important to realize that you don't have to decide right after you understand what the person is suggesting. You can do it later, when you have some time to think about it or talk it over with others. Realizing that you have time to think something over will make you less defensive and a better listener. First listen to understand, and then decide what you want to do about what you've heard.

In the mall, one of our colleagues saw an example of defensive listening. He was walking behind a woman who had an eight- or nine-year-old son. As they walked past the sporting goods store, the kid looked over and saw a beautiful red bicycle outside the store. He stopped in his tracks and said to his mother, "Boy, would I like a bike like that." His mother nearly went crazy and started screaming: "I can't believe it! I just got you a new bike for Christmas! Here it is March, and you already want another one! I'm not buying you another $%&*^ thing!" Our colleague thought the mother would nail this kid's head to the cement. Sadly, she didn't distinguish the need to separate listening for understanding from deciding. If she had said to the kid, "Honey, what do you like about that bike?" he might have said, "See those streamers coming out of the handlebars? I really like them." And those streamers could have been a cheap birthday present. After listening to what he liked about the bike, the mother could have said, "Honey, why do you think I can't get you that bike?" The kid was no fool. He probably would have said, "I just got one for Christmas."

Listening without being defensive is also helpful if you make a mistake with a customer. Defending what you've done will only irritate the customer. When customers are upset, all they want is to be heard. In fact, we have found that if people listen to a complaining customer in a nondefensive, attentive way and then ask, "Is there any way we could win back your loyalty?," more often than not the customer will say, "You've already done it. You listened to me."

If a customer makes a good suggestion or is upset about something that makes sense to change, you can add that suggestion to your customer service picture. For example, we got a letter from a man who owns three quick-service restaurants in the Midwest. Some of the restaurant's elderly customers suggested that during certain parts of the day, the restaurant should use tablecloths, have staff take orders at the tables, and deliver the food to the customers at their tables. After thinking about it, the owner realized it was a pretty good idea. Now, between 4 and 5:30 in the afternoon, the tables have tablecloths and candles, and the people behind the counter come out and wait on the customers. The elderly are pouring in to his restaurants during those hours.

When you put together what you want your customers to experience with what they want to have happen, you will have a fairly complete picture of your desired customer service experience.

Deliver Your Ideal Customer Service Experience

You now have a clear picture of the experience you want your customers to have that will satisfy and delight them and put smiles on their faces. Next you must figure out how to get your people excited about delivering this experience, plus a bit more.

As we emphasized in Chapter 2, "The Power of Vision," the responsibility for establishing a shared vision rests with the senior leadership. And that responsibility includes strong images of what excellent customer service looks like. Once your desired customer experience is set and people are committed to it, the implementation aspect of leadership begins. It is during implementation that most organizations get into trouble. The traditional pyramid is kept alive and well, leaving customers uncared for at the bottom of the hierarchy. All the energy in the organization moves up the hierarchy as people try to please and be responsive to their bosses instead of focusing their energy on meeting the needs of their customers. Now the bureaucracy rules, and policies and procedures carry the day. This leaves unprepared and uncommitted customer-contact people to quack like ducks.

Wayne Dyer, the great personal-growth teacher, said years ago that there are two kinds of people: ducks and eagles. Ducks act like victims and go "Quack! Quack! Quack!" Eagles, on the other hand, take initiative and soar above the crowd. As a customer, you can always identify a bureaucracy if you have a problem and are confronted by ducks who quack: "It's our policy. I don't make the rules; I just work here. Do you want to talk to my supervisor? Quack! Quack! Quack!"

Implementation is all about equipping people throughout the organization to act and feel like owners of the vision. It's about allowing people to take a proactive role in carrying out the organization's vision and direction so that they can soar like eagles and deliver great customer service rather than quack like ducks.

Our colleague's experience trying to rent a car in New York is a perfect example of this phenomenon. He is a trustee emeritus at Cornell University. A while back, he was heading to a meeting in Ithaca, New York, the small upstate town where Cornell is located. He wanted to rent a car that he could drop off at Syracuse, which was about an hour and a half away. Those who travel enough know that if you drop off a car at a different place than where you rented it, the company charges a big drop-off fee. You can avoid that drop-off fee if you rent a car that came from where you are going. Knowing this, our colleague asked the woman behind the counter, "Do you have a Syracuse car?"

She said, "You're lucky. I do." Then she went to the computer and prepared his contract.

Our colleague is not a particularly detail-oriented person, but as he was signing his contract, he noticed a $75 drop-off fee. He said, "What's that $75 drop-off fee?"

She said, "I didn't do it. Quack! Quack!"

He said, "Who did?"

She said, "The computer. Quack! Quack!"

He said, "How do we tell the computer it was wrong?"

"I don't know. Quack! Quack!"

He said, "Why don't you just cross it out?"

She said, "I can't. My boss will kill me. Quack! Quack!"

"You mean I have to pay a $75 fee because you have a mean boss?" he asked.

"I remember one time—quack! quack!—my boss let me cross it out."

"When was that?"

"When the customer worked for Cornell. Quack! Quack!"

He said, "That's great. I'm on the Cornell board of trustees!"

She asked, "What does the board do? Quack! Quack!"

"We can fire the president."

"What's your employee number? Quack! Quack!"

"I don't have one."

"Then I can't help you. Quack! Quack!"

It took our colleague 20 minutes of psychological counseling to get out of this drop-off fee. He used to get angry at these frontline people but doesn't anymore because he realizes that it's not really their fault.

Who do you think this woman worked for, a duck or an eagle? Obviously, a duck. If she worked for an eagle, the eagle would eat the duck. We call the supervisory duck the head mallard because this person just quacks higher up the bureaucracy. The supervisory duck tells you all the rules and regulations and laws that apply to your situation. Who do you think the supervisory duck works for? Another duck, who works for whom? Another duck, who works for whom? Another duck. And who sits at the top of the organization? A great big duck. Have you ever been hit by an eagle turd? Obviously not, because eagles soar above the crowd. It's the ducks that make all the mess.

How do you create an organization where ducks are busted and eagles can soar? As we discussed in Chapter 2:

> *The traditional pyramid hierarchy must be turned upside down so that the frontline people who are closest to the customers are at the top.*

As shown in Figure 17.2, now the frontline people can be *responsible*—able to respond to their customers. In this scenario, leaders *serve* and are *responsive* to people's needs, training and developing them to soar like eagles so that they can accomplish established goals and live according to the vision you have of the customer experience.

The Implementation Role of Leadership

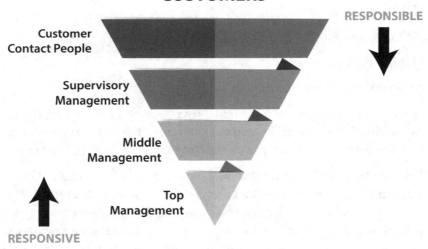

Figure 17.2 The Implementation Role of Leadership

If the leaders in an organization do not respond to the needs and desires of their people, these folks will not take good care of their customers. But when the frontline customer-contact people are treated as responsible owners of the vision, they can soar like eagles and create raving fans rather than quack like ducks.

Permitting People to Soar

One of our consulting partners experienced an eagle incident when he went to Nordstrom one day to get some perfume for his wife. The woman behind the counter said, "I'm sorry; we don't sell that perfume in our store. But I know where I can get it in the mall. How long will you be in our store?"

"About 30 minutes," he said.

"Fine. I'll go get it, bring it back, gift wrap it, and have it ready for you when you leave." This woman left Nordstrom, went to another store, got the perfume our colleague wanted, came back to Nordstrom, and gift wrapped it. You know what she charged him? The same price she paid at the other store. So Nordstrom didn't make any money on the deal, but what did it make instead? A raving fan.

Ken had a beautiful example of the different experiences you can have with organizations depending on whether they are duck ponds or they permit people to soar like eagles. Several years ago, he was heading to the airport for a trip that would take him to four different cities during the week. As he approached the airport, he realized that he had forgotten his driver's license and didn't have a passport with him either. Not having time to go back home to get them and make the flight, he had to be creative.

Only one of Ken's books, *Everyone's a Coach*, which he wrote with legendary football coach Don Shula, has his picture on the cover.[5] So when Ken got to the airport, he ran into the bookstore; luckily, it had a copy of that book. Fortunately, his airline was Southwest Airlines. As Ken was checking his bag at the curb, the porter asked to see his identification. He said, "I feel badly. I don't have a driver's license or passport. But will this do?" And he showed him the cover of the book.

The man shouted, "This man knows Shula! Put him in first class!" (Of course, Southwest doesn't have first class—they didn't even have business select at the time.) Everybody out by the curb check-in started to high-five Ken. He was like a hero. Then one of the baggage handlers said, "Why don't I go in the terminal with you? I know the folks in security. I think I can get you through there, too."

Why did that happen? Herb Kelleher—who cofounded Southwest—and colleagues Colleen Barrett and Gary Kelly, who followed him in the executive suite, not only want to give customers the lowest possible price, but they also want to give them the best possible service. They set up the whole organization to empower everyone—right down to the frontline baggage check folks—to make decisions, use their brains, and be customer maniacs so they can create raving fans. These customer-focused leaders feel that policies should be followed but that people can use their brains in interpreting them. Why do they ask for identification at the airport? To make sure that the person getting on the plane is the same person as the name on the ticket. That was an easy decision for the Southwest Airlines frontline person.

Wallowing in a Duck Pond

The next airline Ken had to fly on before his office could overnight his driver's license was one of the airlines that always seems to be in financial trouble. The baggage handler at the curbside check-in looked at Ken's picture on the book and said, "You've got to be kidding me. You'd better go to the ticket counter."

When Ken showed the book to the woman at the ticket counter, she said, "You'd better talk to my supervisor." Ken was moving up the hierarchy fast. He thought maybe pretty soon he would get to the mayor and then finally to the governor. Quack! Quack! Quack! In this troubled airline, the hierarchy was alive and well. All the energy was moving away from pleasing the customers and toward serving the hierarchy—following the policies, procedures, rules, and regulations to the letter.

Giving Your People Wings

As we briefly mentioned in Chapter 3, during the reign of Horst Schulze, one of the founders of the Ritz-Carlton Hotels, after orientation and extensive training at each Ritz-Carlton property, every employee was given a $2,000 discretionary fund that they could use to solve a customer problem without checking with anyone. They didn't even have to tell their boss. Horst loved to collect stories about people using this empowerment to make a difference. One of his favorites is about a businessman who was staying at one of the Ritz-Carlton properties in Atlanta. That day he had to fly from Atlanta to Los Angeles and then from Los Angeles to Hawaii, because the next day at 1:00, he was making a major speech to his international company. He was a little disorganized as he was leaving. On his way to the airport, he discovered that he'd left behind his laptop computer, which contained all the PowerPoints he needed for his presentation. He tried to change his flights, but he couldn't. So he called the Ritz-Carlton and said, "This is the room I was in, and this is where my computer was. Have Housekeeping get it and overnight it to me. They have to guarantee delivery by 10 tomorrow morning, because I need it for my one o'clock speech."

The next day Schulze was wandering around the hotel, as he often did. When he got to Housekeeping he said, "Where's Mary?" Her coworkers said, "She's in Hawaii." He said, "Hawaii? What's she doing there?"

He was told, "A guest left his computer in his room, and he needs it for a speech today at one o'clock—and Mary doesn't trust overnight carrier services." Now you might think that Mary went for a vacation, but she came back on the next plane. And what do you think was waiting for her? A letter of commendation from Horst and high fives around the hotel. That's really empowering people and giving them wings.

You might wonder if this story is true. The answer is yes. If you create an environment where the customers rule and your people can use their brains to take care of customer needs, stories like this become commonplace, even legendary. People who spread these stories—including your customers—sometimes love to embellish them. For example, a well-known story developed about Nordstrom's "no questions asked" return policy. It was rumored that somebody returned snow tires to Nordstrom and, even though they didn't sell them, the store took them back. When cofounder Bruce Nordstrom was asked about this, he laughed; Nordstrom actually does sell snow tires—in its Alaska store.

*****

As we have argued, if leaders empower, train, and love their people, the people will take good care of the customers, who then will become raving fans—leading to high performing, profitable organizations. As you'll learn in the next section, such organizations have the right kind of leadership.

Companion Online Resource

Visit www.LeadingAtAHigherLevel.com to access the free virtual conference titled "Treat Your Customers *Right.*" Use the password "Customers" for your free access.

SECTION IV

Have the Right Kind of Leadership

Chapter 18 Servant Leadership 287

Chapter 19 Determining Your Leadership
Point of View 313

18

Servant Leadership

Ken Blanchard, Scott Blanchard, and Drea Zigarmi

When people lead at a higher level, they make the world a better place because their goals are focused on the greater good. This requires a special kind of leader: a servant leader.

Robert Greenleaf first coined the term "servant leadership" in 1970 and published widely on the concept for the next 20 years.[1] Yet it is an old concept. Two thousand years ago, servant leadership was central to the philosophy of Jesus, who exemplified the fully committed and effective servant leader.[2] Mahatma Gandhi, Dr. Martin Luther King, Jr., Nelson Mandela, and Mother Teresa are more recent examples of leaders who have exemplified this philosophy.

What Is Servant Leadership?

When people hear the phrase servant leadership, they are often confused. They immediately conjure up thoughts of the inmates running the prison or trying to please everyone. Others think servant leadership is only for church leaders. The problem is that they don't understand leadership. They think you can't lead and serve at the same time. Yet you can if you understand—as we have emphasized a number of times—that leadership has two parts: vision and implementation. In the visionary role, leaders help define the direction. Once direction is clear, it is the leaders' responsibility to communicate what the organization stands for and wants to accomplish.

Max Dupree, legendary chairman of Herman Miller and author of *Leadership Is an Art*, compared this role to that of a third-grade teacher who keeps repeating the basics. "As a top manager, when it comes to vision and values, you have to say it over and over and over again until people get it right, right, right!"

As you now know, the responsibility for this visionary role falls to the hierarchical leadership. Kids look to their parents, players look to their coaches, and people look to their organizational leaders for direction. *The visionary role is the leadership aspect of servant leadership.* (See Chapter 2, Figure 2.1.)

Once people are clear on where they are going, the leader's role shifts to a service mind-set for the task of implementation—the second aspect of leadership.

How do you make the vision happen? *Implementation* is where the servant aspect of servant leadership comes into play.

As we emphasized in Chapter 17, "Serving Customers at a Higher Level," most organizations and leaders get into trouble in the implementation phase. With self-serving leaders at the helm, the traditional hierarchical pyramid stays firmly in place. When that happens, who do people think they work for? The people above them. The minute you think you work for the people above you, you are assuming that person—your boss—is *responsible* and your job is being *responsive* to that boss and to his or her whims or wishes. Now, "boss watching" becomes a popular sport, and people get promoted on their upward-influencing skills. As a result, all the energy of the organization is moving up the hierarchy, away from customers and the frontline people who are closest to the action. What you get is a duckpond.

When there is conflict between what customers want and what the boss wants, the boss wins. You have people quacking like ducks. "Would you like me to get my supervisor?" Servant leaders know how to correct this situation by philosophically turning the pyramid upside down during implementation.

When servant leaders turn the pyramid upside down, who is at the top of the organization? The customer contact people. Who is really at the top of the organization? The customers. Who is at the bottom? The "top" management. (See Chapter 2, Figure 2.2.)

As a result, who works for whom when it comes to implementation? You, the leader, work for your people. This one change, although it seems minor, makes a major difference—the difference between who is responsible and who is responsive.

When you turn the organizational pyramid upside down, rather than your people being responsible to you, they become responsible—able to respond to customers—and your job as the leader/manager is to be responsive to your people. This creates a very different environment for implementation. If you work for your people as servant leaders do, what is the purpose of being a manager? To help your people become eagles rather than ducks and soar above the crowd—accomplishing goals, solving problems, and living according to the vision.

With their emphasis on bringing out the magnificence in people, the two leadership approaches we are best known for around the world— *The One Minute Manager®* and SLII®—are both examples of the skillset required to put servant leadership into action.

After all, what's the first secret of The One Minute Manager? One minute goals. All good performance starts with clear goals—which is clearly part of the leadership aspect of servant leadership. Once people are clear on goals, an effective One Minute Manager wanders around and tries to catch people doing something right so they can deliver a One Minute Praising—the second secret. If the person is doing something wrong or not performing as well as agreed upon, a One Minute Re-Direct is appropriate—the third secret. When effective One Minute Managers deliver praisings and re-directs, they are engaging in the servant aspect of servant leadership—they are working for their people to help them win—accomplish the goals.

SLII® also has three aspects that generate both great relationships and results: goal setting, diagnosis, and matching. Once clear goals are set, an effective SLII® leader focuses on the servant aspect of servant leadership, working with a direct report to diagnose the development level—competence and commitment—on each specific goal. Together they then determine the appropriate leadership style—the amount of directive and supportive behavior—that will match the person's development level on each task so that the manager can help accomplish their goals.

Thus, both *The One Minute Manager* and SLII® are clear examples of putting servant leadership in action. Both approaches recognize that vision and direction—the leadership aspect of servant leadership—are the responsibility of the traditional hierarchy. They also recognize that implementation—the servant aspect of servant leadership—entails turning the hierarchy upside down and helping everyone build a high performing organization.

To emphasize the power of putting servant leadership to work, Ken Blanchard and Renee Broadwell edited *Servant Leadership in Action: How You Can Achieve Great Relationships and Results*, a collection of essays written by forty-four renowned servant leadership experts and practitioners—prominent business executives, authors, and spiritual leaders. As John Maxell writes in the book's foreword:

The only way to create great relationships and results is through servant leadership. It's all about putting other people first.

Applying Servant Leadership

To help you realize that servant leadership can occur in any organization, consider the following example from the Department of Motor Vehicles (DMV). The DMV has such a multitude of people to take care of—basically, everybody with a driver's license—that it's no surprise they sometimes treat you like a number instead of a person. In most states, after you have passed your initial tests, you can avoid the DMV for years if you fill out the proper form and mail it in.

Ken Blanchard had avoided his local DMV like the plague. But several years ago, he lost his driver's license about three weeks before he was scheduled to leave on a trip to Europe. He knew he had to go to the DMV and get a new license to back up his passport on his trip. So he said to his executive assistant, "Dana, would you put three hours on my calendar next week sometime so I can go to the DMV?" In Ken's experience, that's about how long it usually took to get anything done there. He'd wait for a long time, and then they'd tell him he was in the wrong line, he'd filled out the wrong form, or he'd done something that meant he had to start all over.

As a result, Ken headed over to the DMV with low expectations. (Remember, he hadn't been there in years.) He knew immediately something had changed when he walked in the front door because a woman charged him and said, "Welcome to the Department of Motor Vehicles! Do you speak English or Spanish?"

"English," Ken replied.

She said, "Right over there." The guy behind the counter smiled and said, "Welcome to the Department of Motor Vehicles! How may I help you?" It took Ken nine minutes to get his replacement license, including having his picture taken. He said to the woman who took his picture, "What are you all smoking here? I mean, this isn't the Department of Motor Vehicles that I used to know and love."

She asked, "Haven't you met the new director?"

"No," he said.

So she pointed to a desk behind all the counters, right out in the open. Clearly, the director had no privacy. His office was in the middle of everything. Ken went over, introduced himself, and said, "What's your job as the director of the Department of Motor Vehicles?"

What the man said is the best definition of management we've ever heard:

> *"My job is to reorganize the department on a moment-to-moment basis, depending on citizen (customer) need."*

The director obviously had a compelling vision for this department. The point of the DMV's business was to serve the citizens and their needs, and to serve them well.

What did this director do? He cross-trained everybody in every job. Everyone could handle the front desk; everyone could take the pictures. You name it—everyone could do it! Even the people in the back, who normally weren't out in front, could do every job. Why? Because if suddenly there was a flood of citizens, why have people in the back doing bookkeeping, accounting, or secretarial work when there were customers who needed help? So he'd bring them out when they were needed.

The DMV director also insisted that nobody go to lunch between 11:30 and 2:00. Why? Because that's when the most customers showed up. Ken told this story at a seminar one time, and a woman came up to him at the break and said, "Where is your Department of Motor Vehicles? I can't believe what you've been telling us." She continued, "I recently waited in line for about forty-five minutes at our DMV, and I was almost at the front of the line when the woman announced, 'It's break time.' We had to stand around for fifteen minutes while they all went for coffee and stretched their legs."

That didn't happen at this "new" DMV, where the director had created a motivating environment. Those team members were really committed. Even employees Ken recognized from past visits who had joined in on the "fun" of abusing the customers were now excited about serving.

Often you see people at one point, excited about their work. Then you see them three months later, and they're discouraged. In 90 percent of these cases, the only thing that has changed is that they've gotten a new boss. Someone who jerks them around, who doesn't listen to them, who doesn't involve them in decision making, and who treats them as if they really are *subordinates*. The reverse is also true. People can be unhappy in a job situation when suddenly a new leader comes in and their eyes brighten, their energy increases, and they are really ready to perform well and make a difference.

When leaders make a positive difference, people act like they own the place, and they bring their brains to work. Their managers encourage their newfound initiative. Another example from the "new" DMV punctuates this point.

Great Leaders Encourage People to Bring Their Brains to Work

Just about the time Ken had his inspiring experience with the DMV, Dana Kyle, his executive assistant at the time, decided to buy a big motor scooter and bop around southern California. When she got this beauty, somebody told her, "You have to get a license." She had never thought about needing a license for a motor scooter. So, she went to the DMV to do the right thing. The woman behind the counter went into the computer and found Dana's name and driving record. It turns out that Dana had a perfect driving record. She never had a traffic violation.

"Dana," the woman said, "I noticed that in three months you have to retake your written driving test. Why don't you take both tests today?"

Caught off guard, Dana said, "Tests? I didn't know I was supposed to take any tests." And she started to panic.

The woman smiled reassuringly and said, "Oh, Dana, don't worry. With your driving record, I'm sure you can pass these tests. And besides, if you don't, you can always come back."

Dana took the tests. She went back to the woman, who graded them. Dana fell one correct answer short of passing each test, so officially she failed both. But, in a kind way, the woman said, "Oh, Dana. You are so close to passing. Let me try something. Let me re-ask you one question on each test to see if you can get it right so I can pass you." Not only was this a wonderful offer, but the fact was, each question had only two possible answers. So the woman said, "Dana, you chose B. What do you think would be the right answer?"

When Dana said, "A," this helpful woman said, "You're right! You pass!"

Ken once told this story at a seminar, and a bureaucrat came racing up to the platform during the break. He started yelling, "Why are you telling this story? That woman broke the law! Your assistant failed both of those tests!"

So Ken went back to see his DMV director friend. He told him about this bureaucrat, and the director said, "Let me tell you one other thing. When it comes to decision making, I want my people to use their brains more than rules, regulations, or laws. My person decided that it was silly to make someone like your assistant Dana, with her perfect driving record, come back to retake a test on which she missed only one question. I guarantee you, if she had missed four or five questions, my person wouldn't have given her the same deal. And to show you how important I think this is, *I would back that person's decision with my job.*"

Would you like to work for this kind of leader? You'd better believe it. Why? Because he is a servant leader. In Rick Warren's best-selling book *The Purpose Driven Life*, the first sentence is "It's not about you."[3] Just like our DMV director, servant leaders realize that leadership is not about them. It's about what and who they are serving. What's the vision, and who's the customer? The vision answers Hayes and Stevens' question, "What's the point?" As the authors of *The Heart of Business* insist, "profit can be a by-product of the pursuit of a higher purpose and even part of the planned process in pursuit of that higher purpose, but it should never be the purpose and motive itself."[4] If profit is your reason for being an organization, it will eventually drive your people and customers to be self-serving, too. As we argued in Chapter 17, everyone has a customer. Who is a manager's customer? The people who report to that manager. Once the vision and direction are set, managers work for their people.

What Kind of Leadership Impacts Performance the Most?

To find out what kind of leadership has the greatest impact on performance, Scott Blanchard and Drea Zigarmi worked with Vicky Essary to study the interaction between organizational success, employee success, customer loyalty, and leadership.[5] In their yearlong study, which included an exhaustive literature review of hundreds of studies from 1980 to 2005, they examined two kinds of leadership: *strategic leadership* and *operational leadership.*

Strategic leadership is the "what" that ensures everyone is going in the same direction. It's where the answer to the question "What's the point of your business?" is found. Strategic leadership includes activities such as establishing a clear vision, maintaining a culture that aligns a set of values with that vision, and declaring must-do initiatives or strategic imperatives that the organization needs to accomplish. Vision and values are enduring, whereas strategic imperatives are short-term priorities that could last a month or two, or a year or two. An example of a strategic initiative is David Novak, former chairman and CEO of Yum! Brands, declaring a customer mania focus for all the company's restaurants around the world. Strategic leadership is all about the vision and direction aspect of leadership, or the *leadership* part of servant leadership.

Operational leadership is everything else. It provides the "how" for the organization. It includes the policies, procedures, systems, and leader behaviors that cascade from senior management to the frontline employees. These management practices create the environment that employees and customers interact with and respond to on a daily basis. Operational leadership is all about the implementation aspect of leadership, or the *servant* part of servant leadership.

Blanchard and Zigarmi discovered that employee success included things like employee satisfaction (I am happy), employee loyalty (I will stay at my job), employee productivity (how I am performing), perceptions of one's relationship with his or her manager and the teamwork in the environment, and more tangible measures, like absenteeism, tardiness, and vandalism. They identified all these factors as *employee passion.*

When it came to customers, their reactions to the organization's environment fell into three bodies of research: satisfaction (I am happy with how this organization serves me), loyalty (I will continue doing business with this organization), and advocacy (I am willing to speak positively about my experience with this company). The net result of these three factors they labeled *customer devotion.*

Blanchard and Zigarmi combined all the hard measures of organizational success (profitability, growth over time, and economic stability) and soft measures (trust in the company and a sense of its integrity) into a concept they called *organizational vitality*. In many ways, organizational vitality depicts that quadruple bottom line—being the provider of choice, employer of choice, investment of choice, and corporate citizen of choice—we discussed in Chapter 1, "Is Your Organization High Performing?"

If leadership is the engine that drives a high performing organization, Blanchard and Zigarmi were interested in how the two aspects of leadership—strategic leadership and operational leadership—interact with and impact employee passion, customer devotion, and organizational vitality. Figure 18.1 shows the leadership-profit chain of events.

The Leadership-Profit Chain

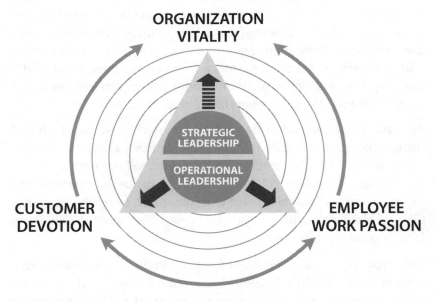

Figure 18.1 The Leadership-Profit Chain

Interestingly, Blanchard and Zigarmi found that while strategic leadership is a critical building block for setting the tone and direction, it has only an indirect impact on organizational vitality. The real key to organizational vitality is operational leadership. If this aspect of leadership is done effectively, employee passion and customer devotion will result from the positive experiences and overall satisfaction people have with the organization.

It is also interesting to note that positive employee passion creates positive customer devotion. At the same time, when customers are excited about and devoted to the company, it has a positive effect on the work environment and the employees' passion. People love to work for a company where customers are raving fans. It makes them gung ho, and together the customers and employees directly impact organizational vitality.[6]

The big-picture conclusion from the research of Blanchard and Zigarmi is that the *leadership* part of servant leadership (strategic leadership) is important—because vision and direction get things going—but the real action is with the *servant* aspect of servant leadership (operational leadership). If the vision and direction are compelling and motivating, and leaders do a good job of implementing them in the eyes of the employees and customers, organizational vitality and success are ensured.

To do a good job, effective servant leaders must be environmentalists whose job is to create and maintain a culture that turns on employees so that they can turn on customers. These leaders do that by looking down the traditional hierarchy and saying, "What can I do for you?" rather than their people looking up the hierarchy and saying, "What can we do for you?"

As John Maxwell writes in his Foreword to *Servant Leadership in Action:*

"I get a kick when I hear people say, 'It's lonely at the top.' To me, if it's lonely at the top, it means nobody is following you. If that's true, you'd better get off the top and go where the people are—and then, in my terms, bring them to the top with you."

When managers focus only on organizational indicators of vitality— such as profit—they have their eyes on the scoreboard, not the ball. Profit, a key aspect of organizational vitality, is a by-product of serving the customer, which can be achieved only by serving the employee. *Profit really is the applause you get for creating a motivating environment for your people so they take care of your customers.*

If the servant aspect of servant leadership has a greater impact on organizational vitality, how do leaders develop their serving qualities?

Being a Servant Leader Is a Question of the Heart

As Robert Greenleaf is often quoted, "A servant leader is a servant first and a leader second."[7] Yet most of our work in the past focused on leadership behavior and how to improve leadership style and methods. We were attempting to change leaders from the outside. In recent years, though, we have found that effective leadership is an inside job. It is a question of the heart. It's all about leadership character and intention. Why are you leading? Is it to serve or to be served? Answering this question truthfully is so important. You can't fake being a servant leader. In *The Servant Leader*, Ken Blanchard and Phil Hodges contend that if leaders don't get the heart right, they simply will never become servant leaders.

The most persistent barrier to being a servant leader is a heart motivated by self-interest that looks at the world as a "give a little, take a lot" proposition. Leaders with hearts motivated by self-interest put their own agenda, safety, status, and gratification ahead of those affected by their thoughts and actions.

In a sense, we all entered this world with a self-focus. Is there anything more self-centered than a baby? A baby doesn't come home from the hospital asking, "How can I help around the house?" As any parent can attest, all children are naturally selfish; they have to be taught how to share.

You finally become an adult when you realize that life is about serving rather than being served.

The shift from self-serving leadership to leadership that serves others is motivated by a change in heart.

Driven Versus Called Leaders

When we talk about servant leadership and ask people whether they are a servant leader or a self-serving leader, no one admits they're a self-serving leader. Yet we observe self-serving leadership all the time. What's the difference?

In his book *Ordering Your Private World*, Gordon MacDonald discusses an interesting distinction that can help us understand the difference between servant leaders and self-serving leaders.[8] McDonald contends that there are two kinds of people: "driven" people and "called" people. Driven people think they own everything. They own their relationships, they own their possessions, and they own their positions. Driven people are self-serving. Most of their time is spent protecting what they own. They run bureaucracies and believe the sheep are there for the benefit of the shepherd. They want to make sure that all the money, recognition, and power move up the hierarchy and away from the frontline people and the customers. They're great at creating "duck ponds."

Called people are very different. They think everything is on loan—their relationships, possessions, and position. Do you know your relationships are on loan? One of the tough things about 9/11 was that some loans got called in early. If you knew you might not see someone important in your life tomorrow, how would you treat that person today? Margie Blanchard has a wise saying: "Keep your I-love-yous up to date."

Called people understand that possessions are only temporary, too. In tough economic times, a lot of people get uptight about losing their toys. They think "He who dies with the most toys wins." The reality is, "He who dies with the most toys dies." It's great to have nice things when things are going well, but you might have to give up some of them in hard times. Possessions are on loan.

Called leaders also understand that their positions are on loan from all the stakeholders in the organization, particularly the people who report to them. Since called leaders don't own anything, they figure their role in life is to shepherd everybody and everything that comes their way.

Self-serving leaders give themselves away in two ways. The first is how they receive feedback. Have you ever tried to give feedback to someone up the hierarchy, and that person killed the messenger? If that has ever occurred, you were dealing with a self-serving leader. They hate feedback. Why? Because if you give them any negative feedback, they think you don't want them to lead anymore. And that's their worst nightmare because they *are* their position. The second giveaway for self-serving leaders is their unwillingness to develop other leaders around them. They fear the potential competition for their leadership position.

Called leaders have servant hearts, and they love feedback. They know the only reason they are leading is to serve, and if anybody has suggestions on how they can serve better, they want to hear them. They look at feedback as a gift. When they receive feedback, their first response is, "Thank you. That's really helpful. Can you tell me more? Is there anybody else I should talk to?"

Called leaders also are willing to develop others. They think leadership is not the province of just the formal leaders. To them, leadership should emerge everywhere. Since they believe their role in life is to serve, not to be served, they want to bring out the best in others. If a good leader rises, servant leaders are willing to partner with that person and even step aside and take a different role if necessary. They thrive on developing others and the belief that individuals with expertise will come forward as needed throughout the organization.

Robert Greenleaf said it well: "The true test of a servant leader is this: Do those around the servant leader become wiser, freer, more autonomous, healthier, and better able themselves to become servant leaders?"[9]

The Plight of the Ego

What keeps people from becoming servant leaders? The human ego. We believe that ego can stand for edging good out and putting yourself in the center. That's when we start to get a distorted image of our own importance and see ourselves as the center of the universe. The greater good is a foreign thought.

Our ego gets in the way in two manners. One is *false pride*, when you start thinking more of yourself than you should. That's when you start pushing and shoving for credit and thinking leadership is about you rather than those who are led. You spend much of your time promoting yourself. Your ego also gets in your way through *self-doubt* or *fear*—thinking less of yourself than you should. You are consumed with your own shortcomings and are hard on yourself. You spend a great deal of time protecting yourself. With both false pride and self-doubt, you have a hard time believing you are okay. To borrow the title from an old song, you are "looking for love in all the wrong places." Now you think that, as Robert S. McGee warns, "your self-worth is a function of your performance plus others' opinions."[10] Since your performance varies from day to day and people are often fickle, with that belief your self-worth is up for grabs every day.

It's easy to understand that self-doubt comes from lack of self-esteem, because people afflicted with it on a daily basis act as if they are worth less than others. It is less obvious with people who have false pride, because they behave as if they are worth more than others. According to research reported by Thomas A. Harris in *I'm OK, You're OK*, people with false pride, who act as if they are the only ones who are okay, are really trying to make up for their lack of self-esteem. They overcompensate for their "not okay" feelings by trying to control everything and everybody around them. In the process, they make themselves unlovable to those around them.

It's interesting to see how false pride and self-doubt play out in managers. When managers are addicted to either ego affliction, it erodes their effectiveness. Managers dominated by false pride are often called "controllers." Even when they don't know what they are doing, they have a high need for power and control. Even when it's clear to everyone that they are wrong, they keep on insisting they are right. These folks aren't much for supporting their people, either. If everyone is upbeat and confident, controllers throw out the wet blanket. They support their bosses over their people because they want to climb the hierarchy and be part of the boss crowd.

At the other end of the spectrum are fear-driven managers, who are often characterized as "do-nothing bosses." They are described as "never around, always avoiding conflict, and not very helpful." They often leave people alone even when those people are insecure and don't know what they are doing. Do-nothing bosses don't seem to believe in themselves or trust in their own judgment. They value others' thoughts more than their own—especially the thoughts of those they report to. As a result, they rarely speak out and support their own people. Under pressure, they seem to defer to whomever has the most power.

If any of this sounds a bit too close for comfort, don't be alarmed. Most of us have traces of both false pride and self-doubt because the issue is really ego. We are stuck, all alone, focusing only on ourselves. The good news is that there is an antidote for both.

Ego Antidotes

The antidote for false pride is humility. True leadership—the essence of what people long for and want desperately to follow—implies a certain humility that is appropriate and elicits the best response from people.

Jim Collins supports this truth in *Good to Great*.[11] He found two characteristics that describe great leaders: *will* and *humility*. Will is the determination to follow through on a vision/mission/goal. Humility is the capacity to realize that leadership is not about the leader; it's about the people and what they need.

According to Collins, when things are going well for typical self-serving leaders, they look in the mirror, beat their chests, and tell themselves how good they are. When things go wrong, they look out the window and blame everyone else. On the other hand, when things go well for great leaders, they look out the window and give everybody else the credit. When things go wrong, these servant leaders look in the mirror and ask questions like "What could I have done differently that would have allowed these people to be as great as they could be?" That requires real humility.

One of the keys, therefore, to becoming a servant leader is humility. We have found two compelling definitions of humility. The first one appeared in a book by Ken Blanchard and Norman Vincent Peale, *The Power of Ethical Management*:[12]

People with humility don't think less of themselves; they just think about themselves less.

People who are humble have solid self-esteem.

The second definition of humility comes from Fred Smith, author of *You and Your Network*:[13]

People with humility don't deny their power; they just recognize that it passes through them, not from them.

Too many people think that who they are is their position and the power it gives them. Yet that's not true. Where does your power come from? It's not from your position; it's from the people whose lives you touch. As Richard N. Bolles noted in *What Color Is Your Parachute?*, most people would like to make the world a better place.[14] But how many actually have a plan for how they will do that? Very few. And yet we all can make the world a better place through the moment-to-moment decisions we make as we interact with the people we come into contact with at work, at home, and in the community.

Suppose as you leave your house one morning, someone yells at you. You have a choice: You can yell back, or you can hug the person and wish her a good day. Someone cuts you off on your way to work. You have a choice: Will you chase him down and give him an obscene gesture, or will you send a prayer toward his car? We have choices all the time as we interact with other human beings. Humility tames your judgmental nature and motivates you to reach out to support and encourage others. That's where your power comes from.

What's the antidote for fear? It's love. Do you have kids? Do you love your kids? Does this love for your kids depend on their success?

If they're successful, you love them; if they're not, you won't? Few people would agree with this. You love your kids unconditionally, right? What if you accepted that unconditional love for yourself? You know God doesn't make junk. He unconditionally loves each one of us. Did you know that you can't control enough, sell enough, make enough money, or have a high-enough position to get any more love? You have all the love you need. All you have to do is open yourself to it.

What Servant Leaders Do

The Secret: What Great Leaders Know and Do[15]—a book Ken Blanchard wrote with Mark Miller, well-known author and vice president of high performance leadership for Chick-fil-A—illustrates that great leaders *serve*. This book is built around the acronym SERVE. In fact, Chick-fil-A organizes its management training program around the five fundamental ways in which every great leader serves. And since Chick-fil-A has less than 5 percent turnover among its restaurant managers in more than 1,100 restaurants, this program has a pretty good track record.

S stands for See the Future. This has to do with the visionary role of leaders that we discussed in detail in Chapter 2, "The Power of Vision." Leadership is about taking people from one place to another. We can't say enough about the importance of having a compelling vision. Once a clear vision is established, goals and strategies can be developed within the context of the vision.

E stands for Engage and Develop People. That's what Section II, "Treat Your People Right," was all about. We took you on a transformational journey from self leadership to one-on-one leadership, to team leadership, to organizational leadership. As a leader, once the vision and direction are set, you have to turn the hierarchical pyramid upside down and focus on engaging and developing your people so that they can live according to the vision. You also must take care of your customers in a way that creates customer maniacs and raving fans.

R stands for Reinvent Continuously. Reinventing continuously has three aspects. First, great leaders reinvent continuously on a personal level. They are always interested in ways to enhance their knowledge and skills. The very best leaders are learners.

Great leaders find their own approach to learning—some read, some listen to audio books or downloads, some spend time with mentors. They do whatever it takes to keep learning. We believe if you stop learning, you stop leading. As Ken often says, "If you stop learning, you might as well lie down and let them throw the dirt on you because you're already dead."

We feel that everyone in every organization, every year, should have at least one learning goal. What do you hope will be on your resume next year that's not on it this year? For example, maybe you want to learn Spanish this year, since more and more of your customers are Spanish-speaking. You might want to learn some new computer program that will make your life simpler and help you retrieve the information you need to make effective decisions. Whatever it is, focus on learning something new every year.

Second, leaders must work to instill the desire for improvement into the people doing the day-to-day work. The leader may champion this cause, but the people make it happen—or not.

The third part of Reinvent Continuously is the idea of structural invention. Many people assume that an organizational structure is permanent. In many cases, the organizational structure no longer serves the business—the people are serving the structure. Great leaders don't change the structure just to have something to do. They understand that their organizational structure should be fluid and flexible. That belief is key to creating the energizing structures and systems that are characteristic of high performing organizations. Other, less proficient leaders tend to let the structure drive their decisions rather than adapting the structure to meet the business's ever-changing demands.

Don Shula, the famous NFL coach and coauthor with Ken Blanchard of *Everyone's a Coach*, was a great believer in this. He said great teams are "audible-ready." Suppose a football quarterback calls "halfback right." When he gets to the line of scrimmage, he sees that the defense is all to the right. He doesn't turn to the halfback and say, "Hold on;

I think they'll kill you." He decides to call a new play. Why? Because the structure and what they've set up are no longer appropriate. Shula always felt it was important to realize that you don't call an audible for nothing. It's good to have a plan; it's good to have your structure in place. But always be watchful and determine whether it's serving you, your customers, and your people well. If it's not, change it.

V stands for Value Results and Relationships. Great leaders—those who lead at a higher level—value both results and relationships. Both are critical for long-term survival. Not either/or, but both/and. For too long, many leaders have felt that they needed to choose. Most corporate leaders have said it's all about results. In reality, there are two tests of a leader. First, does he or she get results? Second, does he or she have followers? By the way, if you don't have followers, it's very hard to get long-term results.

The way to maximize your results as a leader is to have high expectations for both results and relationships. If leaders can create a motivating environment for their people so they can take care of their customers, profits and financial strength are the applause they get for a job well done. You see, success is both results and relationships. It's a proven formula.

E stands for Embody the Values. As we emphasized in Chapter 8, "Building Trust," all genuine leadership is built on trust. Trust can be built in many ways. One way is to live consistently with the values you profess. If I say customers are important, my actions had better support that statement. If I choose to live as if customers are unimportant, people will have reason to question my trustworthiness. In the final analysis, if my people deem me untrustworthy, I will not be trusted—or followed as a leader. Embody the Values is all about walking your talk. The leader, above all, has to be a walking example of the vision. Leaders who say, "Do as I say, not as I do" are ineffective in the long run.

The SERVE acronym builds a wonderful picture of how servant leaders operate. But it's a tough act to follow. Continually doing a good job in each of these areas is a significant task, but it's worth it. Servant leadership is about getting people to a higher level by leading people at a higher level.

Servant Leadership: A Mandate or a Choice

We believe that servant leadership has never been more applicable to the world of leadership than it is today. Not only are people looking for deeper purpose and meaning as they meet the challenges of today's changing world, but they are also looking for principles that actually work. Servant leadership works.

As Blanchard and Zigarmi found in their research, when the "what" (the *leadership* aspect of servant leadership) gets things started in the right direction and the "how" (the *servant* part of servant leadership) excites employees and customers, organizational vitality and success are almost guaranteed. If that's true, why wouldn't everyone—even self-serving leaders who are focused only on making money or their own power, recognition, and status—want to be a servant leader? Doesn't servant leadership benefit their motives, too?

The answer is yes, but not for long. Self-serving motivations can't be hidden forever. Your heart will be exposed. As Blanchard and Zigarmi found, there is a direct correlation between bad senior leadership and organizational failure. What happened at Enron, WorldCom, and other companies speaks volumes.

Servant leadership is not just another management technique. It is a way of life for those with servant hearts. In organizations run by servant leaders, servant leadership becomes a mandate, not a choice, and the by-products are better leadership, better service, a higher performing organization, and more success and significance.

Servant leadership provides better leadership. Organizations led by servant leaders are less likely to experience poor leadership. In studying bad leadership, Barbara Kellerman found seven different patterns, falling along a continuum ranging from ineffective to unethical leadership. Ineffective leadership just does not get the job done because of incompetence, rigidity, and lack of self-control or callousness. Unethical leadership, in contrast, is about right and wrong. "Unethical leadership can be effective, just as ineffective leadership can be ethical," Kellerman states. (*Editor's Note: In other words, it is possible for unethical leadership to get the job done.*) "But unethical leadership cannot make even the most basic claim to decency and good conduct, and so the leadership process is derailed."[16]

Organizations led by servant leaders ward off unethical leadership. When the vision and values are clearly defined, ethical and moral dilemmas are less likely to emerge. Drea Zigarmi, coauthor of *The Leader Within*,[17] contends that a moral dilemma exists when no guidelines for decision making exist, forcing an individual to rely on his or her own values and beliefs. An ethical dilemma arises when the organization has clearly established guidelines for behavior and the individual must consciously decide to either go along with or violate those guidelines.

Organizations work more effectively if clear vision and values are established up front, as they are under servant leadership. When unethical leadership occurs, it is often the result of the moral confusion created by the organization's lack of clearly established guidelines that a compelling vision provides.

Servant leadership provides a cure for ineffectiveness as well. Suppose someone who is unqualified accepts a leadership position. What will it take for this person to become effective and get the job done? The key is humility. True servant leadership embraces a humble sincerity that brings out the best in leaders and those they serve. Because servant leaders have solid self-esteem, they are willing to admit when they have a weakness or need assistance. Put in positions over their heads, they can reach out to their people for help.

We had a beautiful example of this in our own company. Because of a leadership crisis, we needed Debbie Blanchard, one of the owners, to take over our sales department. The only sales experience she had was working at Nordstrom in the summer while in college. When she had her first meeting with all her salespeople, her humility showed through. She told them that she needed their help if she were to be effective. She flew around the country, met with her team, found out what their needs were, and figured out how she could help them. Responding to her humility, the salespeople reached out to make sure she had the knowledge she needed to be effective. With Debbie at the helm, that year the sales department produced the highest sales in the history of the company, far exceeding its annual goals.

Servant leadership provides better service. Organizations led by servant leaders are more likely to take better care of their customers. As we've pointed out, if you don't take care of your customers today, somebody is waiting, ready, and willing to do it. Again, the only thing your competition can't steal from you is the relationship your people have with your customers. Under servant leadership these relationships can really grow because the people closest to the customer are given the power to soar like eagles rather than quack like ducks. As we pointed out in Chapter 17, the great customer service experiences created by Southwest Airlines and the Ritz-Carlton were a direct result of servant leadership. Leaders like Herb Kelleher and Horst Schulze set up their organizations to empower everyone—including the frontline people—to make decisions, use their brains, and be servant leaders who could carry out the vision of high-quality customer service.

Servant leadership helps create a high performing organization. When we discussed HPO SCORES® in Chapter 1, we said that if becoming a high performing organization is the destination, leadership is the engine. And the kind of leadership we want is servant leadership. The one HPO SCORES® element that best characterizes a servant leader is *Shared Power and High Involvement*. It goes hand in hand with leaders who realize it's not about them.

Is being a servant leader just about being nice for the sake of niceness? No—it works. Practicing shared power and high involvement strongly impacts financial results through productivity, retention, and employee satisfaction. Using U.S. Department of Labor data and surveys of over 1,500 firms from various industries, Huselid and Becker found that such participative practices significantly improved employee retention and financial performance and increased productivity. In fact, they were able to quantify the financial impact of participative practices with enough confidence to say that each standard deviation in the use of participative practices increased a company's market value between $35,000 and $78,000 per employee.[18]

The servant leaders in high performing organizations understand that day-to-day decision making should occur closest to the action and on the front lines by those directly involved with the customer. Being involved in decisions that affect their lives reduces people's stress and creates a healthier, happier workforce. Involvement in decision making increases their ownership and commitment as well as effectiveness.

For example, Chaparral Steel does not use quality inspectors. The people in their plants are responsible for the products they produce and the quality of those products. Given the power and responsibility for decision making, they act as they are expected to: as owners.

Servant leaders in high performing organizations involve their people at all levels and from multiple areas of the business in complex and strategic decision making. Research demonstrates that decisions and action plans are more effective when people whose commitment is required are part of the planning.[19] Effectiveness increases in quality, quantity, and implementation. These kinds of decisions are often made in a team environment where everyone involved is in the room at the same time, able to benefit from and react to each other's thinking and to arrive at "collective wisdom." W.L. Gore, a company whose watchwords are "commitment, empowerment, and innovation," recognizes the importance of personal contact. Gore even goes so far as to limit the size of its facilities. They will build a new plant rather than expand one where associates would lose contact with each other.

High performing organizations do not depend on a few peak performers to guide and direct, but have broadly developed leadership capacities. This allows for self-management, ownership, and the power to act quickly as the situation requires. Pushing decision making to those closest to the action is an empowering practice. Servant leaders in high performing organizations create environments where people are free to choose to empower themselves.

Servant leaders think differently than self-serving leaders. It is not possible to share power without believing that people can and will manage power and decision making responsibly if given the proper training, information, and opportunity. It is also not possible to create a high involvement culture without including everyone. Servant leaders in high performing organizations not only appreciate but capitalize on cultural diversity; style diversity; social diversity; and diversity in race, religion, sexual orientation, and age. They realize that effective decision making, problem solving, and innovation come from utilizing different perspectives.

Servant leadership brings more success and significance. In his classic book *Halftime*, Bob Buford reveals that most people, later in life, want to move from success to significance—from getting to giving.[20] Organizations led by servant leaders are more likely to create environments where people at all levels can experience both success and significance.

Too many leaders today focus only on success. They think success depends only on how much wealth they have accumulated, the amount of recognition they have received, and their power and status. Nothing is inherently wrong with any of those things, as long as you don't identify those things as who you are. As an alternative, we'd like you to focus on the opposite of each of those as you move from success to significance. What's the opposite of accumulating wealth? It's generosity of time, talent, treasure, and touch (reaching out to support others). What's the opposite of recognition? It's service. What's the opposite of power and status? It's loving relationships.

We've found over the years that when you focus only on success, you never reach significance. That's the problem with self-serving leaders—they never get out of their own way. On the other hand, if you focus on significance—generosity, service, and loving relationships—you'll be amazed at how much success will come your way. Take Mother Teresa. She couldn't have cared less about accumulating wealth, recognition, and status. Her whole life was focused on significance. And what happened? Success came her way. Her ministry received tremendous financial backing, she was recognized all over the world, and she was given the highest status wherever she went. She was the ultimate servant leader. If you focus on significance first, your emphasis will be on people. Through that emphasis, success *and* results will follow.

An amazing story of significance occurred during the 100-yard dash at the Special Olympics several years ago in Spokane, Washington. Nine contestants waited anxiously for the starting gun to fire. When it did, they raced toward the finish line as fast as they could, given their physical disabilities. About a third of the way down the track, one of the boys fell. He tried to get up, but he fell again. In frustration, he lay on the track, sobbing. While six of the other racers continued to push toward the finish line and possible victory, two of the youngsters, hearing the sobs of their opponent, stopped, turned around, headed back toward their fallen competitor, and helped him up. The three boys held hands, walked down the track, and crossed the finish line together, well after the others had finished the race. The crowd was surprised. When they realized what had happened, they rose in unison and gave these youngsters a longer and louder ovation than they'd given the winner of the race.

Life is all about the choices we make as we interact with each other. We can choose to be self-serving or serving. Most of the youngsters in the race chose to focus on their own success—victory—but two tossed aside their dreams in favor of serving someone else. The crowd responded with enthusiasm because we all yearn to live at a higher level, and these young people modeled what that means. They made a different choice—they were true servant leaders.

We hope you make these kinds of choices. Life constantly presents leaders with opportunities to choose to love and serve one another. Someone once said to Margie Blanchard, "You've lived with Ken for over 50 years. What do you think leadership is all about?" She said:

*"Leadership is not about love—it **is** love."*

She continued, "It is loving your mission, it's loving your people, it's loving your customers, and it's loving yourself enough to get out of the way so that other people can be magnificent."

That's Margie's Leadership Point of View. What's yours? In the next chapter, we'll help you figure that out.

19

Determining Your Leadership Point of View

Margie Blanchard, Pat Zigarmi, and Ken Blanchard

All right, you've heard from us. Throughout this book, we have essentially shared with you our leadership point of view—our beliefs and values about leading people. A core belief of the authors of this book is that as leaders we need to focus on serving others, not being served. In every chapter we have challenged you to lead at a higher level—where the people you lead are inspired to give their best.

Now it's your turn. The goal of this chapter is to help you develop your own leadership point of view. Not only will this help you clarify your thoughts on leadership, it will also prepare you to share your leadership point of view with others. A leadership point of view essentially describes a picture of today and the future where there is consistency between your values, your words, and your actions as a leader. You could call it "a course on you!"

Why is developing a clear leadership point of view important? Ken Blanchard was sold on this idea after reading Noel Tichy's book *The Leadership Engine.* Noel's extensive research has shown that effective leaders have a clear, teachable leadership point of view and are willing to share it with the people they work with.[1] A leadership point of view teaches people what you expect from yourself and them so that together you and the organization can succeed.

Blanchard's work on creating your leadership point of view became a course in the Master of Science in Executive Leadership (MSEL) program jointly offered by The Ken Blanchard Companies® and the

College of Business at the University of San Diego. When you reflect on, write about, and share your leadership point of view, Ken and Margie Blanchard—who teach the course—have found that you get a clearer picture about your intentions as a leader. Writing your leadership point of view invites you to think deeply about your leadership legacy and how you want to be seen and remembered as a leader. The reflection itself may not change your day-to-day interactions with those you lead, but it will shift your intentions. It will help you find what Bill George calls your "True North,"[1] and it can serve as a compass that leaders can use to align their actions with their values.

Elements of a Leadership Point of View

In reflecting and writing your leadership point of view, you are asked to

- Identify key people and events that have shaped and influenced your leadership point of view.

- Describe your leadership values.

- Share your expectations for yourself and others.

Key People

In identifying key people, you are asked to think about the influencers in your life who have had a positive (or in some cases negative) impact on you. Ask these questions:

- Who mentored you? Taught you? Inspired you? Helped you believe in yourself?

- What did you admire or not admire about each of these key people?

- What did you learn from each of these people that shaped your leader behavior?

When we ask people who most impacted their lives, they often mention first the leaders they have worked with. But then, with time, they start to talk about their parents, grandparents, friends, coaches, and teachers. When Ken Blanchard is asked about the key people in his life, he is quick to mention his mother and father:

"My mom was the ultimate positive thinker. She told everyone that I laughed before I cried, I smiled before I frowned, and I danced before I walked. With those kinds of messages, how could I have ended up anything but a positive thinker? Mom also helped me keep things in perspective. She said, 'Ken, don't act like you're better than anybody else. But don't let anyone act like they're better than you either. Remember, there's a pearl of goodness in everyone.'

"My dad was a career naval officer who retired as an admiral. He was a powerful leadership role model for me. He didn't think leadership was choosing between people or results. I learned from him that leadership was a 'both/and' relationship—both people and results were important to him. He taught me that position power and 'my way or the highway' are not the way to lead. I'll never forget when I was elected president of the seventh grade and came home all excited. Dad said, 'It's great, Ken, that you are president of your class. But now that you have a position, don't use it. Great leaders are followed not because they have position power, but because they're respected and trusted as individuals.' He always supported and involved his people, yet he demanded high performance.

"The one-two punch I received from my mom and dad gave me a positive outlook on life and people."

By now you should have a sense why, in crafting your leadership point of view, thinking about who influenced your life and your beliefs about leadership is a good starting point.

Key Events

In identifying key events in your life—whether from your childhood, school years, or earlier career—think about the situations that impacted you most. Ask these questions.

- What events do you remember as if they occurred yesterday?

- What have been the turning points in your life?

- What experiences in your past prepared you for a leadership role?

- What did you learn from each experience?

When we ask people about the key events in their life that impacted them most, they usually focus on the big milestones.

What were the major transitions? Where were the sliding doors—those moments in time where you made a choice to go one way versus another and that, as Robert Frost said, "made all the difference"? In choosing a key event that impacted her life, Pat Zigarmi relates this story in sharing her leadership point of view:

"My value of justice was shaped by the movements for civil rights, women's rights, and equal opportunity that marked my lifetime. I have always wanted underdogs to win. I have wanted people to believe in their potential to be magnificent, and I have challenged bias whenever I had the opportunity to do so. In college, as an officer of my southern-roots sorority I went to a national convention to protest the exclusion of blacks from my sorority and the next fall we defiantly pledged a black woman. In 1986, I persuaded my company, The Ken Blanchard Companies® to let me come back to work with an infant—in a program we called Infant at Work (or, more affectionately, Infinite Work!). I didn't want to have to choose between my passion for my child and my passion for work, and I didn't want someone to choose for me. I believed I knew what was right and just for me. I have always admired pioneers for equality and justice. And, I have always admired generosity of spirit which my dad exemplified and which I see as a component of justice."

Some people will combine a key event and a key person who influenced their leadership point of view. For example, one of our colleagues writes

"The best story I can give you about a key event in my life and a key person is this. When I was in the 8th grade, I applied for the yearbook committee. I had a tough year personally and was getting a lot of sympathetic love from the faculty. However, when the faculty did not place me on the yearbook committee, I was shocked. I went to my dad for comfort. As he held me in his arms while I cried, I uttered, 'It's because I'm black.' My father answered softly, but matter-of-factly, 'No, it's because you were not good enough. You failed to put the effort in to achieve your goal. Simply put, it's your fault. You failed to prioritize this goal, and now you won't be on the yearbook committee.' As I sat on my father's lap, I learned an important lesson: Success comes from the effort you put into achieving your goal's tasks. Excellence is about never finding an excuse for your failure to exert effort."

Reflecting about the key people and events in your life sets the stage for thinking about the next step in writing your leadership point of view: identifying and defining your values.

Values

The values you hold will determine how you behave as a leader. That's why values are an important element of your leadership point of view.

Values are core beliefs that you feel strongly about. It has been said that

---

The most important thing in life is to decide what's most important.

The key people and key events in your life shape your values, which is why people don't have the same values.

Here is a list of personal values. As you look at it, you'll probably find that you value most or all of them, which is why we have to spend some time in really thinking about what's most important. If a value that is not listed here is important to you, feel free to include it.

truth	wisdom
power	commitment
courage	recognition
excitement	learning
creativity	honesty
happiness	originality

service	respect
freedom	order
integrity	spirituality
peace	cooperation
loyalty	humor
security	resources
love	excellence
fun	responsiveness
relationships	success

In identifying your values, you might start with a long list. Start by choosing ten to twelve. Then begin to narrow the list. Hold each value up against the others and see if you can pick out your three to five most important values. You might want to look back at your stories about key people and key events in your life and think about the values reflected in those stories. If you're having trouble narrowing down your top values, you might combine a couple. For example, Ken combined two words to create "spiritual peace" as his number-one value, followed by "integrity," "love," and "success."

Remember to choose values that mean the most to you personally—not just the ones that you think make you look good.

The next step in clarifying your values is to define them. To be able to live consistently with a value, you have to be able to explain what that value means to you. For example, let's take the value "justice." Pat can remember a conversation in which three people defined that value differently. For Pat, it meant equal access to opportunity. For another person, it meant fair process. For the third, it meant "getting my due share."

Unless the people in your life understand exactly what you mean by each of your values, they won't have much meaning. This is especially true of words, like "justice," that can have several definitions.

For example, let's take a value that has many meanings, like "love." Ken defines this value by describing how it feels as well as how he expresses it to others. According to Ken:

> "I value love. I know I am living by this value anytime
> I feel loving toward myself and others, anytime I express
> compassion, anytime I show love to others, and anytime
> I receive the love of others."

Here is a colleague's description of her value of "involvement." Put yourself into one of her team member's shoes as you read it, and you'll see the power of sharing the roots of the value—why it's important—and the power of knowing how the leader defines it and hopes it plays out in day-to-day interactions. Notice how the definition of the value begins to spill over into "expectations for self and others," which is the last component of a leadership point of view presentation.

> "My next value is 'involvement'—I learned how important
> feeling involved in the decision making meant to me as our
> family dealt with my mom's illness. My dad ensured that
> my voice was heard and my opinion was valued. Because
> I have always wanted to 'be at the table' and influence
> decisions that were being made that impacted me, I have
> always assumed others want to be involved and influence
> as well. When I lead I expect people to speak up. For me,
> involvement means creating a sense of partnership—we
> are in this together. In every meaningful decision I have
> to make, I want to involve the people it impacts the most,
> ensuring alignment. I commit to making the tough calls
> when necessary, but not without listening first. And I expect
> those I work with to speak their mind, make sure their voice
> is heard."

Here are three of Pat's five values so you can get a feel for what it means to expand on the definition of the value:

> "I value 'competence and creativity,' which means I am
> very appreciative of someone who is masterful at what
> they do, no matter what it is. I admire fine craftsmanship

and artisanship and virtuosity—whether in an athlete, musician, chef, artists, coach, or business leader. I respect people who are talented at what they do. That usually means that they are constantly reinventing the space they work in.

"I value 'flexibility,' which I define as adaptability, versatility, and resilience—the ability to pivot in the face of change, to take a new course in the face of new information. Flexibility also involves having the courage to try. I have always been focused on trying to expand people's perspectives and helping them find the courage to try something new. Another image that comes to mind with the word 'flexibility' is 'willow-like.' There is incredible strength in a willow, but it bends and then rebalances. Flexibility implies inquisitiveness and openness to change. It is the opposite of rigidity. I am at my best when I am open to change, when I consider alternatives, when I remember that there are multiple paths to the same end.

"Another value I have is 'joyfulness.' Those who know me best have always appreciated my playfulness, glimpsing it even through my intensity. Joyfulness for me means expressiveness. My face has always been an open book. You know what I am thinking by watching my face. Joy connotes warmth for me. It is why I love Christmas so much. Because you can gift joy...cook an old family recipe, decorate the tree with a treasured ornament, honor an old tradition or make a new one, find the right gift, be generous in sharing food and creating memories. I have always had a knack for making memories that involve wonder or appreciation or laughter or tenderness. At the root of joy, for me, is optimism. I never believe things won't turn out for the best."

Again, with all of these examples, the table is set for writing the third part of a leadership point of view: expectations for yourself and others.

Expectations for Yourself and Others

Clarifying your expectations for yourself and others is the last step in crafting your leadership point of view. These expectations should flow naturally from the people and key events that have influenced you and your values. Your expectations really are the essence of your leadership point of view. When you share your leadership point of view with others, they may be engaged in your storytelling, but what they really want to know is how they can work with you more easily.

What You Expect from Yourself

Let's look at some of the expectations Ken has for himself that he shares with others.

> "I believe my role as your manager is to help you win—to help accomplish your goals. I want you to get an A. If I am behaving according to my expectations of myself, I will be cheering you on. If progress is not being made, I will be redirecting your efforts and helping get you back on course by either providing direction or support or both. In other words, you should know when you are getting 'wrong answers' so that we can discuss what would make a 'good answer.' If I am living up to my expectations of myself as a leader, everything I do with you will be geared toward helping you produce good results and, in the process, feel good about yourself."

What People Can Expect from You

Letting people know what they can expect from you underscores the idea that good leadership is a partnership. It gives people a picture of how things will look as you work together.

For example, one of the students in the MSEL program at the University of San Diego described what his people could expect from him:

> "Knowing that I like building things will help you understand what you can expect from me. In fact, I look at many different things in the context of building. I like building houses. I like building my family. I like building

businesses and I like building and developing people. I'm happy to roll up my sleeves to help build most anything. It's what I enjoy most. So, you can expect that I will give you plenty of my time, I will listen to you when you see the need for a sounding board, and I will help you access what you already know by asking thoughtful questions.

"Just the other day, I noticed that Jack, one of my team members, had stayed late at work and was looking a little frustrated. When I asked him how things were going, he shared that our building permits for the new office were held up, putting the whole project behind. Through our conversation, he figured out another person to call and approach to take. He had the answer all along; I just helped him ask different questions."

Your leadership point of view should also let others know how you will set an example for the values and behaviors you are encouraging. As most parents know, people learn from your behavior, not from your words. Leaders must walk their talk.

For example, another MSEL student made clear how he would set an example for his people:

"All of you know that I released our company's top salesperson about nine months ago for questionable activities. He thought that he was untouchable due to his status as a top-producing account executive. However, no one, including me, is above the ethical standards that are expected of someone working at our company."

What You Expect from Your People

Because we believe that effective leadership is a partnership and that effective leaders work side by side with their team members, it is imperative that you let people know what you expect from them. This gives people a picture of how they can be successful under your leadership.

In sharing your expectations, it's helpful to think of an example of someone behaving consistently with what you expect. Real examples are better than platitudes. Think about an example or two illustrating someone doing what you expect.

Here is an example from one of the students in the MSEL program at the University of San Diego. Notice how he shines a spotlight on a manager who is living according to his expectation of ethical behavior:

> "My expectations of you can be combined into a saying known as the Golden Rule: *Do unto others as you would have them do unto you.* What do I mean by that? I expect you all to act ethically in everything you do. You'll have many opportunities to take shortcuts and do things that will result in short-term gains. Plenty of business examples in recent years have shown how disastrous this can be. I expect you to stand tall on this issue and to not allow anyone to think that you tolerate fraud or anything unethical. You manage hundreds of employees. While each of them may not know you that well, they need to know how important integrity is to you. For example, Ruth, I love how in your department you are continually asking the question, 'Is this the right thing to do?'"

Developing Your Own Leadership Point of View

Now you can create your own leadership point of view.

First, don't try to craft your leadership point of view overnight. Spend some significant time thinking about key people, key events, and your values. Let your reflections marinate.

Then write or record what you've been thinking about. Think in terms of stories. People remember and respond more to stories than to a list of general principles about effective leadership. The stories personalize you and allow people to find common ground with you. Lists of attributes or qualities of effective leadership don't explain you the way stories do. Stories help the people you lead figure out why you show up the way you do. When people know your stories, they can more easily understand your intentions. Stories have beginnings, middles, and endings. Be sure to include the details that will make your stories about key people and events come alive. It is also important to point out your leadership learnings from each story. These learnings can be a line of sight to your values.

When you write or record your values, be sure to fully define them, as we discussed earlier, so that people know exactly what you mean by those values.

Once you've developed a draft, consider test-driving it with a coach or others you trust. Ask them to share feedback with you. What resonated? What was insightful? What was confusing? Where is more work needed to make the narrative more compelling? Did the coach or your colleagues think you clearly explained your values and how you expect those values to play out in interactions with your team members and colleagues?

Listen to and evaluate the feedback you're getting. Rewrite what you've written. Sit with it and rewrite it again. Consider which approach works best for you. There is really no single right way to organize a leadership point of view presentation.

- Some people start with a brief bio—highlighting key people and events—and then distill their leadership values and expectations for themselves and others from the stories they have shared.

- Others begin with sharing their values and then showing how key people and key events formed those values.

- Some people start with expectations for themselves and others and then share their values, which are rooted in stories about key people and events.

When you present your leadership point of view, you can convert your long version to an outline that will make your presentation less formal and more conversational. That would be our strong recommendation, because that way your story will come from your heart. But you can also read it. Since a leadership point of view presentation is not a speech about effective leadership, but a deeply personal narrative, having it written out can provide a sense of security and help you regroup if your emotions are triggered during your presentation, which can happen.

Throughout this chapter we've provided you with examples of what the description of a key person, key event, or value might look like. Now we want to share a couple of completed leadership point of view examples.

The first is a leadership point of view presentation. The reason we say presentation is that she shared it with the people who work with her. We highly recommend you do the same because while your leadership point of view is about you, it's not *for* you. It's for your people, to help them work more effectively with you.

Notice that in this example, the leader sets the context, explaining why she is sharing her leadership point of view.

> "You all know I am in a Master's Program in leadership—it has caused me to do a lot of thinking about my background and values and what experiences have shaped me into the person I am today. I'd like to share some of the most influential experiences of my life with you, in hopes that it will enable us to work even better together as a team and clarify to you my expectations as a coach, colleague, and coworker.

> "Some of you may know my background more than others. I was an only child. My parents were high school sweethearts who married. A few years later I was born, and shortly thereafter my dad was transferred and we moved away from the comfort and security of family and close friendships. After the move, their marriage started to suffer, and my mother became depressed. While my parents didn't fight, there was a sadness that was palpable even to a small child. I learned that the best way for me to survive was to be a 'good' girl.

> "The way I did that was I tried very hard to not cause problems or create more pain for them and learned at an early age to avoid conflict and to subvert my own

emotional needs. I'm sure you all remember the fairytale of Snow White and the poison apple—in the story the Evil Queen gives Snow White an apple to put her to sleep. In my version, there was no Evil Queen, just me feeding myself an apple and slowly numbing and putting myself to sleep.

"I knew even as a young girl to ensure my own survival, it was my job to become the adult, to calm my mother and make everything be 'OK.' So I took another bite of the apple. After the divorce I lived with my mom and her boyfriend, who didn't like children or females. (So I had two strikes against me.) When I was 9 my mom remarried and left the country. When that happened, I went to live with my father, who was also in the process of remarrying. For the nine months before they were married, I was shuttled between my dad's house, his girlfriend's house, and my grandparents' house. When he remarried, I joined a new family with three stepsiblings. By this point, I was very good at playing the role of the good girl. What this meant was that I didn't express my anger toward my mom about leaving me, my fear of joining a new family, or my sadness that I didn't seem to be anyone's priority. I took another bite of the apple.

"This pattern of avoiding emotional conflict and trying to please others by being whoever I thought they wanted me to be continued into my adult life. I married a man with many great qualities, but communication and dealing with conflict were not among them. He took conflict personally, ignored and blamed me for what wasn't working in our life. So I took more bites of the apple, until the point that I found myself numb and sleepwalking through my own life, but now with two teenage daughters in tow. I'm not sure exactly what caused me to wake up...my Prince Charming comes later in the story; maybe it was life's kiss that awoke me.

"While I knew I had made my girls a priority, what I hadn't done is role model for them what a healthy, happy life and loving marriage looked like. I ended up getting a divorce (after 25 years). I'm still not sure how I had the courage to go through it, but I believe my desire to live a full life helped me to overcome my stagnation and fear. What I'm learning is that I need to connect my heart with my mind and to pay attention to my own needs, dreams, and desires and that you always have choices. From my reflections on my developmental history, the values that have become clear to me are:

"Value #1—Authenticity—What authenticity means to me is that my mind, heart, body, and soul are all working together and going in the same direction. I'm still learning to say what I am feeling, especially when I'm scared and fear I may lose a relationship by being honest. My expectation is that you should challenge me when you don't agree or when you don't feel I'm making the right decision.

"Rachelle, I'm in awe of your ability to face conflict head-on and ask questions when you don't agree with a job evaluation I've completed. When you do that, you guide us to better outcomes for both the employee and company.

"Value #2—Accountability—What accountability means to me is that we are responsible for ourselves, whether we like it or not. What you do with your life, and what you have done already, is up to you. We are not victims. We have choices to make and have to continually choose to take ownership and responsibility for our lives. For me, this also means taking the actions you need to achieve the results you want—taking time for self-care, like therapy (when needed), exercise, rest, and developing yourself.

"Sarah, I so appreciated when you came to me and shared how much the work travel was having a negative effect on your life and that you needed a change. I'm sure that was hard for you, but you gave me an opportunity to find a solution that works for both you and the company.

"Value #3—Humor—Laughing and having fun with others matters to me. I love to laugh, and humor helps me get through (or diffuse) tense situations. Humor also helps me feel connected with all of you and provides a way to deal with stress. I'm enjoying the opportunity to make up for the playtime I missed out on as a child.

"Joanne and Roxanne, I've had so much fun on our skits as the 'Fixie Chicks.' For me, it's not just 'okay' to be playful and have fun—it's expected.

"These are the values that I'm choosing for the last half of my story...authenticity, accountability and humor...and while it's the last half, it's also a new beginning. I've met an awesome man (maybe my Prince Charming?) that I can be myself with and don't have to pretend. I'm learning to speak my mind without fear of reprisal, and I'm having fun. I'm on a journey, and I want you to speak your truth so we can learn and grow on this journey together.

"I want to close with a quote by Brené Brown: *'If you own this story you get to write the ending.'* We each own our story, and I'm looking forward to sharing that brave, new ending with you."

Our final example of a complete leadership point of view comes from Colleen Barrett. Colleen is President Emerita of Southwest Airlines and the recipient of dozens of business awards and honors, including the Tony Jannus Award; honorary doctorates from St. Mary's College and Grand Canyon University; and listings in The World's 100 Most Powerful Women award from *Forbes* and The Top 50 Leaders from *Fast Company.* Her leadership point of view comes across loud and clear in the book she wrote with Ken Blanchard, *Lead with LUV: A Different Way to Create Real Success.*

My Background

"I grew up poor, with an alcoholic father and a mother who raised the kids. My mother was the most influential person in my life. She was uneducated and didn't have money, but she had a huge heart. Her hard work and determination set a great example for me, and she was a great people person as well. Although she didn't actually use the expression, she modeled the Golden Rule. Her guiding belief in life was that as long as you were respectful of others and treated people the way you would like to be treated, you would get that back in kind. My alcoholic dad was not a good role model. I learned a lot from that, as well. Good teachers or bad teachers—you can learn from both.

What I've Learned

"A series of setbacks across my life also have shaped my leadership point of view. When I was a freshman in high school, my home burned down. I have survived breast cancer and a number of personal attacks. These challenges taught me to think about my priorities and not to judge others, because you never know what's going on in their lives.

"An incident in high school taught me why it's not a good idea to judge others. I was working as the receptionist at a paper company. My supervisor told me to minimize my interaction with the big, burly truck drivers who delivered the paper because she thought they were 'too scruffy, too dangerous, too tough.' But after my house burned down, the truck drivers got together and bought me a winter coat. They knew more about what was going on with me than my manager did. That experience also taught me to reach out when people are going through horrendous times. Every time an employee has a fire or is battling cancer, I reach out by sending a care package or note.

My Values

"My life purpose is to make a positive difference by fighting for a good cause. For example, Southwest Airlines is a cause. We did something no airline has ever done. In 1971, when flying was for the elite, we wanted to open up the skies to everyone. We believed flying could be fun. Only 13 percent of Americans were flying regularly when we started; today, 97 percent are. We got people flying with low fares at night and on weekends. My values actually mirror Southwest's values. Every day I want to show a servant heart, demonstrate a warrior spirit, and project a fun, loving attitude. The warrior spirit value plays out in my passion for causes and people.

"As I said, my mom had a tremendous impact on my values, particularly her hard work and do-unto-others philosophy. Mom encouraged me to believe I could do anything I wanted to do and that in the process I would make a positive difference. She believed that I could be whatever I wanted to be if I worked hard. I share her values of hard work and determination, patience and tolerance.

"I believe that in leading and motivating people, you treat them with respect, practice the Golden Rule, suspend judgment, and love people for who they are. I also believe in teaming, which translates into my desire to be inclusive and egalitarian.

What You Can Expect from Me

"I will set an example for you by following our philosophy of leadership at Southwest Airlines: Treat your people right, and good things will happen. I will do my best to be a servant leader who ensures that you have a good, strong work environment and the tools to do your jobs. I will do my best to ensure that you feel loved, appreciated, and supported so that you can in turn share that same warmth, caring, and fun spirit with our passengers.

"I think if you were to talk to any of my people they would tell you, 'She's a bottom-line-oriented person, and she's always going to tell you what she thinks. Whether you like it or not, you're going to hear it.' That doesn't bother me because I want people to expect that from me. I do have a few nicknames; one of them is 'Mom.' I think people know I will be there for them; I'm their biggest supporter; I believe in them and trust them; I won't judge them. But it goes both ways.

What I Expect from You

"I won't expect you to do anything I won't do myself. I expect a give-and-take relationship. We both need to give back when it's needed.

"I learned about the beauty of give-and-take relationships from my mentor, Herb Kelleher. When I was a young secretary, we had a mailer that had to get out. Everything that could go wrong with it went wrong. It had to be in the mail the next day, but the print machine broke down and the postage was somehow wrong. All the envelopes had to be stuffed and retyped—and this was back when you couldn't just push a button and it would happen. It was 8:00 at night, and we had to start all over. Herb sat right there with me until 4:00 in the morning, on the floor, licking envelopes and putting stamps on them, because we didn't have a postage machine. I'll never forget it. He could have thought it was my fault that the mailing had gone wrong, but he didn't. He just jumped right in there with me. That was a valuable lesson for me about leading and motivating people and how important it was to work side by side with the people you lead.

"I also expect open communication. I don't like surprises. I like to hear bad news first so we can fix the situation. If I don't hear about it, we can't fix it. I want you to see problems, use good judgment, and bring me solutions. I believe in absolute truthfulness. And I want passion; I want you to believe in what you do and to care.

"I want all decisions to be made from a servant's heart. After all, Southwest is in the customer service business. We just happen to provide airline transportation. So if people don't want to serve others, they're not bad people—but they don't belong at Southwest Airlines. For example, we have pilots who have paid for hotel rooms for passengers without money who had to get off at different cities than they'd intended for the night. The pilots don't call and ask, 'Is it okay? Will I get reimbursed?' They do these things because that's the kind of people they are. They are generous and open-hearted. They are there to serve others."

Become a Higher Level Leader

A leadership point of view is intended to capture your voice. It is a signature. It is designed to help you claim and share your unique perspective on leadership. How you tell your story may look like the above examples or be totally different. The goal is to reflect and share how you want people to experience you as a leader so that you are more connected and effective.

In writing *Leading at a Higher Level*, we've done our best to give you the leadership point of view that we have been developing over the last forty years. So, as you develop your own leadership point of view, don't be hard on yourself. This might be your first time thinking about your beliefs about leading and motivating people. Feel free to incorporate any of the ideas you have learned in these pages.

The world needs more leaders who are leading at a higher level. As we said in the introduction, our dream is that someday everyone will work with leaders who are leading at a higher level. We dream of the day when self-serving leaders are history, and leaders serving others are the rule, not the exception.

You can be a leader who makes a positive difference on our planet, so go out and do it! We're counting on you.

Endnotes

Introduction

1. Matt Hayes and Jeff Stevens, *The Heart of Business* (Bloomington, IN: Author House, 2005).

2. Robert Greenleaf, *Servant Leadership: A Journey into the Nature of Legitimate Power and Greatness*, 25th Anniversary Edition (New Jersey: Paulist Press, 2002).

Chapter 1

1. Ken Blanchard and Don Shula, *Everyone's a Coach* (Grand Rapids, MI: Zondervan 1995).

2. John Elkington uses the phrase "triple bottom line accounting" in his 1998 book, *Cannibals with Forks*. Our use of the phrase "quadruple bottom line" has a different focus: success with customers, employees, investors, and the environment.

3. Ken Blanchard and Sheldon Bowles, *Raving Fans: A Revolutionary Approach to Customer Service* (New York: William Morrow, 1993).

4. For more information on the HPO SCORES® model and the research conducted, see "High Performing Organizations: SCORES®" by Don Carew, Fay Kandarian, Eunice Parisi-Carew, and Jesse Stoner, Ken Blanchard Companies, 2001.

5. The HPO SCORES® Profile is a psychometrically sound organizational assessment, with strong validity and reliability, that provides feedback on the extent to which the practices in your organization are similar to those in high performing organizations. Developed by Don Carew, Fay Kandarian, Eunice Parisi-Carew, and Jesse Stoner, The HPO SCORES® Profile is published by The Ken Blanchard Companies®.

6. Supplement to the HPO SCORES® quiz.

Chapter 2

1. Jesse Stoner, *Visionary Leadership, Management, and High Performing Work Units* (doctoral dissertation, University of Massachusetts, 1988).

2. Jesse Stoner and Drea Zigarmi, "From Vision to Reality" (Escondido, CA: The Ken Blanchard Companies®, 1993). The elements of a compelling vision were also described by Stoner in "Realizing Your Vision" (Provo, UT: *Executive Excellence*, 1990).

3. Charles Garfield and Hal Bennett, *Peak Performance: Mental Training Techniques of the World's Greatest Athletes* (New York: Warner Books, 1989).

4. Ken Blanchard and Michael O'Connor, *Managing by Values* (San Francisco: Berrett-Koehler, 1997).

5. Ford Motor Company documents indicate that company officials had data that Firestone tires installed on Explorer sport-utility vehicles had little or no margin for safety in top-speed driving at the tire pressures that Ford recommended. The papers were part of a collection of documents that Congressional investigators released before the third round of Congressional hearings investigating Ford's and Bridgestone/Firestone Inc.'s handling of tire failures.

6. Jim Collins and Jerry Porras, *Built to Last: Successful Habits of Visionary Companies* (New York: HarperCollins, 1994).

7. Research studies described in *Leaders: The Strategies for Taking Charge* by Warren Bennis, 1985, and *The Leadership Challenge* by Kouzes and Posner, among others.

8. *New York Times*, August 2, 1995.

9. Ken Blanchard and Jesse Stoner, *Full Steam Ahead: Unleash the Power of Vision in Your Work and Your Life* (San Francisco: Berrett-Koehler, 2003).

Chapter 3

1. The Sarbanes-Oxley Act of 2002 is a U.S. federal law also known as the Public Company Accounting Reform and Investor Protection Act of 2002. It's commonly called SOX or SarbOx.

2. Edward Lawler, *Creating High Performance Organizations: Practices and Results of Employee Involvement and Total Quality Management* (San Francisco: Jossey-Bass, 1995).

3. http://thecro.com/category/topics/100-best-corporate-citizens/

   In a more recent and rigorous research study, S. R. Silver investigated the relationship between organizational empowerment and "hard" measures of team performance for 50 teams of applied research engineers. The study found that organizational empowerment had a positive impact on the quality, timeliness, and financial outcomes of the team's performance.

   S. R. Silver, "Perceptions of Empowerment in Engineering Workgroups: The Linkage to Transformational Leadership and Performance," unpublished doctoral dissertation, 1999, Washington, D.C., George Washington University.

   In a highly rigorous study, S. E. Siebert, S. R. Silver, and W. A. Randolph analyzed data collected from 375 employees in 50 work teams in one division of a Fortune 100 manufacturer of high-technology office and printing equipment. They determined that a climate of empowerment was positively related to manager ratings of work unit performance and job satisfaction.

   S. E. Siebert, S. R. Silver, and W. A. Randolph, "Taking Empowerment to the Next Level: A Multiple-Level Model of Empowerment, Performance, and Satisfaction," *Academy of Management Journal* 47 (2004).

4. T. W. Malone, "Is Empowerment Just a Fad? Control, Decision Making, and IT," *Sloan Management Review*, Winter (1997): 23–35.

5. Inaugural address of John Fitzgerald Kennedy, January 20, 1961.

6. Ken Blanchard, John Carlos, and Alan Randolph, *Empowerment Takes More Than a Minute* (San Francisco: Berrett-Koehler, 1996).

7. As described in the HPO SCORES® model in Chapter 1, "Is Your Organization High Performing?"

8. Jim Harris, "Five Principles to Revitalize Employee Loyalty and Commitment," R&D Innovator 5, No. 8 (August 1996).

9. Thomas H. Davenport and Laurence Prusak, *Working Knowledge* (Boston: Harvard Business School Press, 2000).

10. Jim Harris, Ibid.

11. Ken Blanchard, Alan Randolph, and Peter Grazier, *Go Team: Take Your Team to the Next Level* (San Francisco: Berrett-Koehler, 2005).

12. Ken Blanchard, Jim Ballard, and Fred Finch, *Customer Mania!: It's Never Too Late to Build a Customer-Focused Company* (New York: Simon & Schuster/Free Press, 2004).

13. Barney Bunnell and Marcelina Gilliam, two of the shift leaders, presented this story with Don Carew at the 2000 Blanchard Client Conference. They received a standing ovation.

Chapter 4

1. Situational Leadership® was originally created by Ken Blanchard and Paul Hersey at Ohio University in 1968. This leadership model gained prominence in 1969 in the authors' classic text *Management of Organizational Behavior*, now in its tenth edition. In the early 1980s Ken Blanchard and the founding associates of The Ken Blanchard Companies®—Margie Blanchard, Don Carew, Eunice Parisi-Carew, Fred Finch, Drea Zigarmi, and Patricia Zigarmi—created SLII®. *Leadership and the One Minute Manager*, coauthored by Ken Blanchard, Drea Zigarmi, and Patricia Zigarmi, presents the SLII® model in parable format, making it easily accessible for managers everywhere.

2. Derived from Leadership Behavior Analysis II (LBAII), an instrument designed to measure both self and others' perceptions of leader flexibility, as well as the leader's effectiveness at choosing an appropriate leadership style. Drea Zigarmi, Carl Edeburn, and Ken Blanchard, *Getting to Know the LBAII: Research, Validity, and Reliability of the Self and Other Forms*, 4th Edition (Escondido, CA: The Ken Blanchard Companies®, 1997).

3. The application of the original SLII® model was advanced when Don Carew and Eunice Parisi-Carew developed the team leadership program; Susan Fowler and Laurie Hawkins championed Self Leadership; and Drea Zigarmi, Pat Zigarmi, and Judd Hoekstra focused energy on organizational leadership.

Chapter 5

1. Marques-Quinterio and Curral, "Goal Orientation and Work Role Performance: Predicting Adaptive and Proactive Work Role Performance Through Self-Leadership Strategies," *The Journal of Psychology* (2012).

2. See the HPO SCORES® model in Chapter 1, "Is Your Organization High Performing?"

3. Ken Blanchard, Jim Ballard, and Fred Finch, *Customer Mania!: It's Never Too Late to Build a Customer Focused Company* (New York: Simon & Schuster/Free Press, 2004).

4. Jim Belasco and Ralph Stayer, *Flight of the Buffalo: Soaring to Excellence, Learning to Let Employees Lead* (New York: Warner Books, 1994).

5. Robert Slater, *The New GE: How Jack Welch Revived an American Institution* (New York: McGraw-Hill, 1993).

6. Based on the Self Leadership program, which was developed to teach SLII® skills to direct reports and other associates.

7. Ken Blanchard, Susan Fowler, and Laurence Hawkins, *Self Leadership and The One Minute Manager* (New York: William Morrow, 2004).

8. Baltasar Gracian, *The Art of Worldly Wisdom*, 1647.

Chapter 6

1. Ken Blanchard and Garry Ridge, *Helping People Win at Work: A Business Philosophy Called "Don't Mark My Paper, Help Me Get an A"* (Upper Saddle River, NJ: Pearson-Prentice Hall, 2009).

2. Jim Belasco and Ralph Stayer, *Flight of the Buffalo: Soaring to Excellence, Learning to Let Employees Lead* (New York: Warner Books, 1994).

3. Doing an Internet search for "handling performance problems" provides excellent insight into the content of the literature and training programs.

4. Marjorie Blanchard and Garry Demarest, *One on One Conversations* (Escondido, CA: The Ken Blanchard Companies®, 2000).

Chapter 7

1. Ken Blanchard and Spencer Johnson, *The One Minute Manager* (New York: William Morrow, 1982 and 2003).

2. An introduction to the research on goal setting can be found in E. A. Locke and G. P. Latham, *Goal Setting: A Motivational Tool That Works* (New Jersey: Prentice Hall, 1984). Two excellent quick summaries can be found in Gary P. Latham, "The Motivational Benefits of Goal Setting" (New York: *Academy of Management Executive,* 2004, Vol. 18, No. 4, pp. 126–129). Also see Stephan Kerr and Landauer Steffen, "Using Stretch Goals to Promote Organizational Effectiveness and Personal Growth" (New York: *Academy of Management Executive,* 2004, Vol. 18, No. 4, pp. 134–138).

3. Scott Meyers, *Every Employee a Manager* (New York: McGraw-Hill, 1970).

4. Gerard Seijts and Gary Latham, "Learning Versus Performance Goals: When Should Each Be Used?" (New York: *Academy of Management Executive,* 2004, Vol. 18, No. 4, pp. 124–131).

5. David McClelland, J. W. Atkinson, R. A. Clark, and E. L. Lowell, *The Achievement Motive* (Princeton: Van Nostrand, 1953).

6. "Management by Wandering Around" was developed by executives at Hewlett-Packard in the 1970s. It was popularized in a book written by Tom Peters and Robert Waterman in the early 1980s, *In Search of Excellence*. Their research revealed that managers of the most successful companies in America stayed close to the customers and the people doing the work; they were involved in rather than isolated from the business's daily routines.

7. Ken Blanchard and Margret McBride, *The Fourth Secret of the One Minute Manager: A Powerful Way to Make Things Better* (New York: William Morrow, 2008). William Morrow originally published this book in 2003 as *The One Minute Apology*.

Chapter 8

1. "Employee Trust & Workplace Performance," *Journal of Economic Behavior and Organization*, Vol. 116, August 2015, pp. 361–378.

2. "Americans Still Lack Trust in Company Management Post Recession," Maritz.com, July 8, 2011, https://www.businesswire.com/news/home/20100414006552/en/Managing-Era-Mistrust-Maritz-Poll-Reveals-Employees.

3. MasteryWorks survey discussion can be found online at http://www.masteryworks.com/newsite/clientimpact/impact_archives_oct09.htm.

4. https://vtshrm.shrm.org/sites/vtshrm.shrm.org/files/Blanchard-Building-Trus.pdf.

5. Ken Blanchard, Cynthia Olmstead, and Martha Lawrence, *Trust Works: Four Keys to Building Lasting Relationships* (New York: William Morrow, 2013).

6. https://www.rollingstone.com/culture/news/steve-jobs-in-1994-the-rolling-stone-interview-20110117

7. https://www.bkconnection.com/home/find-what-you-need/welcome-authors?redirected=true

8. http://www.patagonia.com/footprint.html

9. https://www.wsj.com/articles/why-one-company-invites-all-employees-to-board-meetings-1509028866

10. https://www.americanbanker.com/news/reputation-reboot-how-synovus-got-its-good-name-back

Chapter 9

1. "Coaching: A Global Study of Successful Practices," American Management Association, 2008, www.amanet.org/research/.

2. Goldsmith, "Retain Your Top Performers," Marshall Goldsmith Library online (http://www.marshallgoldsmith.com/articles/retain-your-top-performers/).

3. Madeleine Homan and Linda J. Miller, *Coaching in Organizations: Best Coaching Practices from The Ken Blanchard Companies*® (Hoboken, NJ: John Wiley & Sons, 2008).

Chapter 10

1. *The Chronicle of Evidence-Based Mentoring*, June 2016, https://chronicle.umbmentoring.org/four-ways-mentoring-benefits-mentor/.

2. Ken Blanchard and Claire Díaz-Ortiz, *One Minute Mentoring: How to Find and Work with a Mentor—and Why You'll Benefit from Being One* (New York: William Morrow, 2016).

3. Ibid.

4. Ken Blanchard, *It Takes Less Than a Minute to Suit Up for the Lord* (Mechanicsburg, PA: Executive Books, 2004).

Chapter 11

1. https://trainingmag.com/trgmag-article/work-team-training-and-performance-gaps/.

2. http://marketing.bersin.com/rs/976-LMP-699/images/HRTechDisruptions2018-Report-100517.pdf

3. C. Southers, E. Parisi-Carew, and D. Carew, *Virtual Teams Handbook* (Escondido, CA: The Ken Blanchard Companies®, 2002).

4. J. V. Johnson, W. Stewart, and E. M. Hall, "Long Term Psychological Work Environment and Cardiovascular Mortality," *American Journal of Public Health* (March 1996).

5. J. Despain and J. B. Converse, *And Dignity for All* (New Jersey: Financial Times/Prentice-Hall, 2003).

6. B. Tuckman, "Developmental Sequence in Small Groups," *Psychological Bulletin*, 1964; R. B. Lacoursiere, *The Life Cycle of Groups: Group Development Stage Theory* (New York: Human Science Press, 1980); J. Stoner and D. Carew, "Stages of Group Development and Indicators of Excellence" (unpublished manuscript, 1991); S. A. Whelan and J. M. Hochberger, "Validation Studies of Group Development Questionnaire" (Thousand Oaks, CA: Small Group Research, 1996).

7. Adapted from R. B. Lacoursiere, Ibid.

8. ABC Video Enterprises, *Do You Believe in Miracles?*, 1981. Also, Disney's *Miracle* is a 2004 film that tells the story of Herb Brooks and the 1980 U.S. hockey team.

Chapter 12

1. http://www.sandiegouniontribune.com/sdut-wildfire-cedar-anniversary-fire-2013oct24-htmlstory.html

2. https://www.nature.org/about-us/working-with-companies/companies-we-work-with/dow/2016-collaboration-report.pdf

3. Ken Blanchard and Garry Ridge, *Helping People Win at Work* (Upper Saddle River, NJ: Pearson, 2009).

4. For more information about the Thomas Kilmann Instrument, visit http://www.kilmanndiagnostics.com/overview-thomas-kilmann-conflict-mode-instrument-tki.

Chapter 13

1. https://www.entrepreneur.com/article/274636

2. Ibid. (©2018 Google LLC All rights reserved. Google and the Google logo are registered trademarks of Google LLC.)

3. http://www.nytimes.com/2011/03/13/business/13hire.html Patagonia's vision, Patagonia Works, 2017, http://www.patagoniaworks.com/press/2017/4/26/rose-marcario-statement-on-trump-national-monuments-executive-order. Property of Patagonia, Inc. Used with permission.

4. https://www.dallasnews.com/business/southwest-airlines/2018/01/19/southwest-airlines-named-among-worlds-10-admired-companies-fortune

5. https://www.entrepreneur.com/article/249174

6. https://hbr.org/2008/03/is-yours-a-learning-organization

7. https://www.shrm.org/resourcesandtools/hr-topics/employee-relations/pages/power-of-employee-engagement.aspx

8. https://www.talkdesk.com/blog/top-10-customer-centric-companies-of-2014

9. Ibid.

10. http://www.businessinsider.com/the-8-worst-companies-for-customer-service-2014-7

11. https://economictimes.indiatimes.com/news/company/corporate-trends/best-companies-to-work-for-2014-adobe-encourages-a-culture-of-free-spirited-innovation/articleshow/37517605.cms?intenttarget=no

12. http://www.businessinsider.com/chevron-best-oil-company-to-work-for-2013-2

13. https://blog.kissmetrics.com/googles-culture-of-success/

14. https://hbr.org/2014/01/how-netflix-reinvented-hr

15. M.A. Huselid, "The Impact of Human Resource Management Practices on Turnover, Productivity, and Corporate Financial Performance," *Academy of Management Journal*, Vol. 38 (1995).

16. http://www.tmcnet.com/channels/customer-support-software/articles/87080-how-southwest-airlines-became-model-customer-loyalty.htm

17. https://www.shrm.org/resourcesandtools/hr-topics/
employee-relations/pages/power-of-employee-engagement
.aspx

18. https://www.investopedia.com/university/carly-
fiorina-biography/

19. https://www.shrm.org/resourcesandtools/hr-topics/labor-
relations/pages/ford-uaw.aspx

Chapter 14

1. International Consortium for Executive Development
Research.

2. Gene E. Hall and Susan Loucks, "Teacher Concerns as a
Basis for Facilitating and Personalizing Staff Development,"
Lieberman and Miller, eds., *Staff Development: New Demands,
New Realities, New Perspectives* (New York: Teachers College
Press, 1978).

3. SAP stands for Systems, Applications, Products. It is a main-
frame system that provides users with a soft real-time business
application.

4. In an interesting development, in 2005 SBC Communications purchased AT&T, thus reuniting the venerable phone
company with three of its offspring. (SBC was composed of
Southwestern Bell, Pacific Telesis, and Ameritech.) The merged
company is named AT&T, Inc.

Chapter 15

1. For some of the pioneering work on change leadership, see
Warren Bennis, *Managing the Dream: Reflections on Leader-
ship and Change* (New York: Perseus Book Group, 2000); John
Kotter, *Leading Change* (Boston: Harvard Business School Press,
1996); and Daryl R. Conner, *Managing at the Speed of Change*
(New York: Random House, 1993).

2. John Maynard Keynes, *The General Theory of Employment,
Interest, and Money* (New York, NY: Harcourt Brace, 1965).

3. Blanchard Change Readiness Survey can be viewed at: http://www.blanchardinternational.com.au/static/uploads/files/lptc-pw-look-inside-wfhrpszpvrrm.pdf

4. Indiana Department of Child Services website: www.in.gov.dcs.

Chapter 16

1. Notable scholars who have contributed to our understanding of culture include Edgar Schein, Jim Collins, John Kotter, James Heskett, Max DePree, Richard Lieder, Stephen Covey, and Jim Kouzes.

2. Ken Blanchard and Sheldon Bowles, *Gung Ho!: Turn On the People in Any Organization* (New York: William Morrow, 1998).

3. This first release of the valued behaviors is called "initial" because it is extremely likely that revision of the values or behaviors will occur as the culture change begins to take hold. In the refinement phase, the senior leadership team continually assesses whether the initial valued behaviors need clarification or modification to better define what a good citizen looks and acts like in their organization.

Chapter 17

1. Rick Sidorowicz, "Back to the Beginning—Core Values," *The CEO Refresher* (Ontario, Canada: Refresher Publications, Inc., 2002).

2. Marshall Goldsmith, "Retain Your Top Performers," Marshall Goldsmith Library online (www.marshallgoldsmithlibrary.com/cim/articles_display.php?aid=162).

3. Ken Blanchard and Sheldon Bowles, *Raving Fans: A Revolutionary Approach to Customer Service* (New York: William Morrow, 1993).

4. Thomas Peters and Nancy Austin, *A Passion for Excellence* (New York: Random House, 1995).

5. Ken Blanchard and Don Shula, *Everyone's a Coach* (Grand Rapids, MI: Zondervan, 1995).

Chapter 18

1. A collection of Greenleaf's most mature writings on the subject can be found in *The Power of Servant Leadership* (San Francisco: Berrett-Koehler, 1998). The Greenleaf Center for Servant Leadership (www.greenleaf.org) is a source of all his writings.

2. Ken Blanchard and Phil Hodges, *Lead Like Jesus: Lessons from the Greatest Leadership Role Model of All Time* (Nashville, TN: Thomas Nelson, 2005).

3. Rick Warren, *The Purpose Driven Life: What on Earth Am I Here For?* (Grand Rapids, MI: Zondervan, 2002).

4. Matt Hayes and Jeff Stevens, *The Heart of Business* (Bloomington, IN: Author House, 2005).

5. Scott Blanchard, Drea Zigarmi, and Vicky Essary, "The Leadership-Profit Chain," *Perspectives* (Escondido, CA: The Ken Blanchard Companies, 2006).

6. Ken Blanchard and Sheldon Bowles, *Gung Ho!: Turn On the People in Any Organization* (New York: William Morrow, 1998).

7. Robert K. Greenleaf, *Servant Leadership: A Journey into the Nature of Legitimate Power and Greatness* (Mahway, NJ: Paulist Press, 1977).

8. Gordon MacDonald, *Ordering Your Private World* (Nashville: Nelson Books, 2003).

9. Robert Greenleaf, *The International Journal of Servant Leadership*, Vol. 1, No. 1 (Spokane, WA: 2006).

10. Robert S. McGee, *The Search for Significance* (Nashville, TN: W. Publishing Group, 2003).

11. Jim Collins, *Good to Great: Why Some Companies Make the Leap—and Others Don't* (New York: Harper Collins, 2001).

12. Ken Blanchard and Norman Vincent Peale, *The Power of Ethical Management* (New York: William Morrow, 1988).

13. Fred Smith, *You and Your Network* (Mechanicsburg, PA: Executive Books, 1998).

14. Richard Bolles, *What Color Is Your Parachute?* (New York, NY: Ten Speed Press, 1970, 2018).

15. Ken Blanchard and Mark Miller, *The Secret: What Great Leaders Know and Do* (San Francisco: Berrett-Koehler, 2004 and 2009).

16. Barbara Gellerman, "How Bad Leadership Happens," *Leader to Leader*, No. 35 (Winter 2005).

17. Drea Zigarmi, et al., *The Leader Within: Learning Enough About Yourself to Lead Others* (Upper Saddle River, NJ: Prentice-Hall, 2004).

18. M. A. Huselid, "The Impact of Human Resource Management Practices on Turnover, Productivity, and Corporate Financial Performance," *Academy of Management Journal*, 38 (1995).

19. E. Trist, "The Evolution of Socio-Technical Systems," Ontario Quality of Working Life Centre, 1981.

20. Bob Buford, *Halftime* (Grand Rapids, MI: Zondervan, 1997).

Chapter 19

1. Noel Tichy, *The Leadership Engine: How Winning Companies Build Leaders at Every Level* (New York: HarperCollins, 1997).

Acknowledgments

This is one of the biggest and most significant writing projects in which I have ever been involved. As I indicate in the Introduction, this book pulls together the thinking from The Ken Blanchard Companies® over the past 40 years. This certainly wasn't a solo flight. Many people contributed to bringing to reality the dream of *Leading at a Higher Level*.

Let me start with my coauthors. The idea for creating an organization where *we could work with people we love and care about and make a difference in organizations* was born in the early 1970s by eight of us who were faculty members or doctoral students at the University of Massachusetts in Amherst. This group, including **Margie** and me, **Don Carew**, **Eunice Parisi-Carew**, **Fred Finch**, **Laurie Hawkins**, **Drea Zigarmi**, and **Pat Zigarmi**, is what we call the Founding Associates of The Ken Blanchard Companies®.

In the early 1980s, this group created SLII®, which is the cornerstone of the Blanchard leadership programs. These Founding Associates are the people I went to when I first thought of writing this book. Without their encouragement and important contributions, this book would have remained a dream.

After the Founding Associates got underway on the book, we invited a number of other consulting partners and associates to join us in writing it because of the major part they have played in the development of our work. Big hugs and appreciation to **Scott Blanchard**, **Randy Conley**, **Kathy Cuff**, **Garry Demarest**, **Claire Díaz-Ortiz**, **Chris Edmonds**, **Susan Fowler**, **Bob Glaser**, **Vicki Halsey**, **Judd Hoekstra**, **Fay Kandarian**, **Linda Miller**, **Alan Randolph**, **Jane Ripley**, and **Jesse Stoner**, who have made important contributions to this book.

One other writer was instrumental in this book's becoming a reality. Without **Martha Lawrence**, the executive editor on my team, we would still be talking about this book. She made it happen. She nurtured every section, every chapter, and every word. Martha and I could never do what we do without the support of the other members of our team: **Margery Allen**, **Anna Espino**, and **Renee Broadwell**.

They all light up my life. Plus, heartfelt thanks to our talented artist, Patrick Peña, whose illustrations grace this book.

Another Blanchard person has been key to the creation of this book. **Richard Andrews** is a miracle worker when it comes to writing win-win contracts. He has been a champion in making sure that our intellectual property is protected.

A huge thank-you to the top-notch publishing team at Pearson: **Laura Norman**, **Lori Lyons**, and **Karen Gill Davis**.

I have had the pleasure of coauthoring books with a number of other authors. Several deserve special mention:

Spencer Johnson, my coauthor on *The One Minute Manager*, the book that catapulted my career and our company to a new level.

Sheldon Bowles, my coauthor on *Raving Fans* and *Gung Ho!*, two bestsellers that have taken our company in new directions.

Jim Ballard, a key writing partner who worked with me on *Managing by Values* (coauthored with Michael O'Connor), *Everyone's a Coach* (coauthored with Don Shula), and *The Heart of a Leader*. We also wrote two books together: *Whale Done!* (coauthored with Thad Lacinak and Chuck Thompkins) and *Customer Mania!* (coauthored with Fred Finch). Jim has made me a better writer and has been a constant spiritual encourager.

Bob Lorber, my coauthor on *Putting the One Minute Manager to Work*, the follow-up book that started The One Minute Manager Library.

Margret McBride, my coauthor on *The One Minute Apology* and the literary agent who introduced me to mainstream publishing.

Norman Vincent Peale, my coauthor on *The Power of Ethical Management* and a wonderful inspiration for my spiritual growth.

Phil Hodges, my coauthor on *Leadership by the Book* (with Bill Hybels), *The Servant Leader*, and *Lead Like Jesus*, books that began my writing about Jesus as one of the greatest leadership role models of all time and led to our founding of the Lead Like Jesus ministries.

My work with Spencer, Sheldon, Jim, Bob, Margret, Norman, and Phil is cited throughout this book. They all have had a major impact on my thinking and my life.

About the Authors

Ken Blanchard

With a passion to turn every leader into a servant leader, **Ken Blanchard** shares his inspiring insights with audiences around the world through speeches, consulting services, and bestselling books. Universally characterized by his friends, colleagues, and clients as one of the most influential and compassionate leadership experts in the world, Ken is respected for his lifetime of groundbreaking research and  thought leadership. In fact, few people have influenced the day-to-day management of people and companies more than Ken Blanchard.

He is the cofounder and chief spiritual officer of The Ken Blanchard Companies®, an international management training and consulting firm that he and his wife, Margie Blanchard, established in 1979 in San Diego, California. He is also cofounder of Lead Like Jesus, a worldwide organization committed to helping people become servant leaders. He is a trustee emeritus of the Board of Trustees at his alma mater, Cornell University, and he also teaches students in the Master of Science in Executive Leadership Program at the University of San Diego.

Ken's impact as an author is far reaching. *The One Minute Manager®*—the iconic 1982 classic that he coauthored with Spencer Johnson—sold more than 15 million copies and in 2015 was revised and released as *The New One Minute Manager®*. Ken has authored or coauthored 65 books whose combined sales total more than 22 million copies. His groundbreaking works—including *Raving Fans, The Secret,* and *Leading at a Higher Level,* to name just a few—have been translated into 47 languages. In 2005 Ken was inducted into Amazon's Hall of Fame as one of the top 25 bestselling authors of all time.

Ken has received many awards and honors for his contributions in the fields of management, leadership, and speaking, including the Council of Peers Award of Excellence from the National Speakers Association, induction into the HRD Hall of Fame by *Training* magazine and Lakewood Conferences, the Golden Gavel Award from Toastmasters International, and the Thought Leadership Award by ISA—The Association of Learning Providers.

Born in New Jersey and raised in New York, Ken received his master's degree from Colgate University and his bachelor's and doctorate degrees from Cornell University. He lives with his wife, Margie, in San Diego, California.

Marjorie Blanchard

Dr. Marjorie "Margie" Blanchard has earned a reputation worldwide as a compelling motivational speaker, an accomplished management consultant and trainer, a best-selling author, and an entrepreneur. She was the corecipient, with her husband, Dr. Ken Blanchard, of the Entrepreneur of the Year award from Cornell University.

Coauthor of *The One Minute Manager Balances Work and Life* and *Working Well: Managing for Health and High Performance*, as well as contributor to *Servant Leadership in Action: How You Can Achieve Great Relationships and Results*, Dr. Blanchard is well versed in a variety of topics. She often speaks on leadership, work/life integration, managing change, and life planning. As cofounder and past president of The Ken Blanchard Companies, she works diligently with Ken, developing the company into one of the world's premier management consulting and training companies.

For fifteen years, Dr. Blanchard was head of the firm's Office of The Future—a think tank charged with helping to shape the future of both the training industry and the company. Today she directs the Blanchard Institute, a public nonprofit committed to building resilience in our youth through strong self-leadership skills.

Dr. Blanchard received her bachelor's and master's degrees from Cornell University and her doctorate from the University of Massachusetts. Along with Ken, she teaches a course in leadership for the Master of Science in Executive Leadership program at the University of San Diego.

Madeleine Homan Blanchard

Madeleine Homan Blanchard is a Master Certified Coach for The Ken Blanchard Companies®; a cofounder of Blanchard® Coaching Services; and a co-creator of the Coaching Management System, Blanchard's Internet platform that supports large-scale coaching initiatives. With her deep understanding of human behavior and her humor, she inspires leaders to use coaching concepts to increase their effectiveness in their professional and personal lives.

Madeleine has more than 30 years of experience in the coaching profession and specializes in consulting with companies that want to establish a coaching culture. She can design large-scale implementations, provide mentoring and executive coaching, and teach leaders to leverage the best of coaching technology. Her areas of expertise are leadership presence and effectiveness, self-awareness and impact with others, and strategic focus. Madeleine is a coauthor of Blanchard's coaching skills program, Coaching Essentials®, and the books *Leverage Your Best, Ditch the Rest: The Coaching Secrets Executives Depend On*; *Coaching in Organizations*; *Leading at a Higher Level*; and *Coaching for Leadership: The Practice of Leadership Coaching from the World's Greatest Coaches*.

A pioneer in the coaching profession, Madeleine was a senior leader and founding advisory board member of Coach University and a founding board member of The International Coach Federation. Prior to her career at The Ken Blanchard Companies, she founded Straightline Coaching, a company devoted to the success and satisfaction of creative geniuses. She spent two years as the director for a coaching program that was rolled out to 2,100 individuals at Goldman Sachs.

Madeleine received her master's of science degree in neuroleadership from Middlesex University and her bachelor's degree in theater and performance studies from Georgetown University. She is a Certified Mentor Coach and a graduate of Coach University.

Scott Blanchard

Scott Blanchard is a stimulating author, motivational speaker, accomplished corporate trainer, and passionate champion of coaching in the workplace. He founded Coaching.com, a Web-enabled corporate coaching and personal development service. Under his leadership, his organization is revolutionizing corporate coaching by offering the most advanced, accessible, and research-driven services in the industry.  His personal philosophy is based on a fundamental shift occurring in the discipline of leadership: Great leaders do not succeed by doing what they are good at; instead, they succeed by getting things done with and through others.

Blanchard is senior vice president of The Ken Blanchard Companies®. As a Blanchard family member and part owner, he represents the "next generation" charged with leading the business into the future.

Blanchard is the coauthor of *Leverage Your Best, Ditch the Rest*, a book on corporate coaching. As a senior consulting partner for more than six years, he has led major training interventions at numerous Fortune 500 companies.

Blanchard was educated at Cornell University and received his master's degree in organizational development from American University in Washington, D.C.

Donald K. Carew

Dr. Don Carew is a founding associate of The Ken Blanchard Companies® and a professor emeritus at the University of Massachusetts Amherst. He is an accomplished and respected management consultant, trainer, educator, and author whose primary academic and consulting interests are in the areas of leadership and building high performing teams and organizations.

Dr. Carew met Ken Blanchard when they were young faculty members at Ohio University in 1966. Don moved to the University of Massachusetts in 1969, and Ken joined the faculty in 1970. It was Don Carew's and Eunice Parisi-Carew's research on group development that led the Founding Associates of The Ken Blanchard Companies® to enhance the SLII® model so that it could be used with groups and teams as well as with individuals.

In addition to being a full-time faculty member at the University of Massachusetts, Dr. Carew has been a faculty member at Trenton State University, Princeton University, and the University of San Diego. He is coauthor of two best-selling books: *The One Minute Manager Builds High Performing Teams*, with Ken Blanchard and Eunice Parisi-Carew, and *High Five*, with Ken, Eunice, and Sheldon Bowles. He is also a coauthor of the article "High Performing Organizations: SCORES®."

Dr. Carew holds a bachelor's degree in business from Ohio University, a master's degree in human relations from Ohio University, and a doctorate in counseling psychology from the University of Florida. He is an associate of the NTL Institute and a licensed psychologist in Massachusetts.

Eunice Parisi-Carew

Dr. Eunice Parisi-Carew is the coauthor of three best-selling books: *The One Minute Manager Builds High Performing Teams*, with Ken Blanchard and Don Carew; *High Five*, with Ken Blanchard, Don Carew, and Sheldon Bowles, and *Collaboration Begins with You*, with Jane Ripley and Ken Blanchard. She is also cocreator of the High Performing Teams product line offered by The Ken Blanchard Companies®.

An accomplished consultant, trainer, speaker, and practitioner, she has worked with large and small national and international organizations, including Merrill Lynch; AT&T; Hyatt Hotels; Transco Energy Company; and the Environmental Protection Agency. Team building, leadership, organizational culture, and personal development are her focus areas.

Dr. Parisi-Carew has directed the graduate program in team dynamics at the University of Hartford, and she was a part-time faculty member at American University. She is currently teaching team leadership part-time at the University of San Diego business school. She is also a faculty member at NTL Institute and has served on their board of directors.

Dr. Parisi-Carew has served The Ken Blanchard Companies as vice president of professional services and as senior researcher with the Office of the Future, which studies trends that occur three to five years out and how they might impact leaders, organizations, and business practices.

She received her doctorate in the behavioral sciences from the University of Massachusetts and is a licensed psychologist and certified international OD consultant.

Randy Conley

Randy Conley is the vice president of client services and trust practice leader for The Ken Blanchard Companies®. He oversees Blanchard's client delivery operations and works with organizations around the globe, helping them build trust in the workplace. Trust Across America named him a Top Thought Leader in trustworthy business behavior, and he is a founding member of the Alliance of Trustworthy Business Experts. Inc.com named Randy a Top 100 Leadership Speaker & Thinker, and the American Management Association included him in its Leaders to Watch in 2015 list. Randy is the author of the award-winning "Leading with Trust" blog (www.leadingwithtrust.com) and a contributing author of the books *Trust, Inc.: Strategies for Building Your Company's Most Valuable Asset* and *Trust, Inc.: 52 Weeks of Activities and Inspirations for Building Workplace Trust.* He holds a master's degree in executive leadership from the University of San Diego and enjoys spending time with his family, cycling, and playing golf. You can follow Randy on Twitter @RandyConley.

Kathleen Riley Cuff

Kathy Cuff is an energetic motivational speaker, trainer, and consultant for many organizations. The enthusiasm and humor she brings to every presentation are complemented by her positive attitude and sincere commitment to meeting the specific needs of each client.

For twenty-two years Cuff has been with the Ken Blanchard Companies®, where she now serves as a senior consulting partner. Drawing from her broad base of experience in leadership, management, and customer service, she has designed and implemented training and consulting projects for a client list that includes Charles Schwab, Medtronic, TaylorMade-Adidas Golf, and W.L. Gore.

She is the coauthor of *Legendary Service: The Key is to Care* and The Ken Blanchard Companies'® Legendary Service customer service program, as well as coauthor of the revised Raving Fans® program.

Cuff received her degree from San Diego State University and has participated in numerous educational seminars and programs over the years.

Garry Demarest

Garret Demarest is a highly skilled educator with more than forty years of experience managing, teaching, counseling, and consulting in a variety of occupational settings. His special areas of expertise are leadership training, human development, interpersonal skills training, values-based organizational culture development, team development, and empowerment. More recently he has become inspired in helping leaders formulate and present their leadership point of view.

With his diverse background, Garry is especially effective in helping individuals combine human values and interpersonal skills with leadership and effective management. He is vitally concerned with raising self-esteem in the workplace, addressing the needs of a diverse workforce, and empowering people toward greater levels of self-responsibility. He is committed to developing the leader within every individual and leading at higher level.

As a consultant and trainer, Garry has worked with a variety of small and medium-sized businesses in building organizational values-based cultures, leadership training, team building, customer service, and employee wellness. An associate with The Ken Blanchard Companies® since 1988, he previously served as a dean of students and a college counselor and administrator. He has also managed two hospital-based wellness programs.

His forty years of experience with the Myers-Briggs Type Indicator® have given Garry a unique understanding of individual differences and the ability to use those differences to create strong working relationships and teams.

Garry received a bachelor's degree in hotel administration from Cornell University and a master's degree in education from Michigan State University.

Claire Díaz-Ortiz

Claire Díaz-Ortiz is an author, speaker, and technology innovator who has been named one of the 100 Most Creative People in Business by *Fast Company*. She was an early employee at Twitter, where she spent five and a half years, and is the author of seven books, including *Twitter for Good: Change the World One Tweet at a Time; Design Your Day: Be More Productive,*

Set Better Goals, and Live Life on Purpose; Hope Runs: An American Tourist, a Kenyan Boy, a Journey of Redemption; and with Ken Blanchard, *One Minute Mentoring: How to Find and Work With a Mentor—and Why You'll Benefit from Being One.* She writes a popular business blog at ClaireDiazOrtiz.com and is the cofounder of Hope Runs, a nonprofit organization operating AIDS orphanages in Kenya.

S. Chris Edmonds

Chris Edmonds is an expert on creating high performing, values-aligned organizational cultures. He serves as an executive coach for senior leaders engaged in culture change initiatives, helping them understand their responsibility to clarify expectations, refine systems, consistently demonstrate desired values, and hold leaders and staff accountable for demonstrating those values.

His clients include American Honda, Clorox, Deloitte, Federal Reserve Bank, Genentech, IBM, Merck, New Belgium Brewery, Northwest Airlines, Pfizer, Taylor Corporation, T-Mobile, Toyota Motor Corporation, and YMCA of the USA.

Mr. Edmonds coauthored Blanchard's culture change process, which is based on Ken Blanchard's bestselling book *Gung Ho!*®. The process was recognized as one of the Top Ten Training Programs of 2000 by *Human Resource Executive* magazine.

A graduate of Whittier College with a degree in education, Mr. Edmonds holds a secondary teaching credential from California Lutheran College. He received his master's degree in human resource and organizational development from the University of San Francisco. He is a faculty member of the Master of Science in Executive Leadership program at the University of San Diego.

Fred Finch

Dr. Fred Finch is the author of *Managing for Organizational Effectiveness: An Experiential Approach*. A founding associate of The Ken Blanchard Companies®, he has been a consultant and leadership educator at Harvard University, Merrill Lynch, IBM, Shell International, and many other high-profile organizations. He received his doctorate from the Graduate School of Business at the University of Washington. He served as a professor of management and organizational behavior for 14 years in the Graduate School of Management at the University of Massachusetts.

Dr. Finch is coauthor with Ken Blanchard and Jim Ballard of *Customer Mania! It's Never Too Late to Build a Customer-Focused Company*. This book grew out of a study of Yum! Brands, the world's largest quick-service restaurant corporation, with 850,000 employees in more than 100 countries. He is also coauthor with Pat Stewart of Frontline Leadership, a popular training program for frontline leaders.

Susan Fowler

Susan Fowler is coauthor with Ken Blanchard and Laurence Hawkins of *Self Leadership and the One Minute Manager*, published in 2005. With Ken Blanchard and Laurence Hawkins, she created and is the lead developer of Self Leadership®, a best-of-class self leadership and personal empowerment program.

Fowler received the Lifetime Achievement Award for creative training designs from the North American Society for Games and Simulations. As a senior consulting partner with The Ken Blanchard Companies®, Fowler has consulted with Pfizer, Harley Davidson, MasterCard, AMF Bowling, Dow Chemical, KPMG, Black & Decker, SC Johnson, TJX Retailers, the National Basketball Association, and dozens of other clients. Prior to that, she gained worldwide seminar presentation experience with CareerTrack.

Fowler brings a unique perspective to her programs from her extensive experience in advertising and television and radio broadcasting. She received her degree in marketing from the University of Colorado. As one of the world's foremost experts on personal empowerment, she has delivered training seminars, workshops, and keynote speeches to more than 50,000 people in over 20 countries and in all 50 states.

Her publications include *Optimal Motivation: Why Motivating People Doesn't Work...and What Does; Overcoming Procrastination; Mentoring; The Team Leader's Idea-a-Day Guide* (coauthored with Drea Zigarmi); and *Empowerment* (coauthored with Ken Blanchard). Fowler also serves as an adjunct professor in the University of San Diego's Master of Science in Executive Leadership program.

Robert Glaser

Robert Glaser is a regional consulting partner at The Ken Blanchard Companies® and has been a member of the consulting partner group for 13 years. He has a 30-year track record of successfully facilitating leadership development, team development, strategic planning, performance consulting, organizational change, and organizational culture change.

Prior to joining Blanchard, Glaser worked for more than 20 years in a Fortune 500 restaurant chain based in San Diego, where he was the director of management and leadership development.

Glaser is an adjunct faculty member at the University of San Diego's Master of Science in Executive Leadership program. He is also coauthor of Blanchard's Gung Ho!® culture change program and process.

He has extensive international and cross-cultural experience and served for four years in the Peace Corps in Ghana and Uganda.

Glaser received his bachelor's degree in social science from California State University at Chico and his master's degree in leadership studies from the University of San Diego.

Lael W. Good

Lael Good serves as a lead consultant on many of Blanchard's largest multinational client initiatives, including Coca-Cola, Diageo, Mars/Masterfoods, MTN South Africa, Nokia, Pfizer Pharmaceuticals, Royal Dutch Shell, SAP, and Skanska. She is one of the most requested and respected consulting partners because her unique skill set enables her to work with global organizations in places as diverse as Western and Eastern Europe, Central and Latin America, Africa, China, India, and the Middle East.

She is coauthor of two Blanchard programs—Team Leadership, with Don Carew and Eunice Parisi-Carew, and The Leadership Bridge: SLII® and MBTI®, with Tom Hill and Ken Blanchard. She also is an expert on the dynamics of high performing teams.

Working with global clients, Good provides customized design, delivery, and sustainability solutions. Her capabilities in and knowledge of organizational development and instructional design complement her natural ability to influence and involve people in solving their own problems.

Good received her bachelor's degree in counseling from the University of Arizona and her master's degree in counseling psychology from the University of Wyoming.

Dr. Vicki Halsey

Dr. Vicki Halsey is a spirited speaker, author, coach, and trainer whose lively presentations promote learning and captivate audiences worldwide. Her mission of inspiring others to claim their greatness is achieved through blending solutions that meet the needs of all learners.

As vice president of applied learning for The Ken Blanchard Companies®, Dr. Halsey specializes in partnering with organizations to design, deliver, and coach people through interactive workshops, keynotes, webinars, and blended classroom and virtual trainings. She is the coauthor of Blanchard's Legendary Customer Service program as well as the award-winning blended SLII® training. Her clients include Fortune 100 companies such as Nike, Gap, Wells Fargo, Oracle, and Procter & Gamble. In addition, Dr. Halsey is cocreator of the highly acclaimed Master of Science in Executive

Leadership and EMBA degree programs for the University of San Diego and Grand Canyon University, respectively.

She is the author of *Brilliance by Design: Creating Learning Experiences That Connect, Inspire, and Engage.* She is also a coauthor of *Legendary Service: The Key Is to Care; The Hamster Revolution: How to Manage Your Email Before It Manages You;* and *The Hamster Revolution for Meetings: How to Meet Less and Get More Done.*

Laurence Hawkins

Dr. Laurence Hawkins is one of the founding associates of The Ken Blanchard Companies®, as well as an internationally renowned management consultant and motivational speaker. With Ken Blanchard and Susan Fowler, he coauthored the Self Leadership program, which focuses on empowerment and taking initiative when you're not in charge. He is also the coauthor with Ken and Susan of *Self Leadership and the One Minute Manager*, published in 2005.

Dr. Hawkins has concentrated much of his work on aerospace, particularly Lockheed Martin and McDonnell Douglas, and pharmaceutical giants such as Pfizer, Merck, and GlaxoSmithKline. He has focused his career on applying the Blanchard standards of SLII®, Team Leadership, and Self Leadership in the international arena, concentrating on Europe, South America, and Saudi Arabia. More recently, he has been teaching the tools, concepts, and philosophy of self leadership to clients in China and Korea—countries where obedience is rapidly shifting to a culture of entrepreneurship and taking initiative.

Dr. Hawkins received his bachelor's degree in American history and literature from Williams College and his master's and doctorate degrees in leadership and organizational behavior from the University of Massachusetts Amherst.

Judd Hoekstra

Judd Hoekstra is one of Blanchard's experts in organizational change and is coauthor of its Managing a Change consulting methodology and training program. His approach to change is based on a shared commitment to Dr. Don Carew's principle that people have a right to be involved in decisions that affect their lives and the concept that those who plan the battle rarely battle the plan.

He is the coauthor of *Who Killed Change?: Solving the Mystery of Leading People Through Change* and *Crunch Time: How To Be Your Best When It Matters Most.*

Prior to joining Blanchard in 2001, Hoekstra served as a strategy execution consultant with Fourth Floor Consulting. Before that, he was a change management consultant with Accenture. He was primarily responsible for helping client executives lead their organizations through large-scale changes. His experience crosses a number of industries; his clients have included The Dow Chemical Company, Allstate Insurance Company, Anheuser-Busch, and Commonwealth Edison.

Hoekstra received his bachelor's in business management and marketing from Cornell University and graduated from the Advanced Business Management Program at Kellogg Graduate School of Management. He and his wife, Sherry, live in the Chicago area and are the proud parents of Julia and Cole.

Fay Kandarian

Dr. Fay Kandarian has worked as both an internal and an independent organizational change consultant over the past 20 years. She has been a consulting partner with The Ken Blanchard Companies® since 1998.

Her extensive line, staff, and executive experiences provide constant reference points that inform her consulting. Her areas of expertise include whole systems change, executive coaching, strategic planning, intervention design, leadership and team development, communications skills, and process consultation.

While doing doctoral research at Columbia University's Department of Organization and Leadership, Dr. Kandarian studied and developed proficiency in using large-group interventions as a new paradigm for organization development and large-scale change. She researched Polarity Management (B. Johnson, 1996) as a training intervention to help teach systems thinking skills. She later introduced Polarity Management's "both/and" thinking to The Ken Blanchard Companies®.

Working with fellow HPO team members Jesse Stoner, Eunice Parisi-Carew, and Don Carew, she helped create the HPO SCORES® Model and coauthored the article "High Performing Organizations: SCORES®."

She holds a bachelor's from George Washington University, a master's in business from the University of New Haven, and a master's and doctorate in education from Columbia University.

Linda Miller

Linda J. Miller is an executive coach, trainer, and keynote speaker who has a passion for people taking effective, intentional action. She helped launch Corporate Coach U, a leader in organizational coach training. Since 2000, she has served as global liaison for coaching with The Ken Blanchard Companies®. In 2002, Miller coauthored Coaching Essentials for Leaders, a coach training program that encourages leaders to use coaching skills to create strong business alliances.

Miller also coaches executives and helps organizations establish internal coaching cultures. Her client list includes leaders and their teams from Adobe, Alltel, Boeing, Deloitte, Duke Energy, Franklin Templeton, KPMG, Nissan, Pfizer, SAP, Scotia Bank Wells Fargo, and the University of Washington. She co-led a team that moderated thirteen of the Arizona state legislative debates in collaboration with the Arizona Clean Elections Commission during the 2008 election cycle.

As a founding recipient of the Master Certified Coach designation from the International Coach Federation, Miller has been featured in numerous articles and television news segments on coaching. She is coauthor with Madeleine Homan Blanchard of *Coaching in Organizations: Best Coaching Practices* from The Ken Blanchard Companies®.

Alan Randolph

Dr. Alan Randolph is an internationally respected and highly accomplished management educator, researcher, and consultant. His work focuses on empowerment, leadership, teamwork, and project management issues for both domestic and international organizations in the public and private sectors. He has worked in a variety of countries, including most recently Peru, Brazil, China, Germany, France, and Poland.

Dr. Randolph is a professor emeritus of management and international business at the Merrick School of Business at the University of Baltimore. He also is a senior consulting partner with The Ken Blanchard Companies®. He has developed a variety of leadership and empowerment educational products. He has also published numerous articles in practitioner and academic journals such as *Harvard Business Review* and *Sloan Management Review*.

Dr. Randolph has written and coauthored a number of books, including *Go Team!: Take Your Team to the Next Level, Checkered Flag Projects: 10 Rules for Creating and Managing Projects That Win!, Empowerment Takes More Than a Minute,* and *The 3 Keys to Empowerment: Release the Power Within People for Astonishing Results.*

Jane Ripley

Jane Ripley is co-founder of WiredLeaders .com, a leadership development company focusing on collaboration. Her work life has been shaped by three significant experiences relating to leadership and collaboration: watching her father struggle in his career, serving as an officer in the British Army, and working with The Ken Blanchard Companies®.

In 2012, Ripley enrolled at the Kingston Business School to earn an MSC in business psychology. For her dissertation, she chose the topic of collaboration and a case study approach based within an analytical instruments company, which had "implemented" collaboration but was not seeing the hoped for results. Her research led to the writing of *Collaboration Begins With You* with Eunice Parisi-Carew and Ken Blanchard.

Jesse Stoner

Dr. Jesse Lyn Stoner is one of the foremost experts on helping leaders create a shared vision and the strategies to achieve it. For over twenty-five years she has worked closely with leaders in hundreds of organizations using collaborative processes to engage the entire workforce in creating their desired future.

Coauthor with Ken Blanchard of the international bestseller *Full Steam Ahead: Unleash the Power of Vision in Your Work and Your Life*—as well as several materials in Blanchard's Team Leadership program—her clients include Honda, Marriott, Skanska, Stanley Black & Decker, SAP and T.J. Maxx.

Jesse writes an award-winning leadership blog; she was named a Leader to Watch by the American Management Association, a Top 50 Leadership Expert by INC magazine, and is a recipient of the Conant Leadership Award. Her writing has been featured in *Harvard Business Review, Huffington Post*, and *Forbes*, and she serves on the board of Berrett-Koehler Publishers.

Dr. Stoner received advanced degrees in psychology and a doctorate in organizational development from the University of Massachusetts.

Drea Zigarmi

Formerly president of Zigarmi Associates, Inc., **Dr. Drea Zigarmi** is the director of research and development for The
Ken Blanchard Companies®. His work has
been critical to the company's success
with its clients. Almost every product that
has been developed at The Ken Blanchard
Companies® over the past 20 years has
Zigarmi's mark on it. He coauthored with
Ken Blanchard the well-known Leader
Behavior Analysis instrument and the
Development Task Analysis form used in
all SLII® seminars.

He has coauthored three books: *The Leader Within: Learning Enough
About Yourself to Lead Others*, *The Team Leader's Idea-a-Day Guide*, and
Leadership and the One Minute Manager.

He received his bachelor's in science from Norwich University. He
earned a master's in philosophy and a doctorate in administration and
organizational behavior from the University of Massachusetts Amherst.

Patricia Zigarmi

Dr. Patricia Zigarmi is a founding
associate of The Ken Blanchard
Companies®. She is a speaker, consultant,
product designer, business developer,
account strategist, trainer, and team
builder for many of Blanchard's clients
and is a mentor to many colleagues at
Blanchard.

Dr. Zigarmi is coauthor of *Leadership
and the One Minute Manager*. She also designed Blanchard's premier product line, SLII®. With her leadership, ongoing initiatives for
SLII® training and coaching have been negotiated with many global
companies and most of the Fortune 500 companies. She is also the
author of Blanchard's Managing a Change program and a number of

performance management products on Giving Feedback and Monitoring and Reviewing Performance.

Dr. Zigarmi has taught Managing a Change for the Masters in Executive Excellence program at the University of San Diego. In addition, she is a member of the San Diego Women's Foundation.

She received her bachelor's in sociology from Northwestern University and her doctorate in leadership and organizational behavior from the University of Massachusetts Amherst.

Services Available

The Ken Blanchard Companies® is the global leader in management training. For 40 years, Blanchard® has been creating the best managers in the world, training over 150,000 people each year. From the award-winning First-time Manager program—based on the best-selling business book, *The New One Minute Manager*®, to SLII®, the most widely taught leadership model in the world, Blanchard is the provider of choice of Fortune 500 companies as well as small to medium businesses, governments, and educational and nonprofit organizations.

Blanchard programs are based on the evidence that people are the key to accomplishing strategic objectives and driving business results. They help people develop excellence in leadership, teams, customer loyalty, change management, and performance improvement. The company's continual research points to best practices for workplace improvement. Its world-class trainers and coaches drive organizational and behavioral change at all levels and help people make the shift from learning to doing.

Leadership experts from The Ken Blanchard Companies® are available for workshops, consulting, and keynote addresses on organizational development, workplace performance, and business trends.

Global Headquarters

The Ken Blanchard Companies

125 State Place

Escondido CA 92029

www.kenblanchard.com

1-800-728-6000 in the U.S.

+1-760-489-5005 from anywhere

Keynote Speakers

Blanchard keynote speakers present enduring leadership insights to all types of management-related events, including corporate gatherings and celebrations, association conferences, sales meetings, industry conferences, and executive retreats. Our network of speaking professionals is among the best in the world at engaging audiences to new levels of commitment and enthusiasm.

Blanchard speaker topics include

- Coaching
- Customer loyalty
- Employee engagement
- Leadership
- Motivation and inspiration
- Organizational change
- Public sector leadership
- Team building
- Women in leadership

To book a Blanchard keynote speaker for your next event, please call:

United States: 800-728-6052
United Kingdom: +44-1483-456300
Canada: 800-665-5023
International: 760-489-5005

Or visit www.kenblanchard.com/speakers to learn more and to book your speaker today.

Social Networking

Keep Up with Ken on Twitter

Receive timely messages and thoughts from Ken. Find out the events he's attending and what's on his mind @KenBlanchard.

Visit Blanchard on YouTube

Watch thought leaders from The Ken Blanchard Companies® in action. Link and subscribe to Blanchard's channel, and you'll receive updates as new videos are posted.

Join Ken Blanchard on Facebook

Be part of our inner circle and link to Ken Blanchard on Facebook at https://facebook.com/KenBlanchard. Meet other fans of Ken and his books. Access videos and photos, and get invited to special events.

Join Conversations with Ken Blanchard

Blanchard's blog, HowWeLead.org, was created to inspire positive change. It is a public-service site devoted to leadership topics that connect us all. This site is nonpartisan and secular and does not solicit or accept donations. It is a social network, where you will meet people who care deeply about responsible leadership. And it's a place where Ken Blanchard would like to hear your opinion.

Visit Ken's Website

Learn about Ken and browse his library of more than 65 books at www.kenblanchardbooks.com.

Helping People Win at Work with SLII®

SLII® is the most widely taught leadership model in the world. SLII® provides leaders with a diagnostic approach for creating open communication and developing self-reliance in those they manage. It is designed to increase the frequency and quality of conversations about performance and development. As a result, competence is developed, commitment is gained, and talented individuals are retained.

SLII® is recognized as both a business language and framework for employee development because it works across cultural, linguistic, and geographic barriers. The foundation lies in teaching leaders to diagnose the needs of an individual or team and then use the appropriate leadership style to respond to the needs of the person and situation.

Based on 40 years of research and corporate adoption, SLII® is proven to help develop leaders who excel at goal setting, coaching, performance evaluation, active listening, and proactive problem solving. By creating the systems needed to track performance and partnering, it has allowed users to clarify individual goals and ensure alignment with the organization's goals. In addition, SLII® has helped companies increase the retention of "star" employees, improve individual and organizational development, and improve job satisfaction and morale at all levels.

Contact The Ken Blanchard Companies® at +1-760-489-5005 to find out how your company can develop competence, gain commitment, and retain talent.

Index

Numbers

9/11, 299

A

ABCD Trust model, 120–121, 124, 121,
    126, 128
    ABCD Trust model supportive
        behaviors, 122
    conversations to restore trust, 123–124
    diagnosing weaknesses, 123
    trust levels, assessing, 122–123
accountability, one-on-one leadership,
    104–105
achieving goals, responsibility for, 31
Adobe, 195–196, 197
After Action Review (AAR) process (U.S.
    Army), 194
Alice in Wonderland, 17–18
alignment conversations, 66
alignment phase (cultural
    transformation), 258–260
Allied Signal, 49–50
Amazon, 195
American Banker, 129
American Management Association, 131
Apollo Moon Project, 21–22
apologies, One Minute Apologies,
    116–117
appraisal process (performance),
    restructuring, 47
assumed constraints, challenging,
    72–73
AT&T, 218–219
autonomy, boundaries for, 45–48

B

Ballard, Jim, 90–91
Bandag Manufacturing, 70–71
Banta Catalog Group, 253
Barrett, Colleen, 282, 328
Bay of Pigs, 117
Becker, Huselid and, 197, 309

behaviors
    connected behaviors, 123
    dependable behaviors, 123
Belasco, Jim, 84
Berrett-Koehler Publishers, 125
Bersin, Josh, 156
Bezos, Jeff, 195
Bird, Larry, 161
blame, placing, performance
    coaching, 95
Blanchard, Debbie, 308
Blanchard, Ken, 3, 5–6, 23, 27, 30–31, 41,
    42–43, 49, 53, 72, 83–84, 90–91,
    103, 116, 119–121, 123, 123–124, 126,
    146–151, 155, 161, 199–201, 218,
    218–219, 235, 250, 267, 271–272,
    281–282, 290, 290–292, 293–294, 298,
    302–303, 304, 305, 312, 313–315,
    319, 328
Blanchard, Madeleine, 142
Blanchard, Margie, 101, 148, 199–201,
    299, 312–314
Blanchard, Scott, 294–297, 307
Blanchard Training & Development,
    200–201
Bock, Laszlo, 196
Bolles, Richard, 303
Boston Celtics, 161
bottom line (quadruple), 4, 9
    corporate citizen of choice,
        becoming, 8–9
    employer of choice, becoming, 4–5
    investment of choice, becoming, 6–8
    provider of choice, becoming, 5–6
boundaries for autonomy, 45–48
Bowater Pulp and Paper, 253
Bowles, Sheldon, 5–6, 30–31, 250,
    271–273
Broadwell, Renee, 290
broken trust, repairing, 126–128
Brown, Brené, 328
Brown, Michael, 45
Buffer, 192
Buford, Bob, 150, 311
bureaucracy, change and, 244

Burr, Donald, 274
Bush, George H. W., 19
business case for change, explaining, 233–236

C

called leaders, servant leadership, 299–300
capable but cautious performers (development level), 55, 58, 60, 79–80
career coaching, 132, 137–140
career stages, tailoring mentoring to, 152–154
Carew, Don, 9, 10, 50, 161, 183–184
Carlos, John, 41
Carlzon, Jan, 274
Carnegie, Dale, 76
Caterpillar Track Type Tractors (TTT) division, 161
Cathy, Truett, 150–151
Cedar Rapids fire (2007), 180
change management
    bureaucracy and, 244
    child support collection case study, 230–233, 234, 236, 238
    concerns, 215
        collaboration concerns, 222, 232
        different people at different levels of concern, 223
        impact concerns, 221, 232
        implementation concerns, 220–221, 231–232
        information concerns, 216, 231, 233
        personal concerns, 216–220, 231, 236
        refinement concerns, 222–223, 232–233
    flexibility, 229–230
    high involvement change strategy, 229
    inclusion, importance in change management, 216–220
    influence in, 226–233
    involvement in, 226–233
    Leading People Through Change Model, 225
        Collaborate on Implementation strategy, 236–241
        Expand Involvement and Influence strategy, 226–233
        Explain the Business Case for Change strategy, 233–236
        Explore Possibilities strategy, 245–246
        Make the Change Sustainable strategy, 241–244

loss of control and resistance to change, 227–228
organizational change, 209
    complexity of, 210–211
    concerns, 215–223
    failure of, 212–213
    leading change, importance of, 209–210
    leading change, journey of change, 214
    necessity for, 211
    reinforcing change, 247
Chaparral Steel, 310
cheering (praising), 31, 110–113, 116
Chevron Chemical, 112, 196
Chick-fil-A, 150, 151, 304
child support collection case study, change management, 230–233, 234, 236, 238
Clinton, Bill, 117
closure and team leadership, 175–176
coaching, 131
    applications of, 132–133
    career coaching, 132, 137–140
    defined, 131–132
    development coaching, 132, 135–137
    internal culture of coaching, creating, 132, 142–144
    as leadership style, 58, 59, 65, 79, 89–90, 92–93, 204
    learning, coaching to support, 132, 140–142
    performance, 82, 90–93, 132, 133–135
        declining performance, 93–95
        decommitment, 94–99
        placing blame, 95
    sweet spot, 133
Coaching in Organizations (Blanchard, Miller), 142
Collaborate on Implementation strategy (Leading People Through Change Model), 236–241
collaboration, 179–180, 189
    change management, 222, 232
    Collaborate on Implementation strategy (Leading People Through Change Model), 236–241
    competition versus, 183–184
    cooperation versus, 180
    coordination versus, 179
    defined, 184
    framework of, 181–182
    hands of, 184, 188
    head of, 184, 187
    heart of, 184–185
    reciprocity and, 184

teamwork versus, 180
UNITE Model, The, 185–189
College of Business at the University of
San Diego, 313–314, 321, 323
Collins, Jim, 302
Collins and Porras, 24
commitment, 55
decommitment, handling,
performance coaching, 94–99
performance planning, 85
communication
alignment conversations, 66
Collaborate on Implementation
strategy (Leading People Through
Change Model), 240–241
open communication, organizational
leadership, 192
shared information, 10
of vision, 28
Compaq, 207
compelling vision, 10, 19, 46
cultural transformation, importance
in, 254
culture of greatness, 24
HPO SCORES®, 193
organizational leadership, 193
picture of the future, 21–22
significant purpose, 20–21
values, 22–24
competence, 54–55, 85
competition versus collaboration,
183–184
concerns (change management), 215
collaboration concerns, 222, 232
different people at different levels of
concern, 223
impact concerns, 221, 232
implementation concerns, 220–221,
231–232
information concerns, 216, 231, 233
personal concerns, 216–220, 231, 236
refinement concerns, 222–223, 232–233
confusion and mentoring relationships,
146–147
connected behaviors, 123
constraints (assumed), challenging, 72–73
control and resistance to change,
loss of, 227–228
conversations (alignment), 66
conversations, restoring trust, 123–124
cooperation versus collaboration, 180
coordination versus collaboration, 179
Cornell University, 218, 278–279
corporate citizen of choice, becoming, 8–9
Corporate Responsibility magazine, 8
Covey, Steve, 276

Crawford, Janet, 253
cross-generational mentoring, 147
Cuff, Kathy, 267
cultural transformation, 249–251
alignment phase, 258–260
compelling vision, importance of, 254
critical success factors in, 261–262
culture by design, 251–252
discovery phase, 256–257
employee surveys, 259–260
immersion phase, 257–258
managing, 255–256
refinement phase, 260–261
"right" culture, the, 251
senior leadership and, 252–253
skepticism about culture, 252–253
culture of coaching (internal), creating,
132, 142–144
culture of greatness, compelling
vision, 24
customer devotion, servant
leadership and, 295
customer experience, Legendary Service
deciding, 272–275
delivering, 277–281
discovering, 275–277
customer results, 11
HPO SCORES®, 195
organizational leadership, 195

D

Daley Freightliner, 273–274
Davis, Bob, 112
De Niro, Robert, 153
decision-making rules, clarifying, 46–47
declining performance, performance
coaching, 93–95
decommitment (performance
coaching), handling, 94–99
"Default to Transparency," 192
delegating as leadership style, 58,
60–61, 63, 65, 80, 89–90, 92–93, 206
Deloitte Consulting LLP, 156
Demarest, Garry, 101
Department of Motor Vehicles (DMV),
232–233, 290–292
dependable behaviors, 123
Depree, Max, 28
Deterding, Mark, 253
developing stage (organizational
development), 205
development (team leadership), stages
of, 162–168

development coaching, 132, 135–137
development levels
   capable but cautious performers, 55,
    58, 60, 79–80
   diagnosing, by self-leaders, 54–55
   disillusioned learners, 55, 58, 59, 61,
    63, 79
   enthusiastic beginners, 55, 58–59, 61,
    79, 89, 92
   flexibility in, 62–65
   goal setting, 61
   matching leadership styles to, 55–58
   organizational leadership
    applying leadership styles to,
     203–206
    developing stage, 205
    diagnosing development levels,
     198–201, 206–207
    high performing stage, 206
    improving stage, 204
    matching leadership styles to,
     201–203, 206–207
    relationships, 198–201
    results, 198–201
    start-up stage, 203–204
   self-reliant achievers, 55, 58,
    60–61, 63, 80, 89, 92, 135–136
   variation by task, 61
diagnosing
   performance planning, 85–88
   team leadership stages of
    development, 162
Díaz-Ortiz, Claire, 146–147, 148–149
direct reports, empowerment and,
   36–37
directing as leadership style, 58–59, 65,
   79, 89–90, 92–93, 203
directing behavior (team leadership), 168
direction of work, providing, 89–90
discovery phase (cultural
   transformation), 256–257
disillusioned learners (development
   level), 55, 58, 59, 61, 63, 79
Disney, Walt, 20, 21, 23
Disney theme parks, 23–24, 254
Disney World, 20
dissatisfaction stage (team leadership),
   165–166, 171–172
Domo Gas, 272–273
do-nothing bosses, 301
Dow Chemical Company, 180
driven leaders, servant leadership,
   299–300
Drucker, Peter, 18
duck ponds (Legendary Service), 282
Dupree, Max, 288

Dyer, Wayne, 278
dynamics (team), team leadership,
   174–175

E

eagles (Legendary Service), soaring like,
   281–282
Education, U.S. Department of, 215
ego, servant leadership and, 300–303
employees
   cheering (praising), 31
   motivation for customer service, 30–31
   passion and servant leadership, 295
   performance and empowerment, 37
   potential, traffic flow case study, 39
   self-direction and empowerment,
    48–50
    surveys, cultural transformation,
     259–260
   teams and empowerment, 49–50
   traffic flow case study, 39
employer of choice, becoming, 4–5
empowerment, 35
   boundaries for autonomy, 45–48
   compelling vision, 46
   decision-making rules, clarifying, 46–47
   defined, 36
   direct reports and, 36–37
   goals, setting, 46
   hierarchical culture versus, 37–38,
    40–41, 48
   obstacles to, 37–38
   organizational learning, 44–45
   performance and, 37, 47
   potential, traffic flow case study, 39
   self-direction, 48–49
   self-leadership, 50–51, 70–71
   sharing information, 41–45
   teams, 49–50
   traffic flow case study, 39
   training, 47–48
   trust, 43–44
Empowerment Takes More Than a Minute
   (Blanchard, Carlos, Randolph), 41
energizing systems/structures, 11
   HPO SCORES®, 195–196
   organizational leadership, 195–196
Enron, 307
Enterprise Rent-A-Car, 194
enthusiastic beginners (development
   level), 55, 58–59, 61, 79, 89, 92
Essary, Vicky, 294
essence versus form (mentoring), 147–148
Everyone's a Coach (Blanchard and
   Shula), 3, 281, 305

Expand Involvement and Influence
strategy (Leading People Through
Change model), 226–233
expectations, leadership point of view,
321–323, 330–331
Explain the Business Case for Change
strategy (Leading People Through
Change model), 233–236
Explore Possibilities strategy (Leading
People Through Change model),
245–246

F

false pride
humility and, 302–303
servant leadership and, 300–303
Fast Company, 328
fear and mentoring relationships, 146
Federal Office of Child Support, 230
feedback
importance of, 106–107
money and, 107
as motivation, 107
Finamore, Joe, 197
Fiorina, Carly, 206–207
Firestone, 24
Fixie Chicks, 328
flexibility
change management, 229–230
in leadership, 62–65
Flight of the Buffalo (Belasco, Stayer), 84
Footprint Chronicles, 125, 192
Forbes, 129, 328
Ford Motor Company, 24, 45, 207–208
form versus essence (mentoring),
147–148
Fortune, 193
four bottom lines, 4, 9
corporate citizen of choice, becoming,
8–9
employer of choice, becoming, 4–5
investment of choice, becoming, 6–8
provider of choice, becoming, 5–6
*Fourth Secret of The One Minute Manager:
A Powerful Way to Make Things Better*
(Blanchard, McBride), 116
Fowler, Susan, 72
Frankfurter, Felix, 62
Freightliner, 273–274
Frost, Robert, 316
*Full Steam Ahead! Unleash the Power
of Vision in Your Work and Your Life*
(Blanchard, Stoner), 27, 235, 272
future (compelling vision), picture of
the, 21–22

G

Gandhi, Mahatma, 287
Garfield, Charles, 21
Garrett, Jane, 269–270
Garrett, Milt, 269–270
Gascoigne, Joel, 192
Gates, Bill, 73
General Electric (GE), 71–72, 255
Generosity Factor, The, 150–151
George, Bill, 313–314
Gerstner, Jr., Louis, 25–26
Give Kids the World, 20–21
giving people wings (Legendary
Service), 282–284
goal setting, 46
development levels and, 61
limiting number of goals, 108
one-on-one leadership, 103–104
limiting number of goals, 108
SMART goals, 108–109
performance planning, 85
responsibility for, 31
goals, responsibility for, 31
Golden Door Spa, 265
Good to Great (Collins), 302
Google, 192, 194, 196, 197
Gore, W.L., 310
Graham, Billy, 269–270
Grand Canyon University, 328
Great Scott Trucking, 273, 274
greatness (culture of), compelling
vision, 24
Greenleaf, Robert, 287, 298, 300
*Gung Ho!: Turn On the People in Any
Organization* (Blanchard, Bowles),
30–31, 250–251

H

Halftime (Buford), 150, 311
Hall, Gene, 215
Halsey, Vicki, 267
Harris, Thomas, 301
Hathaway, Anne, 153
Hawkins, Laurence, 72
heart and servant leadership, 298
*Helping People Win at Work: A Business
Philosophy Called "Don't Mark My
Paper, Help Me Get an A"* (Blanchard,
Ridge), 83–84
Hersey, Paul, 53
Hewlett-Packard, 112–113, 206–207
Hibe, Jim, 273
hierarchical culture, empowerment
versus, 37–38, 40–41, 48

high involvement, 11, 229
high performing stage (organizational development), 206
high trust environments, creating, 121
   ABCD Trust model supportive behaviors, 122
   conversations to restore trust, 123–124
   diagnosing weaknesses, 123
   trust levels, assessing, 122–123
high-performing organizations
   characteristics of, 10–12
   defined, 9
   HPO SCORES®, 10–12, 13–16
   leadership in, 12–13
   quadruple bottom line, 4–9
higher level leadership, 332
Hodges, Phil, 298
Hoekstra, Judd, 225
How to Win Friends and Influence People (Carnegie), 76
HPO (High-Performance Organizations), vision and stock returns, 24
HPO SCORES®, 10–12, 50
   Legendary Service and, 265–267
   organizational leadership
      compelling vision, 193
      customer results, 195
      developing stage, 205
      energizing systems/structures, 195–196
      high performing stage, 206
      improving stage, 204
      ongoing learning, 194
      open communication, 192
      shared information, 192
      shared power, 196–197
      start-up stage, 203
   quizzes, 13–16, 201–202
   servant leadership, 309–310
HR Technology Disruptions of 2018, 156
Hudson River plane crash (2009), 176–177
human resources, mentoring programs, creating, 151–152
humility
   defined, 302–303
   false pride and, 302–303
   servant leadership, 302–303
Huselid and Becker, 197, 309
Hyatt, Michael, 145

I

"I Have a Dream" speech (Martin Luther King, Jr.), 24
"I need" statements, 76–77

IBM, 25–26
I'm OK, You're OK (Harris), 301
immersion phase (cultural transformation), 257–258
impact concerns (change management), 221, 232
IMPACT program (mentoring), tailoring to career stages, 152–153
implementation concerns (change management), 220–221, 231–232
improving stage (organizational development), 204
inclusion, importance in change management, 223–224
Indianapolis 500, 272–273
individual learning
   organizational learning versus, 204
   self-leadership and, 71–72
Infant at Work, 316
influence in change management, 226–233
information
   change management, 216, 231, 233
   sharing information
      empowerment, 41–45
      transparency and, 124–126
integrating style (team leadership), 172
integration stage (team leadership), 166–167
Intern, The, 153
internal culture of coaching, creating, 132, 142–144
investment of choice, becoming, 6–8
involvement
   change management, 226–233
      high involvement, 11
IRS (Internal Revenue Service), 232–233

J

Jobs, Steve, 124
Johnson, Robert, 22–23
Johnson, Spencer, 103, 116
Johnson & Johnson, 22–23
Johnsonville Foods, 71–72
Jones, John, 218, 219
Jones, KC, 161
journey of change, change management, 214

K

Kandarian, Fay, 9, 10, 266
Kelleher, Herb, 282, 309, 331
Kellerman, Barbara, 307

Kelly, Gary, 282
Ken Blanchard Companies®, The, 42–43,
  53, 199, 201, 235, 313–314, 316
Kennedy, John F., 21–22, 38, 117
Keynes, John Maynard, 234
KFC, 49, 71–72
King, Jr., Martin Luther, 24, 287
knowledge power, 75
Kodak, 206
Kyle, Dana, 290, 293–294

L

Labor, U.S. Department of, 197
Lacinak, Thad, 90–91
Lawler, Edward, 37
Lawrence, Martha, 120–121
*Lead with LUV: A Different Way to Create
  Real Success* (Barrett, Blanchard), 328
Leader Within (Zigarmi), *The*, 308
leadership
  coaching as leadership style, 204
  delegating as leadership style, 206
  directing as leadership style, 203
  flexibility in, 62–65
  higher level leadership, 332
  leadership vacuums, 50–51
  one-on-one leadership, 67, 103
    accountability, 104–105
    feedback, importance of, 106–107
    goal setting, 103–104, 108, 108–109
    One Minute Apologies, 116–117
    One Minute Praisings, 110–113, 116
    One Minute Re-Directs, 113–116
    one-on-one meetings, 101
    performance management systems,
      81–100
    performance reviews, 107–108
    performance standards, 105–107
  operational leadership, 294, 295
  organizational leadership, 68, 191
    compelling vision, 193
    customer results, 195
    development levels, 198–207
    energizing systems/structures,
      195–196
    HPO SCORES®, 191–197
    ongoing learning, 194
    open communication, 192
    shared information, 192
    shared power, 196–197
    style of leadership, 198, 201–207
    turnaround, example of, 207–208
  point of view, 313–314

developing, 323–329
  elements of, 314
  expectations, 321–323, 330–331
  higher level leadership, 332
  key events, 315–317
  key people, 314–315
  values, 317–320, 329–330
self-leadership, 50–51, 67, 69–70
  empowerment and, 70–71
  individual learning and, 71–72
  skills of, 72–80
servant leadership, 287
  applying, 290–292
  benefits of, 307–312
  called leaders, 299–300
  customer devotion, 295
  defined, 287–290
  driven leaders, 299–300
  ego and, 300–303
  employee passion, 295
  encouraging, 293–294
  false pride and, 300–303
  heart and, 298
  HPO SCORES®, 309–310
  humility and, 302–303
  Leadership-Profit Chain, 296
  organizational vitality, 295
  performance, 294–298
  SERVE acronym, 304–306
SLII®, 53–54
  diagnosing development levels,
    54–55
  flexibility in leadership, 62–65
  matching leadership styles to
    development levels, 55–61
strategic leadership, 294–295
styles of leadership
  coaching, 58, 59, 65, 79, 89–90,
    92–93
  delegate, 58, 60–61, 63, 63, 65
  delegating, 80, 89–90, 92–93
  directing, 58–59, 65, 79, 89–90,
    92–93
  matching to development levels,
    55–61
  support, 58, 60, 65, 79–80, 89–90,
    92–93
support, as leadership style, 205
team leadership, 67, 155–158
  characteristics of, 159–161
  closure and, 175–176
  directing behavior, 168
  effective approach to, 159
  importance of, 156–158
  integrating style, 172

leadership behaviors, 168–170
momentum and, 173–174
performance, obstacles to, 158
performance strategies, 173–176
power of, 176–177
resolving style, 171–172
stages of development, 162–168
structuring style, 170–171
supporting behavior, 168
team dynamics, 174–175
validating style, 172–173
as transformational journey, 67–68
vision, 29–31
organizational vision, 26–27
shared vision, impact of, 25–26
Leadership Engine (Tichy), *The*, 313
Leadership is an Art (Dupree), 28, 288
Leadership-Profit Chain, 296
Leading at a Higher Level (Blanchard), 332
leading change, organizational change
importance of, 209–210
journey of change, 214
Leading People Through Change model, 225
Collaborate on Implementation strategy, 236–241
Expand Involvement and Influence strategy, 226–233
Explain the Business Case for Change strategy, 233–236
Explore Possibilities strategy, 245–246
Make the Change Sustainable strategy, 241–244
learning
coaching to support learning, 132, 140–142
individual learning
organizational learning versus, 204
self-leadership and, 71–72
ongoing learning, 10–11
HPO SCORES®, 194
organizational leadership, 194
organizational learning
individual learning versus, 204
sharing information and empowerment, 44–45
Lee, Robert, 227–228
Legendary Service, 265
creating, 267–272
customer experience
deciding, 272–275
delivering, 277–281
discovering, 275–277
duck ponds, 282
elements of, 268

giving people wings, 282–284
HPO SCORES®, 265–267
soaring like eagles, 281–282
Legendary Service (Blanchard, Cuff, Halsey), 267
Lewin, Kurt, 209
Lewinsky, Monica, 117
living your vision, 28–29
loss of control and resistance to change, 227–228
low trust, cost of, 119–120

M

MacDonald, Gordon, 299
Make the Change Sustainable strategy (Leading People Through Change model), 241–244
Make-A-Wish Foundation, 20
Malone, Thomas, 37
Management By Wandering Around (Hewlett-Packard), 112–113
managing
cultural transformation, 255–256
performance management systems
establishing, 81–84
partnering as, 100
performance coaching, 82, 90–99
performance delivery, 91
performance planning, 81–82, 85–90
performance reviews, 82, 100, 107–108
top-down management, 156
Mandela, Nelson, 287
Marcario, Rose, 193
Maritz, 119
Marriott hotels, 6
Master of Science in Executive Leadership (MSEL) program, 313–314, 321, 322, 323
MasteryWorks, 119
matching, performance planning, 88–90
Maxell, John, 290, 297
McBride, Margaret, 116
McCarty, Steve, 194
McGee, Robert S., 301
McHale, Kevin, 161
mentoring, 145–146
career stages, tailoring mentoring to, 152–154
confusion and mentoring relationships, 146–147
cross-generational mentoring, 147

essence versus form, 147–148
fear and mentoring relationships, 146
human resources, 151–152
MENTOR model, The, 148–151, 152
mentoring programs, creating, 151–152
new hire mentoring, 147
obstacles to a mentoring relationship, 146–147
partners, choosing, 147
peer-to-peer mentoring, 147
time and mentoring relationships, 146
Merck, 253
Meyers, Scott, 105–106
Miami Dolphins, 3
Microsoft, 45
Miller, Herman, 28, 288
Miller, Linda, 142
Miller, Mark, 304
Minera El Tesoro, 253
Moments of Truth, 274, 275
momentum and team leadership, 173–174
money, feedback and, 107
morale, team leadership, 163–164
Mother Theresa, 73, 287, 311
motivation, feedback as, 107
Motor Vehicles, Department of, 232–233
Mulally, Alan, 207–208

N

NASA, 21–22
Nature Conservancy, 180
Netflix, 196, 197
new hire mentoring, 147
New One Minute Manager (Blanchard, Johnson), *The,* 103
New York Times, 25–26
NFL, 3, 305
Nixon, Richard M., 117
Nordstrom, 254, 266–267, 281, 283–284, 308
Nordstrom, Bruce, 283–284
Novak, David, 49, 295

O

O'Connor, Michael, 23
Ohio University, 53
Olmstead, Cynthia, 120–121
One Minute Apologies, 116–117

One Minute Manager (Blanchard, Johnson), *The,* 113, 116, 200–201, 289–290
One Minute Mentoring: How to Find and Work with a Mentor - and Why You'll Benefit from Being One (Blanchard, Díaz-Ortiz), 146–147
One Minute Praisings, 110–113, 116, 289
One Minute Re-Directs, 113–116, 289
one-on-one leadership, 67, 103
    accountability, 104–105
    feedback, importance of, 106–107
    goal setting, 103–104
        limiting number of goals, 108
        SMART goals, 108–109
    One Minute Apologies, 116–117
    One Minute Praisings, 110–113, 116
    One Minute Re-Directs, 113–116
    one-on-one meetings, 101
    performance management systems
        establishing, 81–84
        partnering as, 100
        performance coaching, 82, 90–99
        performance delivery, 91
        performance planning, 81–82, 85–90
        performance reviews, 82, 100
    performance reviews, 107–108
    performance standards, 105–107
ongoing learning, 10–11
    HPO SCORES®, 194
    organizational leadership, 194
open communication, 10
    HPO SCORES®, 192
    organizational leadership, 192
operational leadership, 294, 295
Ordering Your Private World (MacDonald), 299
organizational change, 209
    bureaucracy and, 244
    child support collection case study, 230–233, 234, 236, 238
    complexity of, 210–211
    concerns, 215
        collaboration concerns, 222, 232
        different people at different levels of concern, 223
        impact concerns, 221, 232
        implementation concerns, 220–221, 231–232
        information concerns, 216, 231, 233
        personal concerns, 216–220, 231, 236
        refinement concerns, 222–223, 232–233
    failure of, 212–213
    inclusion, importance in change management, 216–220

influence in, 226–233
involvement in, 226–233
leading change
  importance of, 209–210
  journey of change, 214
Leading People Through Change
  model, 225
  *Collaborate on Implementation
    strategy, 236–241*
  *Expand Involvement and Influence
    strategy, 226–233*
  *Explain the Business Case for Change
    strategy, 233–236*
  *Explore Possibilities strategy,
    245–246*
  *Make the Change Sustainable
    strategy, 241–244*
necessity for, 211
reinforcing change, 247
organizational culture
compelling vision, importance of, 254
culture by design, 251–252
senior leadership and, 252–253
skepticism about culture, 252–253
transforming, 249–251
  alignment phase, 258–260
  critical success factors in, 261–262
  discovery phase, 256–257
  employee surveys, 259–260
  immersion phase, 257–258
  managing transformation, 255–256
  refinement phase, 260–261
  "right" culture, the, 251
organizational leadership, 68, 191
development levels
  applying leadership styles to, 203–206
  developing stage, 205
  diagnosing, 198–201, 206–207
  high performing stage, 206
  improving stage, 204
  *matching leadership styles to,
    201–203, 206–207*
  relationships, 198–201
  results, 198–201
  start-up stage, 203–204
HPO SCORES®
  compelling vision, 193
  customer results, 195
  developing stage, 205
  *energizing systems/structures,
    195–196*
  high performing stage, 206
  improving stage, 204
  ongoing learning, 194
  open communication, 192
  shared information, 192

  shared power, 196–197
  start-up stage, 203
style of leadership, development levels
  applying leadership styles to, 203–206
  determining, 198
  *matching leadership styles to,
    201–203, 206–207*
turnaround, example of, 207–208
organizational learning
individual learning versus, 204
sharing information and
  empowerment, 44–45
organizational vision, 26–27
**organizational vitality, servant
  leadership and, 295**
**orientation stage (team leadership),
  164–165**

P

Parish, Robert, 161
Parisi-Carew, Eunice, 9, 10, 183–184
partnering
as a performance management
  system, 100
for performance skills (SLII®), 66–67
Patagonia, 125, 192, 193
*Peak Performance: Mental Training
  Techniques of the World's Greatest
  Athletes* (Garfield, Zinabennett), 21
**Peale, Norman Vincent, 148, 150–151,
  302–303**
Peale, Ruth, 148
peer-to-peer mentoring, 147
People Express Airlines, 274
performance
appraisal process, restructuring, 47
coaching, 82, 90–93, 132, 133–135
  declining performance, 93–95
  decommitment, 94–99
  placing blame, 95
dashboards, 244
declining performance, 93–95
empowerment and, 37
one-on-one leadership
  performance reviews, 107–108
  performance standards, 105–107
partnering for performance skills
  (SLII®), 66–67
performance management systems
  establishing, 81–84
  partnering as, 100
  performance coaching, 82, 90–99
  performance delivery, 91

performance planning, 81–82, 85–90
performance reviews, 82, 100,
    107–108
planning, 81–82, 85–86
    diagnosing, 85–88
    goal setting, 85
    matching, 88–90
reviews, 82, 100, 107–108
servant leadership, 294–298
team leadership
    performance, obstacles to, 158
    strategies for, 173–176
personal concerns (change management),
    216–220, 231, 236
personal power, 75
picture of the future, vision as, 21–22
Pizza Hut, 71–72
placing blame, performance
    coaching, 95
planning performance, 81–82, 85–86
    diagnosing, 85–88
    goal setting, 85
    matching, 88–90
point of view (leadership), 313–314
    developing, 323–329
    elements of, 314
    expectations, 321–323, 330–331
    higher level leadership, 332
    key events, 315–317
    key people, 314–315
    values, 317–320, 329–330
points of power, activating, 73–76
Porras, Collins and, 24
position power, 75
potential, developing, traffic flow case
    study, 39
power
    "I need" statements, 76–77
    knowledge power, 75
    personal power, 75
    points of power, activating, 73–76
    position power, 75
    relationship power, 75
    shared power, 11
        HPO SCORES®, 196–197
        organizational leadership, 196–197
    task power, 75
Power of Ethical Management
    (Blanchard, Peale), The, 148, 302–303
Power of Positive Management
    (Blanchard), The, 148
praising (cheering), 31, 110–113, 116
pride (false)
    humility and, 302–303
    servant leadership and, 300–303
proactive, being, 77–80

production stage (team leadership),
    167–168
productivity, team leadership, 163–164
profit, 157
provider of choice, becoming, 5–6
Purpose Driven Life, The (Warren), 294

Q

quadruple bottom line, 4, 9
    corporate citizen of choice, becoming,
        8–9
    employer of choice, becoming, 4–5
    investment of choice, becoming, 6–8
    provider of choice, becoming, 5–6
quizzes, HPO SCORES®, 13–16, 201–202

R

Randolph, Alan, 41
Raving Fans®: A Revolutionary Approach
    to Customer Service (Bowles and
    Blanchard), 5–6, 272
reciprocity and collaboration, 184
refinement concerns (change
    management), 222–223, 232–233
refinement phase (cultural
    transformation), 260–261
reinforcing change, change
    management, 247
relationships
    mentoring relationships, obstacles to,
        146–147
    organizational leadership, diagnosing
        development levels, 198–201
    power of, 75
reports (direct), empowerment and,
    36–37
reprimands. See One Minute Re-Directs
resistance to change, loss of control
    and, 227–228
resolving style (team leadership),
    171–172
responsibility for goals, 31
results
    customer results, 11
        HPO SCORES®, 195
        organizational leadership, 195
    organizational leadership,
        development levels, diagnosing,
        198–201
reviewing performance, 82, 100,
    107–108

Ridge, Garry, 83–84, 256–259
"right" culture and cultural transformation, the, 251
Ritz-Carlton hotels, 49, 282–283, 309
Rolling Stone, 124
Rubrik, 126
rules (decision-making), clarifying, 46–47

S

San Diego wildfire (2003), 180
San Diego, University of, 313–314, 321, 323
SAP, change management, 216, 220–222
Sarbanes-Oxley, direct reports and empowerment, 36–37
Satoro, Ryunosuke, 177
Saturn Corporation (Saturn LLC), 269–270
Schmidt, Tim, 253
Schulze, Horst, 282–283, 309
SeaWorld, 20
Secret: What Great Leaders Know and Do (Blanchard, Miller), *The,* 304
self-direction, empowerment and, 48–50
Self-Leadership and The One Minute Manager (Blanchard, Fowler, Hawkins), 72
self-leadership, 50–51, 67, 69–70
    empowerment and, 70–71
    individual learning and, 71–72
    skills of
        activating points of power, 73–76
        being proactive, 77–80
        challenging assumed constraints, 72–73
self-reliant achievers (development level), 55, 58, 60–61, 63, 80, 89, 92, 135–136
self-serving leaders, 300
Servant Leader (Blanchard, Hodges), *The,* 298
Servant Leadership in Action: How You Can Achieve Great Relationships and Results (Blanchard, Broadwell), 290, 297
servant leadership, 287
    applying, 290–292
    benefits of, 307–312
    called leaders, 299–300
    customer devotion, 295

defined, 287–290
driven leaders, 299–300
ego and, 300–303
employee passion, 295
encouraging, 293–294
false pride and, 300–303
heart and, 298
HPO SCORES®, 309–310
humility and, 302–303
Leadership-Profit Chain, 296
organizational vitality, 295
performance, 294–298
SERVE acronym, 304–306
shared information, 10
    HPO SCORES®, 192
    organizational leadership, 192
shared power, 11
    HPO SCORES®, 196–197
    organizational leadership, 196–197
shared vision, impact of, 24–26
sharing information
    empowerment and, 41–45
    organizational learning, 44–45
    transparency and, 124–126
    trust, 43–44, 124–126
Shula, Don, 3, 281–282, 305
significant purpose, as vision element, 20–21
Sinha, Bipul, 126
skills, partnering for performance skills (SLII®), 66–67
SLII®, 53–54, 289–290
    alignment conversations, 66
    development levels
        diagnosing, 54–55
        flexibility in, 62–65
        goal setting, 61
        matching leadership styles to, 55–61
        variation by task, 61
    flexibility in leadership, 62–65
    leadership as transformational journey, 67–68
    one-on-one leadership, 67
    organizational leadership, 68
    partnering for performance skills (SLII®), 66–67
    self-leadership, 67, 77–80
    team leadership, 67
SMART goals, 108–109
Smith, Fred, 303
Snow White, 325–326
soaring like eagles (Legendary Service), 281–282
Southwest Airlines, 193, 197, 254, 281–282, 309, 328, 329–330, 331

Special Olympics, 311
St. Mary's College, 328
stages of development, team
   leadership, 162
      dissatisfaction stage, 165–166, 171–172
      integration stage, 166–167
      morale, 163–164
      orientation stage, 164–165
      production stage, 167–168
      productivity, 163–164
Star Trek, 21–22
start-up stage (organizational
   development), 203–204
Stayer, Ralph, 84
Stelling, Kessel, 129
Stoner, Jesse, 9, 10, 18–19, 27, 235, 272
strategic leadership, 294–295
structuring style (team leadership),
   170–171
Sullenberger, Chesley "Sully," 176–177
support, as leadership style, 58, 60, 65,
   79–80, 89–90, 92–93, 205
supporting behavior (team leadership),
   168
Survey of Bank Reputations, 129
surveys, cultural transformation,
   259–260
sustainability, Make the Change
   Sustainable strategy (Leading People
   Through Change model), 241–244
sweet spot of coaching, 133
Sykes, Jeffrey, 176–177
Synovus Financial, 129

T

Taco Bell, 71–72
task power, 75
task-specific, development goals as, 61
Tate, Rick, 106
team dynamics, team leadership,
   174–175
team leadership, 67, 155–156
      characteristics of, 159–161
      closure and, 175–176
      directing behavior, 168
      dissatisfaction stage, 165–166, 171–172
      effective approach to, 159
      importance of, 156–158
      integrating style, 172
      integration stage, 166–167
      leadership behaviors, 168–170
      momentum and, 173–174
      morale, 163–164

   need for, 156–158
   orientation stage, 164–165
   performance, strategies for, 173–176
   performance, obstacles to, 158
   power of, 176–177
   production stage, 167–168
   productivity, 163–164
   resolving style, 171–172
   stages of development, 162
      dissatisfaction stage, 165–166,
         171–172
      integration stage, 166–167
      morale, 163–164
      orientation stage, 164–165
      production stage, 167–168
      productivity, 163–164
   structuring style, 170–171
   supporting behavior, 168
   team dynamics, 174–175
   validating style, 172–173
teams, empowerment of, 49–50
teamwork versus collaboration, 180
Texas, University of, 215
Tichy, Noel, 313
time and mentoring relationships, 146
Tompkins, Chuck, 90–91
Tony Jannus Award, 328
Top 50 Leaders, The, 328
top-down management, 156
Toyota Motor Company, 194
Track Type Tractors (TTT) division
   (Caterpillar), 161
Trader Joe's Grocery, 37, 195, 266
traffic flow case study, employee
   empowerment, 39
training, empowerment and, 47–48
Training magazine, 155
transformational journey, leadership
   as, 67–68
transparency, 208
   "Default to Transparency," 192
   sharing information, 124–126
   trust and, 124–126
trust, 119
   ABCD Trust model, 120–121, 124,
      121–124, 126, 128
   benefits of, 120
   broken trust, repairing, 126–128
   connected behaviors, 123
   cost of, 119–120
   dependable behaviors, 123
   elements of trust, 120–121
   high trust environments, creating, 121
      ABCD Trust model supportive
         behaviors, 122

conversations to restore trust, 123–124
diagnosing weaknesses, 123
trust levels, assessing, 122–123
leaders as examples, 128–129
levels of trust, assessing, 122–123
low trust, cost of, 119–120
restoring, 123–124
ripple effect, 128–129
sharing information, 124–126
sharing information and empowerment, 43–44
transparency and, 124–126
Trust Works!: Four Keys to Building Lasting Relationships (Blanchard, Olmstead, Lawrence), 120–121
Twain, Mark, 210
Tylenol, 22–23

U

UNITE model and collaboration, The, 185–189
United States Olympic hockey team (1980), 176
University Associates, 218
University of San Diego, 313–314, 321, 323
University of Texas, 215
UPS (United Parcel Service), 197
U.S. Army After Action Review (AAR) process, 194
U.S. Department of Education, 215
U.S. Department of Labor, 197
USA Today, 6

V

validating style (team leadership), 172–173
values
    leadership point of view, 317–320, 329–330
    as vision element, 22–24
vision
    communicating, 28
    compelling vision, 10, 19, 46
        cultural transformation, importance in, 254
        culture of greatness, 24
        HPO SCORES®, 193

organizational leadership, 193
    picture of the future, 21–22
    significant purpose, 20–21
    values, 22–24
creating, 27–28
defined, 27
HPO stock returns and, 24
importance of, 17–18
leadership and, 29–31
living, 28–29
organizational vision, 26–27
shared vision, impact of, 24–26
vision statements, 18–19

W

Warren, Rick, 294
Watergate, 117
WD-40 Company, 83, 256–259
Welch, Jack, 255
Whale Done!: The Power of Positive Relationships (Blanchard, Lacinak, Tompkins, Ballard), 90–91
What Color Is Your Parachute? (Bolles), 303
wings (Legendary Service), giving people, 282–284
work direction, providing, 89–90
WorldCom, 307
World's 100 Most Powerful Women Award, The, 328
worthwhile work, 30

Y

You and Your Network (Smith), 303
YPO (Young President's Organization), 199
Yum! Brands, 48–49, 71–72, 295
Yum! University, 71–72

Z

Zappos, 193
Zigarmi, Drea, 19, 294, 295–297, 307–308
Zigarmi, Pat, 225, 316–320